GRIPLA

Ráðgjafar

FRANÇOIS-XAVIER DILLMANN, MATTHEW JAMES DRISCOLL,
JÜRG GLAUSER, STEFANIE GROPPER, TATJANA N. JACKSON,
KARL G. JOHANSSON, MARIANNE E. KALINKE, KJARTAN OTTOSSON,
STEPHEN A. MITCHELL, JUDY QUINN, ANDREW WAWN

Gripla er alþjóðlegur vettvangur fyrir rannsóknir á sviði íslenskra og norrænna fræða. Birtar eru útgáfur á stuttum textum, greinar og ritgerðir og stuttar fræðilegar athugasemdir. Greinar skulu að jafnaði skrifaðar á íslensku en einnig eru birtar greinar á öðrum norrænum málum, ensku, þýsku og frönsku. Leiðbeiningar um frágang handrita er að finna í 10. bindi (1998) á bls. 269–278 en þær má einnig nálgast hjá ritstjórum. Allt efni sem birtast á er lesið yfir af sérfræðingum. Fyrstu gerð efnis þarf aðeins að skila í handriti en þegar samþykkt hefur verið að birta það, og það telst frágengið af hálfu höfundar þarf bæði að skila því í lokahandriti og á tölvudisklingi. Upplýsingar um ritvinnsluforrit og leturgerð skulu fylgja. Greinum og útgáfum (öðrum en stuttum athugasemdum o.þ.h.) skal fylgja útdráttur á öðru máli. Hverju bindi Griplu fylgir handritaskrá.

GRIPLA

XX

NORDIC CIVILISATION
IN THE MEDIEVAL WORLD

RITSTJÓRI

VÉSTEINN ÓLASON

REYKJAVÍK
STOFNUN ÁRNA MAGNÚSSONAR Í ÍSLENSKUM FRÆÐUM
2009

STOFNUN ÁRNA MAGNÚSSONAR
RIT 74

Prófarkalestur
HÖFUNDAR OG RITSTJÓRI

Aðstoð við ritstjórn og prófarkalestur
GÍSLI SIGURÐSSON, EMILY LETHBRIDGE, MARGRÉT EGGERTSDÓTTIR,
SVANHILDUR GUNNARSDÓTTIR, SVANHILDUR ÓSKARSDÓTTIR,
ÚLFAR BRAGASON

© Stofnun Árna Magnússonar í íslenskum fræðum
Öll réttindi áskilin

Umbrot
SVERRIR SVEINSSON

Filmuvinna, prentun og bókband
LETURPRENT

Prentþjónusta og dreifing
HÁSKÓLAÚTGÁFAN

Meginmál þessarar bókar er sett með 10,5 punkta Andron Mega Corpus letri
á 13,4 punkta fæti og bókin er prentuð á 115 gr. Munken Pure 13 pappír

PRINTED IN ICELAND

ISSN 1018-5011
ISBN 978 9979 654 06 3

EFNI

Vésteinn Ólason: Introduction ... 7
Jóhann Páll Árnason: A Mutating Periphery:
   Medieval Encounters in the Far North ... 17
Sverre Bagge: Nordic Uniqueness in the Middle Ages?
   Political and Literary Aspects ... 49
Gunnar Karlsson: Was Iceland the Galapagos
   of Germanic Political Culture? ... 77
Richard Gaskins: Creating at the Margins:
   Cultural Dynamics in Early Iceland ... 93
Kirsten Hastrup: Northern Barbarians:
   Icelandic Canons of Civilisation ... 109
Przemysław Urbańczyk: Deconstructing
   the "Nordic Civilization" ... 137
Margaret Clunies Ross: Medieval Icelandic Textual Culture ... 163
Rudolf Simek: The Medieval Icelandic World View
   and the Theory of the Two Cultures ... 183
Torfi H. Tulinius: The Self as Other:
   Iceland and the Culture of Southern Europe in the Middle Ages ... 199
Vilhjálmur Árnason: An Ethos in Transformation:
   Conflicting Values in the Sagas ... 217
Svavar Hrafn Svavarsson: Honour and Shame:
   Comparing Medieval Iceland and Ancient Greece ... 241
Joseph Harris: Philology, Elegy, and Cultural Change ... 257
   Handrit ... 281

INTRODUCTION

THE ARTICLES published in this volume of *Gripla* are based on papers which were delivered at a conference held in Skálholt, 5th–9th September 2007; these articles are supplemented here by three additional contributions by other participants at the conference. The title of the conference was "Nordic Civilisation in the Medieval World". Twenty five participants, from eight countries, represented a range of scholarly disciplines— history, archaeology, anthropology, literary studies, philosophy, and runology. Nine papers were presented at the conference and individual participants responded to each one of them.

The impetus for the Skálholt conference came from Jóhann Páll Árnason's idea to bring together scholars from different fields to discuss the civilisation of the inhabitants of the Scandinavian countries (especially the Icelanders) in the Viking Age and in the Middle Ages. This was with a mind to investigating whether and how this civilisation was distinctive compared with medieval European civilisation. Since Jóhann was not in Iceland on a permanent basis, I approached the historian Gunnar Karlsson and the philosopher Vilhjálmur Árnason (both professors at Háskóli Íslands) in order to organise the conference under the auspices of the Stofnun Árna Magnússon and Háskóli Íslands. We were soon joined by Dr Salvör Nordal at the Siðfræðistofnun Háskóla Íslands (Institute of Ethics at the University of Iceland). It was decided that the conference would be held at Skálholt and that a certain number of scholars working in different academic fields would be invited: some to give papers, and others to respond with prepared critiques or comments. In addition, a number of Icelandic participants were invited to join the discussions.

The relationship between the Scandinavian countries and other parts of Europe in the Middle Ages with regard to the subject of civilisation has been discussed widely in the last few decades, especially in the forum of academic publications. The Roman-Catholic Church exerted a powerful influence on civilisation in the northern and western parts of Europe during the Middle Ages. This civilisation was flanked by wild nature to the west and the north—the Atlantic Ocean and the Arctic Sea—and by the world of the Eastern Orthodox church to the east and Islam to the south. The parts of Europe dominated by the Roman-Catholic church were far from being homogenous regions, however: countries and districts had their own characteristics and cultural peculiarities as well as common features. The particular characteristics of different countries of course had both natural and historical explanations, rooted in social and geographical conditions or circumstances as well as past history. With this in mind, it is worth asking whether the extent to which we look at the Scandinavian countries as some kind of unified whole within Europe in the Middle Ages is an anachronistic illusion created by later history. For a long time, various differences have been evident between the groups of people who combed the Atlantic sea-ways, claimed settled and unsettled islands in the Atlantic and not least, who had fertile dealings with Celtic peoples, when compared to those people who sailed their ships to the Baltic Sea and along Russian rivers, and who established relations with the inhabitants of the continental European mainland. Those in the first group—Icelanders and Norwegians—were quick to accept Christianity and to learn to write in their mother tongue but those in the latter group—which included the Danes, who also had many dealings over the North Sea—wrote mainly in Latin for a long time. Nevertheless, medieval authors describe the Scandinavian region as a region divided in three main parts, as can be seen in volume four of Adam of Bremen's *Gesta Hammaburgensis Ecclesiæ Pontificum*, and in Snorri Sturluson's *Heimskringla*.

Preserved sources, or lack of sources, set the limits for historical investigations. Emphases will differ in critical accounts based predominantly on written texts, and in those that direct their attention towards interpreting the material record that is evident or has been uncovered by archaeologists. There is great variation from one region to another across the Scandinavian countries in so far as the possibilities opened up by the sources are concerned. To a great degree, the wealth of written sources on parchment has its roots in Iceland; archaeological evidence (including runic inscriptions) is especially prominent in central and eastern Scandinavia. These differences

INTRODUCTION

are brought out in the present volume, although the interpretation of written sources with a primary emphasis on Iceland prevails in most of the articles. Anyone attempting to interpret written sources of the past will be faced with the perennial difficulty that the written sources are frequently not recorded by direct witnesses to the events and circumstances they relate. The time which elapses between the date of an event and the written recording of it, and the circumstances of the moment of writing, are inherent parts of the text. This problem presents itself immediately to all those who wish to use Icelandic texts from the thirteenth century as sources of information about the Viking Age; academics' attitudes to this methodological difficulty and how it is approached by different disciplines, can vary. Archaeology differs from the study of texts in that precisely dated material phenomena bear unequivocal witness to specific times and places, but they are seldom easily interpreted or contextualized. When archaeologists have the opportunity, therefore, they frequently must rely on the testimony of written sources to make sense of the material picture; interpretative problems arise in all avenues of historical research.

It is virtually unavoidable that discussion about the civilisation of the Scandinavian countries taking place in Iceland, at the initiative of Icelanders, will be coloured by an Icelandic perspective: consciously and unconsciously, the literary culture of the Icelanders in the Middle Ages and history as recounted in Icelandic books—in sum, the picture of civilisation that they present—is taken as the norm. This is obvious in the greater part of the articles which are published here. In fact, the wealth of medieval Icelandic sources and scholarly tradition has led, and continues to lead, not only Icelanders but many others to rely on Icelandic texts as the foundations for research into investigating what was distinctive about the civilisation of the Scandinavian countries during the Viking Age and the Middle Ages. With one exception (the Rök stone), all of the texts which are analysed in this volume are Icelandic. Despite the considerable extent to which this perspective circumscribes the meaning of the phrase 'Nordic civilisation' in the conference-title, the selection of scholars that were invited to Skálholt may be seen as an attempt to prevent discussion on the subject being dominated by the Icelandic perspective. In the nineteenth century and on into the early decades of the twentieth century, most scholars believed that the Icelandic prose narratives and the old poetry about the

Scandinavian people and their lives were genuine sources for the civilisation of the Scandinavian countries, and furthermore, that these texts bore a general Germanic stamp. This view is now outdated and it is clear that the source value of the medieval writings of the Icelanders is greatly restricted. The texts were determined by the specific circumstances surrounding their production in Iceland and their presentation of the pre-Christian world was moulded by the fact that that they were conceived by Christians in an environment where the church and its ideology dominated textual production to a great extent. This does not mean, however, that these sources—the sagas and the poetry—have no value for research into the history of the Scandinavian countries other than Iceland in the Viking Age and the Middle Ages. Such research, however, calls for strict criticism of the sources.

For many years, Jóhann Páll Árnason, an Icelandic philosopher with an international academic career behind him, has dedicated himself to the academic field known as 'civilisation studies'. As noted earlier, the initiative behind the conference was Jóhann's and therefore his article is printed first here, also because the scope of his article is broad. Jóhann focuses on the origins and nature of the Icelandic 'Commonwealth' and reviews and analyses ideas about its basic characteristics, as formulated by twentieth-century scholars from Arnold Toynbee and Sigurður Nordal to Jesse Byock and Gunnar Karlsson. Jóhann's subject is the distinctive society that came about in Iceland and its development. An important element of Jóhann's interpretation is that even before the country's conversion to Christianity, Icelandic society was different to the Scandinavian monarchies. Jóhann follows Sigurður Nordal in believing that explanations for the Commonwealth cannot be based exclusively on the particular physical conditions in the extensive, very sparsely populated, and previously unsettled land; the establishment of a social organisation, which could not be called a state in the normal sense but rather a political community, was also the result of the ideas and desires of its leaders. However, both these scholars agree that these ideas could not be fully realised because of adverse circumstances. In explaining and defining the political community that evolved in Iceland, Jóhann looks to the ancient Greek polis for comparison, amongst other things. One determining factor in the origin and development of Icelandic society was the relation between politics and religion.

The chieftains' power rested on religion but it also had rational secular objectives which were put into practice with a varying degree of success. The social structure that was formed before the Conversion laid the foundation for the special character of Icelandic society which endured for three hundred years, until the Commonwealth came to an end. Although Iceland was itself without a king, it is important to appreciate the extent to which monarchy was a central concept in the world view of Icelandic society. This comes out very clearly in the literature.

In the next article, Sverre Bagge questions whether or not there are legitimate arguments for talking about a particular Nordic civilisation in the Middle Ages and he suggests that this can be justified on two possible counts: first, the literature of the Icelanders, and second, the 'Scandinavian model' with equality, democracy, welfare and freedom. Bagge believes that it is difficult to adduce sufficiently strong arguments to support the idea that later developments in Scandinavian society towards this model were rooted in medieval culture. After discussing the literature (especially the sagas) and comparing it with literature produced by other nations in the Middle Ages, Bagge concludes that "there is more to suggest a distinct cultural tradition, expressed in saga literature, which in turn is related to the character of Icelandic society, to some extent also to the other Scandinavian countries, notably Norway."

Gunnar Karlsson examines whether the Icelandic political community, prior to the country's submission to the Norwegian crown, was "of its own special kind, rather than just a variant of a medieval European political system." After a short but comprehensive description of various problems and arguments, Gunnar builds on his own extensive research in coming to some conclusions. His verdict is that Icelandic society probably was different but that this was not on account of "the inventiveness or the ideals of the people of Iceland". Rather, it was caused primarily by the country's physical remove from royal power: the Atlantic Ocean protected the society that formed after the settlement of the country. Gunnar thus makes less than Sigurður Nordal and Jóhann Páll Árnason of the likelihood that the social system was the result of the systematic intentions of those who created it.

In an article which brings together many of the subjects and themes of this collection of essays, Richard Gaskins takes his lead from Jóhann Páll and Gunnar and also discusses the views of scholars who were not present at the conference, such as Jón Viðar Sigurðsson and certain anthropologists. Gaskins notes that it is not possible to assume that there was a single consistent system of values in the society depicted in the sagas. It is much more likely that conflict between different ideas and values impelled the development of Icelandic society. Sources for this position are, of course, found in the sagas, where the self-reflection of society itself is expressed: "It is often said that "heroic societies" are static places where reflection has no place ... Perhaps an early Iceland can be seen as an exceptional case study: a heroic society in the process of emerging from that static condition, spreading out over four centuries, and recorded in singular fashion by a contemporary literature of self-reflection."

Kirsten Hastrup also centres her discussion on Iceland but she considers how the outside world perceived Iceland, and how Icelanders perceived themselves, in the light of ideas about civilisation and concepts of centre and periphery. In this context, literature and texts are of primary importance. For both the ancient Greeks and for the Icelanders, literature—certain ur-texts, to use her terminology—defines what civilisation is, and the social status of groups within society. In this respect, Icelandic ideas about civilisation were profoundly European and logocentric although the Icelanders had very different ideas about themselves than the world beyond them.

Being an archaeologist with his roots east of the Baltic, Przemysław Urbańczyk comes to the subject with a different perspective to those of the other participants in this discussion. Urbańczyk is highly critical of the traditional view held by Scandinavians of their own history, and he emphasises how ideas about the unity and uniqueness of Nordic civilisation can obscure multifarious internal differences, as well as the effects of contacts with areas outside Scandinavia.

In the articles just summarised, a number of different approaches are employed and general questions asked about the uniqueness of Scandinavian, and especially Icelandic, civilisation in the Middle Ages. The papers which come next in this volume restrict their focus to texts and textual history to a greater degree than those that precede them, and with one exception (Joseph Harris's contribution), they direct their attention mainly towards medieval Icelandic texts. Margaret Clunies Ross signals this clearly in her title "Medieval Icelandic Textual Culture". Although medieval Icelandic texts are both many and varied and unique in one sense because of the dominance of the vernacular, they were not an isolated product in her view. Rather, they were connected both to other medieval literary traditions in Scandinavian countries and with European medieval literary culture, as is now generally recognised. Poetry in skaldic measures is, of course, one of the best examples of an unusual form but nonetheless it was utilised to communicate the general European world-view in religious poetry. Indigenous and foreign elements intertwine to such a degree in medieval Icelandic texts that attempts to determine their exact proportions are fruitless.

Rudolf Simek discusses the Icelandic world-view in the Middle Ages, responding to an idea that was espoused both by European and Icelandic scholars in the first part of the twentieth century, namely that the worldview of medieval Icelandic culture was of a dual nature. On the one hand, there was the western European and Christian dimension in which context men read, for the most part, the same books; on the other hand, the somewhat different world-view of the farmers was supposed to have been expressed in the writing of the country's history. Simek rejects this and holds only the former world-view to have influenced those who produced texts in Iceland; we can know nothing with regard to the latter, neither in Iceland nor in any other country. Simek does argue, however, that the Icelanders stood somewhat apart because of the unusual knowledge they had pertaining to two areas: firstly, pre-Christian mythology as preserved in skaldic poetry, and secondly, geographical knowledge about the north and the coasts beyond the Atlantic Ocean.

Torfi H. Tulinius places a particular emphasis on the notion that Icelandic texts were founded on European Christian culture, which is woven into narrative accounts and poetry about the world of the past to a greater extent than is visible on the surface; he accordingly presents some examples illustrating this. Torfi believes that ideas about purity and influence are not useful when explanations for medieval Icelandic civilisation are sought; it is more productive to apply a dynamic concept or model that can reveal how Icelandic culture constantly redefined itself and integrated the foreignness of the past with its contemporary secular Christian culture.

The next two authors are Icelandic philosophers, and both wrestle with the problem of defining the moral attitudes of the Icelandic sagas, thereby relating medieval Icelandic literary culture to more general philosophical debate. They each choose a narrow perspective from which to approach the study of Icelandic civilisation—texts which, as a matter of fact, are often regarded as kinds of cultural signifiers or symbols. They then analyse these texts with reference to debates on general philosophical problems or issues. First, Vilhjálmur Árnason deals with the concept of honour in the Icelandic sagas and critiques the different ways in which scholars have gone about approaching this concept. Vilhjálmur comes to the conclusion that two perspectives or viewpoints are at odds with each other in the sagas: an unconditional requirement for vengeance, and the community's need for peace. His article draws on *Njáls saga*, which shows how social order is doomed to failure because no means of release from this conflict exists. Svavar Hrafn Svavarsson compares ideas about honour and shame in medieval Icelandic texts with ancient Greek ideas. He sides with the philosophy that has criticised "the well known formulation of the distinction made by the anthropologist Ruth Benedict in 1947: "True shame cultures rely on external sanctions for good behavior, not, as true guilt cultures do, on an internalized conviction of sin. Shame is a reaction to other people's criticism""; it has frequently been claimed that the ethics of the Icelandic sagas are characterised by the attitudes of a shame culture. Svavar argues that the concepts of 'moral thickness' and 'thinness' are useful in shedding light on the relation between society and ethics in the world of the *Íslendingasögur*, and on how conceptual values therein became established as facts.

Joseph Harris's article, which is last in the volume, expands the focus of the area under discussion since the text on which he concentrates is the runic inscription on the Swedish Rök stone, dated to the first part of the ninth century. This lengthy (for a runic inscription) and complex text is an example of an early attempt to conjoin ancient skills or knowledge of texts with a newer technology, "an early stage in the battle of literacy with orality where, clearly, orality won out". The form and medium of expression of the Rök stone are certainly distinct from the Icelandic texts most frequently referred to in the preceding articles in this collection. Yet both in the text's content and in its form of expression, unequivocal signs of kinship may be discerned which suggest that the concept of a 'Nordic civilisation' is not exclusively the invention of scholars. This is corroborated in the article with frequent references to Egill Skallagrímsson's poem *Sonatorrek*.

When this volume is seen as a whole, certain distinctive features emerge from the cross-disciplinary dialogues. The authors seem to feel that there is a greater need to explain general premises and established research-positions than is normal in scholarly articles. This is quite natural in such a compilation, some going over the foundations laid by prior scholarship will be inevitable, precisely because of the nature of the inter-disciplinary discussion. Someone who comes to one research area from another area can see the shortcomings of the unfamiliar research area more clearly, and can also overlook the multiple nuances that reduce these shortcomings. In this volume, a variety of wide-reaching themes are touched on in order that discussion may continue to move forward, although conclusive answers to the problems may not be found.

The participants at the conference agreed that it would be desirable to publish written papers based on the lectures and discussion in Skálholt. In addition to those who gave papers, the respondents and other participants were invited to contribute material. The Stofnun Árna Magnússonar and the regular editors of *Gripla* approved the idea of publishing the collection of articles as the twentieth volume of *Gripla* and asked me to edit it. In carrying out this work I have benefitted from, and enjoyed, the cooperation of the authors, anonymous reviewers and the *Gripla* editors. Dr Emily Lethbridge worked on language and style in the papers where necessary, and translated some summaries and this introduction.

The Skálholt symposium received financial support from Háskóli Íslands (The University of Iceland), The Icelandic Ministry of Culture and Education, The Nordic Culture Fund, The Royal Gustavus Adolphus Academy for Swedish Folk Culture, and the Clara Lachmann Foundation. Part of the funding granted by the Nordic Culture Fund and the Ministry of Culture and Education was, with their agreement, used to support the publication of this volume. Heartfelt thanks go to each of these organisations.

Vésteinn Ólason

JÓHANN PÁLL ÁRNASON

A MUTATING PERIPHERY: MEDIEVAL ENCOUNTERS IN THE FAR NORTH

> Her gælder det i hvert fald, at vi ikke
> kan vide noget med sikkerhed... Det
> betyder ikke, at der ikke er plads for
> hypoteser eller fortolkning, men at
> disse er noget andet, der går videre
> end det objektive.
> (Meulengracht Sørensen 1991, 222, 226)

IN A PAPER on "Icelandic uniqueness or common European culture?", published a decade ago, Sverre Bagge suggested that a swing of the pendulum was apparent in recent scholarship on medieval Nordic culture in general and its Icelandic branch in particular: after a phase dominated by those who saw the region as "part of the common culture of Western Christendom", earlier views on the importance of pre-Christian traditions and on inventive uses of their legacy were back in favour (Bagge 1997, 418). Although it would be going too far to claim a new consensus on this point, the trend appears to have strengthened, and the following discussion will be based on that assumption. But the ongoing reappraisal of the pre-Christian background and its influence on cultural developments after conversion does not lead to a complete rehabilitation of the older approaches mentioned at the beginning of Bagge's paper; the formerly dominant paradigm was too obviously dependent on uncritical attitudes to sources to be reclaimable. The swing of the pendulum is, of necessity, accompanied by attempts to redefine the terms of reference for exploration of the pre-Christian past.

This approach could begin with general considerations of plausibility. In view of what comparative history tells us about the dynamics and consequences of civilizational expansion into regions with distinctive traditions, the notion of a completely and unilaterally Christianized North seems unconvincing. Adaptations, combinations and syncretisms are more likely. But this elementary observation does not help to clarify the particular patterns that crystallized on the northern periphery of Western Christendom. If we want to test the relevance of civilizational analysis to this issue, it would seem advisable to take note of earlier work in that vein. I will therefore discuss ideas put forward by authors who saw the medieval North from a civilizational angle, although they did not always use that language. The speculative character of their arguments should not deter us from closer examination: they may have asked questions that are still worth pursuing, even when the answers and the presuppositions reflected in them leave something to be desired, and undeveloped insights may be translatable into more adequate terms. This excursion through the history of ideas will be combined with a discussion of substantive issues. But to provide a background to both sides of the argument, a few introductory remarks on some key aspects of the civilizational frame of reference are in order.

The civilizational dimension: Definitions and examples

Civilizational analysis may now be seen as an established and thriving form of historical sociology, with links to classical sources and a formative phase beginning with a more recent revival. No comprehensive account can be attempted in this paper (for a more detailed discussion, see Arnason 2003). A few crucial points should, however, be noted; they will serve as signposts for closer engagement with the main theme.

1. Case studies and comparative analyses have shown that intertwined forms of religious and political life are the most central and revealing criteria for identifying civilizational patterns. Seen from a civilizational perspective, the religious and political spheres are not simply specific parts of a societal whole; rather, they are "meta-institutions" (to use a concept of Durkheimian origin), i.e. fundamental and interconnected components of the framework within which all domains of social life take shape, interact and develop along their own lines. On this level, religion and politics represent the core structures – structuring struc-

tures, to use the more technical language of sociological theory – of culture and power as elements of social life, whose mutually constitutive dynamics are perhaps most evident in processes of state formation.

2. Civilizational approaches have proved particularly instructive in regard to historical breakthroughs and turning-points, and the theoretical perspectives of scholars in the field have to some extent been influenced by their choice of paradigmatic cases. The historical watershed most important for our purposes is the transformation of the Roman world around the middle of the first millennium CE, resulting in the formation of three successor civilizations: Western Christendom, Byzantium and Islam. The post-Roman worlds represent unusually clear-cut cases of institutional cores crystallizing around interrelated religious and political patterns. Each of the three civilizations transformed the legacy of *sacrum imperium* in a distinctive way. The Western Christian separation of papal and imperial authority was crucial to the later course of European history. The Byzantine pattern was based on a much closer relationship between the two poles of authority and a more pre-eminent position of the imperial centre, although the traditional notion of caesaropapism is now rejected by the most knowledgeable historians. The Islamic variant seems to have begun with a vision of unified religious and political authority; a weaker version of this model – the caliphate – then gave way to more conjunctural coalitions of religious and political elites, but the civilizational utopia of a restored union survived as an intermittently active force.

This tripartite post-Roman world was the historical environment of Nordic expansion in the late first millennium. That process brought societies of the Nordic region into contact with three types of more advanced civilizations, but in different ways and with different results. At the same time, the dynamics of expansion went beyond the post-Roman context on two fronts: through contacts with the Inner Eurasian world on the eastern side, through colonization in the North Atlantic on the western one.

3. The three civilizations that divided the Mediterranean world between them can also be seen as exemplary cases of a more general problematic. Sacral rulership (this category seems preferable to the more restrictive

concept of sacred kingship) is both a recurrent phenomenon in otherwise different civilizational settings, and open to a wide range of variations in form as well as content that reflect and affect broader civilizational patterns. It is therefore a particularly promising – but so far not thoroughly explored – topic for comparative civilizational analysis. And there is another side to it: traditions of sacral rulership can function as bridges between different civilizational universes, and the result may be a unilateral transfer or a creative refashioning of older models. Not that the varieties of sacral rulership are uniformly adaptable: the mutual exclusivity of the three post-Roman paradigms is a striking counter-example. But the late Roman Empire, out of which the successor civilizations emerged, was the product of an intercivilizational encounter which transformed both sides. The progressive sacralization of the imperial institution paved the way for the Constantinian turn, which imposed a Christian version of sacral rulership. There was no pre-existing model of the latter, but the invention that began with Constantine's conversion could draw on evolving conceptions of the relationship between divine and human authority within the Christian counterculture, and this emerging tradition was in turn rooted in the civilizational innovation of Jewish monotheism. As has recently been argued, this theme is of key importance for comparative studies of the Nordic region as a civilizational area. Within the limits of this paper, there is no space to discuss Gro Steinsland's work (2000); suffice it to say that – in the present writer's opinion – the idea of sacred kingship in pre-Christian Scandinavia has been successfully rehabilitated. Steinsland's analyses of the specific Nordic version of this near-universal institution are sometimes convincing and always thought-provoking.

4. I have already used the term "intercivilizational encounter"; but the variations and vicissitudes of sacral rulership are only a part of the vast spectrum of phenomena to which this category can be applied. This is a highly significant but relatively neglected topic of civilizational studies. One of the most persistent weaknesses of traditional approaches to that field was a tendency to think of civilizations as mutually closed worlds. In fact, their interaction – at different levels, with more or less mutually formative results – is one of the most fundamental constitu-

tive features of world history. As for more specific forms, the dynamics and consequences of expansion are an especially rewarding theme for comparative studies. Military expansion is a recurrent and prominent aspect of the interaction between civilizations, but it often entails or facilitates intercivilizational encounters of a less coercive kind; in some cases, encounters of epoch-making significance occurred with little or no military involvement.

An Abortive Scandinavian Civilization?

Having noted some basic points about the civilizational frame of reference, let us now consider the case for a Nordic civilization, preceding Christianity or at least in the making when overtaken by Christianization, and begin with what seems to be (although often by hearsay only) the best-known discussion of this issue. Arnold Toynbee's account of "the abortive Scandinavian civilization" is perhaps most noteworthy for the discrepancy between questions and answers. Toynbee's way of posing the problem and defining its context is still instructive, but the conclusion – his attempt to identify the emerging distinctive features of a cultural world overwhelmed by Christianity – is unconvincing, and the main lesson to be learnt from it is negative: if the search for evidence of a Nordic or Scandinavian civilization is to make sense, it must take a different line.

Abortive civilizations – mature enough to leave a historical record, but thwarted by internal or external, natural as well as cultural forces – appear in various places and periods on Toynbee's map of world history, and two such cases are located in the medieval North: the Irish and the Scandinavian. The former was based on a local version of Christianity, and its fate was decided when the Roman Church triumphed in Anglo-Saxon England in the late seventh century. Here we are only concerned with the Scandinavian one. As Toynbee argues, its destinies can only be understood in the context of interaction with the Roman world and its subsequent transformation. This is a valid point, and still a useful reminder of the dimensions of the problem to be discussed; it remains to be seen how the successive phases of the story are treated. At the beginning, Scandinavia is a remote part of the northern periphery, open to some cultural influence (for one thing, the runic alphabet was a reinvention of the Roman model), but much less affected than the neighbouring barbarians. At a later stage, after the tripartite division of the Roman realm, the relationship between central and peripheral regions was redefined: the barbarians most directly drawn into the Roman orbit became key players in the reconstruction of a post-Roman West, and the overall geopolitical reconfiguration shifted the power centre of the region towards the northwest. But it is of some importance for Toynbee's account that – as far as Scandinavia is concerned – this second phase is not a direct continuation of the first. As he sees it, there was a period of segregation before the "re-establishment of contact between the Scandinavians and Western Christendom" (Toynbee 1951, 343). He explains the temporary separation as a consequence of Slavic migration into the vacuum left by Teutonic barbarians gone south. This reflects an exaggerated view of the Slavic impact on Central Europe, and it is also hard to reconcile with Toynbee's own statements about Saxony as a buffer zone between Franks and Scandinavians, destroyed by Charlemagne's conquest. Nor is it clear what happened to Scandinavia during the interval, but Toynbee seems to agree with Axel Olrik's assessment of the isolated "Northman" (sic): "In certain respects he became a barbarian again" (Ibid., 343). There is both a parallel and a contrast to the Irish trajectory; Ireland was also segregated, because of the Roman withdrawal from Britain and the collapse of Romanized culture throughout the island; but in this case, the presence of Christianity provided a civilizing impulse that was lacking in Scandinavia.

It seems clear that developments in parts of the erstwhile northern periphery (the continental, the insular and the peninsular) diverged during the period in question, but Toynbee's account does not do much to clarify the picture. However, the oversimplified notion of a period of segregation is essential to his narrative: a new beginning was needed, and the character of that beginning left its mark on the course of later events. The next round of the interaction between southern civilization and North European barbarism was initiated by the Carolingian Empire. Toynbee judges this new actor on the scene very harshly: it was an "abortive evocation of a ghost" and "a fiasco because it was both grandiose and premature" (Toynbee 1951, 344). The result of its self-destructive *hubris* was to trigger a counter-offensive from the north. Toynbee seems to assume that the spectacle of a richer civilization, represented by an aggressive but conspicuously fragile state, prompted the northerners to move into the European arena. But when he goes on to describe the Viking campaigns as "a supreme effort to overwhelm the civilizations of the South, which they encountered on their warpath, and to establish in their stead a new Scandinavian Civilization erected on barbarian foundations and unencumbered by reminiscences of a traditional style or by traces of a traditional ground-plan" (Ibid., 359), he is vastly overstating his case. There is nothing in his account – nor, for that matter, anywhere else – to support the idea of a civilizational mission inherent in the Viking expansion.

Toynbee does not think that the "new Scandinavian Civilization" ever stood a chance against Western Christendom. The civilizational resources of the adversary were superior and the response was overwhelming. But the North was conquered by the Church, not by the fraudulently restored empire that could never live up to its pretensions. As Toynbee sees it, the self-destructive dynamic of Carolingian imperialism left the field open for a more markedly civilizational – i.e., primarily religious – expansion, and he obviously does not believe that the German re-evocation of the imperial ghost changed this constellation in any basic way. His emphasis on the civilizational character of this final defeat inflicted on northern barbarism leads him to downgrade the role of converted kings and their violent assaults on paganism: the rulers traditionally credited with Christianizing their countries should be seen as figureheads of "a deep and gradual psychological mass-movement which statecraft might bring to a head, but which it could not have initiated and could not arrest" (Ibid., 353). Examples of rulers unsuccessfully using their power to enforce religious change are supposed to validate this claim. But the cases that Toynbee mentions are drawn from very disparate settings, and only a closer study of similarities and differences could justify any firm conclusions. More importantly, the dismissive view of individual monarchs implies a more fundamental disregard for kingship as an institution. It plays no role in Toynbee's discussion of the Scandinavian transformation.

If the outcome of the struggle was a complete absorption of the North into Western Christendom, where is the evidence for civilizational identity or aspirations on the losing side? Toynbee can only refer to reactive developments, temporary turns in a losing battle, and this part of his narrative boils down to two episodes. The description of the first is taken from Axel Olrik's work on Viking civilization: the "spirit of militant reaction... embodied... in the heroic figure of Starkad the Old" (Ibid., 351) represents a civilization on the defensive, and the final betrayal committed by the protagonist symbolizes an inevitable failure. This is a very tenuous foundation for arguments about an intercivilizational encounter, and it tells us nothing about positive beliefs, virtues or achievements of the losers. The second episode – the Icelandic *Kulturkampf*, as Toynbee describes it – is more revealing. In AD 1000, the Icelanders "capitulated" to an "alien civilization" (358), but the conversion was followed by a long-drawn-out rearguard struggle, The main line of defence was "backward-looking scholarship" (358), an antiquarian effort to reconstruct a lost world with intellectual tools borrowed from Christian culture and turned against its spirit. In this context, Toynbee seems to regard saga writing as nothing more than an imaginary extension of scholarship and an integral part of the antiquarian project. It is, in his view, highly significant that the period portrayed by the sagas does not extend beyond the immediate aftermath of conversion. He shows no interest in the particular kind of narratives developed in medieval Iceland, nor in the different directions taken by stories about the Icelandic past and about the Scandinavian world.

The *Kulturkampf* ended with an utter and irreversible defeat. In the fourteenth century, "the paralysis of the Icelandic genius is complete" (Ibid., 358). In fact, Toynbee seems to think that the Icelanders simply went bananas. His quotation from Olrik is worth reproducing *in extenso*: "The nation that once had so sharp an eye for the world of reality falls into slumber – politically, aesthetically, economically – and sleeps its sleep of centuries, full of disturbing dreams, while the elves shriek their shrill laughter from all the cliffs and the giants from all the rocky caves, while the earth quakes, and the fire-mountains shine, and souls fly about the crater of Hekla like black birds" (Ibid. 358, quoting Olrik 1939, 192). The finale, then, was not only a cultural annihilation, but also a "stupefyingly outlandish" (Ibid., 358) mental regression.[1]

---

[1] Follwing Olrik, but with added emphasis, Hauksbók is singled out as an exemplary cultural disaster. In his brief discussion of Toynbee, Sigurður Nordal (1993, II, 65–68) rightly takes him to task for this complete misjudgment. But some other points seem less obvious. Toynbee's view on the relative superiority of Scandinavian civilization (compared to ninth- and tenth-century Christianity) is more nuanced than Nordal appears to have thought.

What was the distinctive spirit of the civilization that lost its bearings so completely? What can justify the reference to twelfth- and thirteenth-century Iceland as attaining the "highest tension and finest harmony" of the "original Scandinavian ethos"? Antiquarianism alone cannot answer the question. When Toynbee finally tackles the issue, his view turns out to be a variation on a very widely shared *topos*: the secular rationalism and unsentimental realism of medieval Icelandic literature. But he introduces this theme through a very wide detour. The supposedly obvious affinities between medieval Icelandic prose and poetry on the one hand, Homeric epic on the other, are taken to reflect a similar civilizational condition; but it is an in-between situation, a mindset characteristic of cultures that have moved out of one world without as yet fully settling into another one: "Both these young civilizations are distinguished by a freedom from the incubus of tradition, which gives them a precocious freshness and originality, and by a freedom from the incubus of superstition, which gives them a precocious clarity and rationalism. Their members are fully aware both of the extent of their human powers, and of these powers' limitations..." (Toynbee 1951, 356). As used here, "tradition" and "superstition" are rubbery notions, but the context helps to clarify Toynbee's point: he is comparing societies that were no longer primitive but not yet at the level of full-fledged civilizations. In the Greek case, the ethos of the transitional phase was incorporated into an exceptionally productive and powerful civilizational pattern (Toynbee suggests as much when he links Herodotus's conception of history to the Homeric epics); in the Icelandic case, it was

---

In an appendix on what might have happened if the Vikings had won (one of the wildest speculations to be found in A Study of History), Toynbee suggests that Icelandic culture might have become the centre of a much larger world, and that "its aesthetic sensibility and intellectual penetration would have been of a rare quality", but he adds the very significant caveat that "its religious temperature would have been sub-normal" (441). Given the increasing importance of religion to Toynbee (it caused his project to explode in midstream), this must have appeared as a disqualifying handicap in a world that already knew universal religions. Toynbee is not as dependent on assumptions about oral tradition as Nordal claims (antiquarian scholarship is not synonymous with unbroken links to orality), and his chronology, although objectionable by today's standards, is not wildly off the mark: he refers to the period between 1150 and 1250 as the heyday of Icelandic culture, and does not propose a more detailed dating for the sagas. That said, Nordal's main objection to Toynbee is convincing: the whole scenario is simply incoherent. If the Icelanders capitulated to an alien civilization 1000 AD, where did the resources for a century-long *Kulturkampf* come from, one hundred and fifty years later?

obliterated after a foredoomed but articulate rearguard struggle; in many other cases, it must have come and gone too quickly to leave a significant record. We are, in other words, dealing with a recurrent phenomenon, inherent in the general dynamics of civilizing processes, but more markedly present in some cases than others. It does not take us very far when it is a question of defining the spirit of a specific civilization.

The Nordic episode in the making of Europe

The above discussion of Toynbee's views on the medieval North led to unequivocal conclusions: his answers do not match his questions. The evidence cited does not confirm speculation about a distinctive civilization in the making and a conceivable rival to the Christian constitution of Europe. This shortcoming becomes even more obvious when considered in light of more recent advances in civilizational analysis. Toynbee made no attempt to identify a configuration of religious and political patterns that would justify a claim to civilizational status.

In view of these unsatisfactory results, another look at Toynbee's background assumptions may be useful. As we have seen, his emphasis on Nordic expansion, its broad geopolitical scope and its interaction with the richer and ultimately more powerful societies of the South was a promising start; but there are some understated aspects that merit more attention. To reiterate a point made in another context: in Toynbee's presentation, the encounter with Western and Eastern Christendom (Islam plays a more shadowy role) overshadows two other arenas of expansion. On the one hand, the eastern flank entered into contact with a vast intercivilizational zone (the future Russia) and its adjacent cultures. On the other hand, expansion into the northwest Atlantic created new societies in previously uninhabited areas, and thus enlarged the Nordic region on an uncontested but challenging frontier. In both cases, broader geohistorical horizons are connected to the internal dynamics of Nordic societies during the period in question. On this latter issue, Toynbee has very little to say: apart from the re-barbarization supposed to have taken place between the *Völkerwanderung* and the Viking Age, there is next to no reference to transformations inside the region. In particular, the question of state formation is left out of account (this is, more generally speaking, a major blank spot in Toynbee's *Study of History*, whereas recent versions of civilizational analysis have taken it more and more seriously). A brief overview of basic facts will highlight the importance of this factor. Patterns and processes of state formation were involved in the changing relationship between Scandinavia and Western Christendom. The conquering and colonizing forays of the Viking Age culminated in a more constructive contribution to state building in different parts of Europe (the Norman inputs have been extensively described and sometimes exaggerated by historians of medieval Europe). As for the ultimately more decisive reverse movement, notions and visions of statehood were crucial to the integration of Scandinavia into Western Christendom; the imported models, grafted onto indigenous trends, were in part directly linked to the Church as a core civilizational institution, in part embedded in the broader civilizational patterns that accompanied Christianization.

State formation was, in short, an eminently significant field of interaction between North and South. But its ramifications also went beyond that context on the two frontiers mentioned above. In the east, the directions and outcomes of state formation were shaped by a very different environment; new approaches to the origins of Russia have highlighted the complexity of this background. It is beyond the scope of the present paper (for a very wide-ranging and rather speculative discussion, see Pritsak 1981). My main concern will be with developments on the other frontier. Questions about the conditions, varieties and limits of state formation also arise in connection with the colonization of the Northwest Atlantic, and here the main case in point is – to anticipate later arguments – the trajectory of the Icelandic Freestate (I follow Borgolte (2002), Byock (2000) and Hastrup (1985) in using this term; it seems more adequate than other labels on offer).

But before moving in this direction, it may be useful to take a look at another interpretation of the medieval North, obsolete in some ways but still of interest because of its attempt to bring the Northwest Atlantic into focus as a historical region. Christopher Dawson's work on the making of Europe can, to some extent, be read as an alternative to Toynbee's project, albeit on a much smaller scale. It is still one of the most articulate Catholic readings of European history. A chapter on "The age of the Vikings and the conversion of the north" (Dawson 1974 [1934], 202–217) deals with the place and role of the Nordic region in the making of a Christian Europe, and it is an outstanding example of a detour made to fit into an orthodox order of things. The framework for Dawson's analysis is a story of two barbarian assaults on Roman-Christian Europe, the *Völkerwanderung* and the Viking raids. As he sees it, the second came closer to destroying the heartland from which a mature Europe was to emerge ("Western civilization was reduced to the verge of dissolution" – 209), but ended with a more definitive victory of Christian faith and its ideas of order. Dawson's description of the background to the second assault still seems instructive: "... an old and in some respects highly developed culture which yet possessed few possibilities for peaceful expansion. During its centuries of isolation, it had carried the art and ethics of war to a unique pitch of development. War was not only the source of power and wealth and social prestige, it was also the dominant preoccupation of literature and religion and art" (Ibid., 203). Nordic ideas of kingship were cast in this cultural mould, and so were the power structures of the kingdoms taking shape on the eve of expansion.

But taken as a whole, Dawson's view of late antique and early medieval history is no longer a serious proposition. New approaches to the *Völkerwanderung*, now seen as an aspect of the transformation of the Roman world, have demolished the original model of the barbarian assault, and *eo ipso* its derivative versions; medievalists now seem to agree that traditional accounts of the ninth- and tenth-century invasions (Viking, Muslim and Magyar), and especially the estimates of their impact, were vastly exaggerated; last but not least, a better understanding of the early medieval "economy of plunder" has somewhat attenuated the contrast between the Vikings and the power elites of the societies which they attacked.

For present purposes, the obsolete framework is less important than a particular twist in Dawson's use of it. He reconstructs the story of the showdown between Christian Europe and its northern barbarians in a way that allows for a very noteworthy sideshow in the Northwest. Nordic – i.e. mainly Norwegian – colonization of the Northwest Atlantic created a "maritime empire" that ultimately extended from Greenland and Iceland to footholds in Ireland, Scotland and England. More importantly, conquest paved the way for cultural transfer and innovation: "In this way, there arose in the ninth century a mixed Celtic-Nordic culture which reacted upon the parent cultures, both in Ireland and in Scandinavia" (Ibid., 211). At first sight, the cultural growth that took place in this part of the northern periphery seems marked by a paradox: on the one hand, the contact with Christian Ireland appears as an essential precondition, but on the other hand, the signal achievement of the Northwest was the sublimation of the traditional Viking spirit into an original culture.

Before considering the transfiguration of this paradox in Icelandic literature (as interpreted by Dawson), let us note that this line of argument focuses attention on two issues that still haunt discussions about the Viking Age and its sequel, but have proved very difficult to tackle in precise terms, let alone to resolve. First, Dawson stresses the emergence of a new *Geschichtsregion* (to use the term favoured by German historians, who have done most to develop comparative approaches to this problematic) in the Northwest Atlantic; it included newly settled territories as well as zones of contact (both through more peaceful exchange) with Anglo-Saxon and Celtic societies. There can be no doubt about the significance of this regional configuration, but sources are so fragmentary that attempts to trace its internal connections can easily take a speculative turn (for an intriguing recent contribution, see Helgi Guðmundsson 1997). The second issue is best seen as a particular aspect of the first, but has had a life of its own. The question of Gaelic and more specifically Irish influence on Nordic culture in general and Icelandic literature in particular is notoriously intractable (for a recent, comprehensive and cautious discussion, see Gísli Sigurðsson 1988). Dawson's statements on this are not as clear as we might desire, but may be worth closer scrutiny. He begins with a very general claim about the influence of the Irish literary tradition on the younger Icelandic one, but cites no concrete examples, and goes on to contrast the "fantastic rhetoric" of Irish narratives with the sobriety and "psychological truth of the Icelandic saga" (Dawson 1974, 212). The former is, in a sense, pre-medieval, whereas the latter is proto-modern. The underlying suggestion is – although Dawson never says it in so many words – that Irish literary culture acted as a catalyst rather than a model: the contact triggered the crystallization of a very different imaginary. A second and much closer encounter with Christianity then led to the introduction of literacy, and in this case, a much more far-reaching adaptation to new modes of thought was inevitable (but it should not be mistaken for a complete substitution). It is not obvious, at least not to the present writer, that later scholarship has come up with a better answer to the Irish question.

To conclude, Dawson's interpretation of the Icelandic sequel to the Celtic-Nordic encounter is best summarized in his own words. It places a stronger emphasis on Eddic poetry than on the sagas (the unstated premise is that oral traditions behind the Older Edda underwent a fundamental reinterpretation in Iceland), and the main thesis has to do with paradigms of the human condition. For Dawson, the Eddic spirit transfigures the heroic ideal and brings the tragic vision of life to unequalled perfection: "The Eddic conception of life is no doubt harsh and barbaric, but it is also heroic in the fullest sense of the word. Indeed, it is something more than heroic, for the noble viragos and bloodthirsty heroes of the Edda possess a spiritual quality that is lacking in the Homeric world. The Eddic poems have more in common with the spirit of Aeschylus than with that of Homer, though there is a characteristic difference in their religious attitude. Their heroes do not, like the Greeks, pursue victory or prosperity as ends in themselves. They look beyond the immediate issue to an ultimate test to which success is irrelevant. Defeat, not victory, is the mark of the hero... There is no attempt, as in the Greek way of life, to justify the ways of gods to man, and to see in their acts the vindication of eternal justice. For the gods are caught in the same toils of fate as men... they have become themselves the participants in the heroic drama. They carry on a perpetual warfare with the powers of chaos, in which they are not destined to conquer" (Ibid., 213).

The *Völuspá* is, unsurprisingly, cited as a prime source. But Dawson seems puzzled by some of its themes and inclined to argue that they are neither Celtic nor Nordic, neither Scandinavian nor Christian. "Above all, it is strange to find in the *Volospa* (sic) an idea which seems to us so difficult and recondite as that of the Eternal Return" (Ibid., 213). Be that as it may, the poem is for him the apogee of pre-Christian Nordic spirituality. At this point, however, the latent thrust of Dawson's analysis comes to the fore: the perfection of Celtic-Nordic culture turns out to be a prelude to Christianity, and a proper understanding of its message makes it possible to grasp the conversion of Iceland as "not merely a matter of political expediency; it was the acceptance of a higher spiritual ideal" (Ibid., 216).

Dawson's Iceland is, in short, the place where the internal evolution of paganism made it most ready for Christianization. In this scenario, there is – in contrast to Toynbee – no *Kulturkampf* and no capitulation, only a mature surrender to superior truth. But Dawson's claim that the conversion was in the spirit of *Völuspá* can also be contrasted with Halldór Laxness's observation that it reflected the spirit of *Hávamál* (Laxness 1946, 34). Of the three, Laxness was probably closest to the view that seems most compatible with contemporary scholarship: that the Icelandic way of embracing Christianity was a judiciously balanced compromise with a changed environment. As such, it obviously did not preclude further acculturation.

The view from Thule: Re-formative dynamics in Iceland

So far, I have discussed interpretations that began with a focus on the Nordic region as a whole and its interaction with the European world into which it was in the end integrated. From such points of view, Iceland appears as the periphery of a periphery, but not only in the sense that it was located on the outer fringe: its history and culture brought the peripheral condition of a much larger area to more articulate expression than elsewhere. At this point, it seems appropriate to turn the perspective around and consider Iceland as a starting-point for reflections that may then throw light on the problematic of a larger historical region. This approach will be explored through a brief and very selective reflection on Sigurður Nordal's *Íslenzk menning*, which has – to the best of my knowledge – never been subjected to the close reading that it merits (I intend to continue that part of the discussion in another paper).

But before tackling interpretive problems, a few words should be said about the historical setting. The patterns of continuity and discontinuity in Icelandic history – from the settlement to the acceptance of Norwegian sovereignty – differ from those of the Nordic kingdoms during the same period, and this point is crucial to the following discussion. There were no less than five major landmarks or turning-points in the history of the Icelandic Freestate. The first was the settlement itself: a fragment of Nordic society, or perhaps more precisely several Nordic societies, as they had developed during the Viking Age, was transplanted to a new environment where both different living conditions and the experience of migration — as well as, to some extent the different cultural backgrounds of the settlers — were bound to affect the directions of social and cultural development in several significant ways. The second, most decisive but also most difficult to grasp and most irresistibly conducive to speculation, was the tenth-century turn to state formation on a geopolitical, social and cultural basis that set the beginnings as well as the long-term dynamics apart from comparable processes in Scandinavia. The third was the conversion to Christianity; in one sense this is the most visible landmark, but there is still room for a good deal of controversy on the meaning of the *siðaskipti*, as well as on the distinction between conversion date and conversion period (proposed by Peter Foote 2004). The fourth shift is more difficult to date, but it was clearly under way in the late twelfth century: a new twist to state formation, in much less regulated and more internecine ways than before, led to the emergence of a few family and territory-based blocs, whose rivalry destroyed the framework of the Freestate. Sigurður Nordal refers to this phase as a "revolutionary time" (Sigurður Nordal 1942, 351, repr. 1993 I, 412). The final episode was the incorporation into an ascendant and expanding Norwegian kingdom; this was a rapid transition, but it is best understood as a process that includes events before and after 1262–1264.

All these discontinuities have been emphasized in recent scholarship on medieval Iceland. They are doubly important for our present concerns. On the one hand, questions about civilizational commonalities and differences between Iceland and the rest of the Nordic world must be posed with due regard to the historical context of ruptures and reorientations. To anticipate a point that will only be adumbrated in this paper, the above picture of Icelandic history casts doubt on the idea of a Scandinavian civilization surviving for some four centuries after the settlement. Rather, the Icelandic experience appears as a very distinctive episode within Western Christendom, turning a peripheral location to political as well as cultural advantage and combining the resources borrowed from more developed civilizational centres with elements of pre-Christian traditions. It is, in other words, better understood as a highly specific and background-dependent variant of the civilization then entering its flourishing phase in Western Europe, rather than the last stand of another civilization on the wane. On the other hand, the representative — and that means, to all intents and purposes, literary — products of Icelandic culture, and especially those to which we may want to attribute a civilizational meaning, must also be understood as attempts to cope with discontinuity and maintain an overarching tradition. This latter point has been stressed in recent scholarship on the sagas (e.g. Vésteinn Ólason 1998, Meulengracht Sørensen 1993).

From settlement to state formation

The third of the abovementioned turning-points is the most crucial. More precisely, the Icelandic mode of conversion explains both sides of the constellation that prevailed during the first quarter of the second millennium CE: a unique situation within Western Christendom and an ability to relate to the pre-Christian past in unorthodox ways. As Gunnar Karlsson (2004) has emphasized, the distinctive historical phenomenon of Christianity without monarchy is the key to the cultural achievements of medieval Iceland. But it was the peculiar structure of the pre-Christian polity that made the Icelandic separation of Christ and king possible, and this will be the main theme of the following discussion. As for the first landmark, there has been much speculation about the characteristics and consequences of the settlement, but for present purposes, the main point is that the settlers took a particularly circuitous road back to the long-term pattern of European state formation. The first step was, as Meulengracht Sørensen (2000, 21) put it, a "re-formation, which took a different direction from the evolution of society in Scandinavian and British lands." The resultant socio-political regime was, as he adds, "both more innovative and more archaic than those of the old countries."

In what sense was the re-formation a new beginning of state formation? Rather than taking that for granted, we should pause to consider the problems involved. Can we speak of a state where there is no governmental apparatus, no executive authority backed up my means of coercion, and no central taxation? The difficulty with labelling the Icelandic regime a state is not unlike the more frequently cited case of the ancient city-states (although the latter were mostly endowed with more salient attributes of statehood); and the problem can, in my opinion, be solved in the same way: through a flexible use of Max Weber's political sociology. As the very extensive discussion of this subject has shown, Weber's unfinished work uses two concepts of the state, and the relationship between them was never clarified. The rational-bureaucratic model of the state, which Weber had in mind when he argued that the state had only existed in the Occident, is still used by historians who claim that Europe – more precisely late medieval and early modern Europe – invented the state and spread it to the rest of the world. It is even less applicable to medieval Iceland than to the Greek *polis*. The much more general definition of the state in terms of a monopoly of legitimate violence within a certain territory can be extended to a much broader spectrum of societies, modern and premodern. But it does not solve our problem: there was, notoriously, no monopoly of violence. At this point, however, we can turn to Weber's complementary concept of political community. It is defined as a community whose collective action consists in imposing an orderly domination by the participants on a territorial domain (which can be more or less clearly demarcated), by means of a readiness for physical violence.

We can take this sketch one step further. If order and violence revolve around a centre endowed with eminent authority (and it has been plausibly argued that human societies cannot do without some kind of such a centre), that centre can be more or less separate from the community, and approximate more or less closely to the criteria already noted as defining features of statehood in the more general sense. It can, in particular, move towards a monopoly of violence; but violence can also be regulated rather than monopolized (even through the incorporation of institutions as centrifugal as the feud). To put it another way, the political centre is an intermediate category between the political community and the state. Explicit construction of a centre comes closer to state formation than the ongoing functioning of a centre embedded in ancestral custom. On the other hand, the explicit project can aim at minimizing the distance between the centre and the political community, and in the process, functions previously or elsewhere identified with state structures may be shifted to other institutions – invented, inherited, or readjusted.

The Icelandic Freestate is best understood in terms of such a self-limiting process of state formation. So are the Greek *polis* and the Roman republic, albeit in very different ways. Such processes are reflexive in a double sense: they involve an explicit project of institution building (the level of articulation and the scope of construction vary widely), and they relate to a world of other states. Both points are relevant to the Icelandic "re-formation." To quote Jesse Byock (2000, 66): "Although it would be going too far to assume that the settlers and their descendants knew exactly what they wanted, available evidence does suggest that the early Icelanders knew quite well what they did not want." What they did not want was what they saw happening to others, and the desire to avoid it led to a limited but operative consensus on what should be done. Comparative reflections will help to clarify what this mix of negative and positive goals amounted to. But to begin with, let us return to Nordal's reflections on the origins of the Icelandic polity. What remains important and merits closer examination is a very distinctive analysis of the relationship between Viking ethos and Icelandic culture, Viking expansion and Icelandic state-building. Nordal begins by noting that Viking assaults and conquests lacked the religious (and, as we might now say, civilizational) dimensions characteristic of Islamic expansion as well as of the crusades (Sigurður Nordal 1942, 76). Nor were they backed up by centralized power structures of the kind that sustained nomad expansion across Eurasia. The Viking pattern enabled an exceptionally large number of people to "exercise independent leadership, assuming responsibility at their own risk" (Ibid., 76).

There was, in short, no civilizational or imperial dynamic at work in Viking expansion.[2] But in Nordal's view, this does not mean that it had no cultural meaning or potential. He argues that visions of a "more aristocratic (*höfðinglegra*) life" than the Vikings could lead at home went beyond mere plundering and could translate into more lasting achievements (Ibid., 76). Obviously, this meant – in the first instance – a quest for more stable forms of power and wealth. But further aspirations, which Nordal links to his key philosophical concept of *þroski* (I will, for present purposes, leave it untranslated), led to efforts to gain access to a more advanced civilization, including its intellectual and aesthetic spheres. The question to be raised at this point is whether such ambitions could, in another context, become a

---

[2] The only exception (a very inconsequential one) is Canute's shortlived early eleventh-century attempt to build a North Sea empire. "Viking empire" is therefore strictly speaking a misnomer; and if it can now be used as a book title (Forte et al. 2006), that says more about the current marketability of empires and Vikings than about anything else.

source of significant variations to the cultural and institutional patterns that prevailed in the surrounding European world. At that level, we would be dealing with civilizational results and ramifications of a process that originally seemed to have no such significance. As I will try to show, this is precisely Nordal's line of argument. In Iceland, the ethos of Viking expansion was transfigured into a spirit of state formation (this term is used by analogy with the "spirit of capitalism", as defined by Weber and others, i.e. to denote inbuilt cultural orientations of institutional dynamics); this set the scene for further combinations of innovation and archaism, including an exceptionally long-drawn encounter between paganism and Christianity.

The Viking ethos, as described by Nordal, was doubly resistant to central authority: the principal actors were small units, rather than expanding states in pursuit of more power, and these units were organized in a relatively egalitarian way. When the conquerors and colonizers came into closer contact with established power structures, these habits gave way to more hierarchical patterns on both levels. But where a shared order had to be created anew, the de-centralized, individualistic and egalitarian trends could remain strong enough to leave their mark on the emerging regime. It is not being suggested that the Icelandic mode of state formation was wholly unique; Nordal notes the beginnings of a similar political culture in the Isle of Man and the Faroe Islands (Ibid., 105). But there were several factors that set Iceland apart. It was not only virgin territory; it was also big enough to make it possible for the project to unfold on an incomparably larger scale than elsewhere; and it was remote enough for external threats to be minimal. Aspirations to autonomy came naturally to the settler community. It should, however, be noted that Nordal is not talking about national independence or sovereignty. As he sees it (Ibid., 98), the awareness of a separate Icelandic identity was comparable to regional identities within the emerging Norwegian, Swedish and Danish kingdoms. But the fact that a comparable collective identity was linked to a higher level of political autonomy made the Icelandic constellation, in the long run, more conducive to nation formation.

So far, I have discussed the cultural matrix of state formation. It is time to consider the formative events as such, i.e. the decisive moves towards common statehood. Nordal's analysis of them is worth reconstructing in some detail; it is a largely and explicitly conjectural account, but to my mind a very plausible one. The story begins with a strong emphasis on the ambitious, deliberate and artificial character of the project that was implemented in the first half of the tenth century (Ibid., 102–108). A common state, however minimal in terms of central authority and coercive machinery, was neither necessitated by external threats nor imposed by internal problems. The settlement was not a collective enterprise; the living conditions of a small community scattered throughout a large island were not conducive to massive conflicts, and there is no obvious reason why the settlers could not have muddled through without a constitutional order – perhaps with local assemblies on a smaller scale – for a much longer time. In Weberian terms, the creation of this order was a rationalizing breakthrough; Toynbee's model of challenge and response is applicable, but it must be added that the response took shape through inventive interpretation of traditions and circumstances. There was, however, another side to the state-building project. Nordal discusses it twice (Ibid., 107 and 123–124), briefly in both cases but with a clear focus on the essentials. Political innovation must, as he sees it, have been backed up by religious authority. To him it seems clear that laws were given a sacral status through a connection to pagan religion (in a broad, quasi-Durkheimian sense), probable that various kinds of belief ("*ýmiss konar átrúnaður*") entered into the details of lawmaking, and possible that the institutional terms *goði* and *goðorð* had an old religious content. This was not a sufficient basis for a hierocracy (this Weberian term seems the most adequate translation of Nordal's *prestaveldi*), and what we know about paganism in Iceland indicates that it was too unstructured (or de-structured) to sustain a model of divine legislation. On the other hand, Nordal suggests (this is the most conjectural part of the argument) that beliefs relating to *landvættir* and other numinous beings (*goðmögn*) may have motivated efforts to consolidate the relationship to a new country, and that a certain reordering of religious life may therefore have accompanied the foundation of a political order.

This description of a constitutive but flexible relationship between religion and politics is obviously to the taste of civilizational analysts. It may be useful to underline the point through a brief comparative excursus. Recent debates on the origins of the Greek *polis* seem to have highlighted two themes. On the one hand, even the early *poleis* were "cities of reason"

(Murray 1990), i.e. political communities shaped by extensive rational reconstruction, and this is particularly evident in the subordination of kinship to principles of a constructed order. On the other had, historians dealing with this period have also found the concept of *polis* religion useful: it stresses the pervasive role of religion in the institutions and practices of the *polis*, without returning to the discredited interpretation of the "ancient city" as a wholly and immutably religious community. Taken together, the two perspectives reveal a constitutive but flexible relationship between religion and politics, comparable – *mutatis mutandis* – to the one suggested above. A religious framework was essential to the continuity and demarcation of the collectivity, but the particular characteristics of this religion gave a very large scope to political action, construction and reasoning. The sources do not allow for more than a highly tentative account of the early *polis*, and that applies even more to the Icelandic Freestate; but with that proviso, and with due regard to the very different circumstances and outcomes, the two historical situations seem comparable. It may be added that in both cases, we seem to be dealing with religious universes in a somewhat de-structured state: they had to a certain extent decomposed under the impact of geopolitical and civilizational upheavals. That said, subsequent developments could not have differed more starkly: *polis* religion was reintegrated and went on to enjoy a very long life, whereas the recomposition that might have accompanied early state formation in Iceland and elsewhere in the North was cut short by the triumph of Christianity.

It would, of course, be very misleading to think of state formation as a spontaneous outgrowth of the changing relationship between religion and politics. No account of the process would make sense without assumptions about agency and strategy, and Nordal is very clear on this point. As he argues, the only plausible explanation of the very big step towards statehood is that "a solid and suitably large coalition of chieftains who already had extensive power" (Ibid., 107) set out to consolidate and coordinate their positions. There must, in other words, have been a bid for more – and more structured – power. This claim is backed up by a detailed attempt to show that one particular family was the core of the coalition. To the best of my knowledge, later scholars have neither refuted the hypothesis nor taken it further. Be that as it may, the result was, and could only be, "an oligarchy, an aristocracy" (Ibid., 108 – "*fámennisveldi, höfðingja-*

veldi"). But it was an oligarchy with a difference. Its architects had to come to terms with the fact that the settler community was a "bad material for an obedient underclass" (Ibid., 120). If the project had aimed at containing the ethos of individualism and equality within a power elite, the result showed that it had to be accommodated on a much larger scale. Nordal argues that the chieftains who embarked on state building must have expected their power to grow, and to translate into effective taxation (Ibid., 120). That did not happen; they had to settle for a *modus vivendi* that may be described as an "aristo-democracy" (Ibid, 120), and for a leadership role built on very fragile foundations.

If this interpretation is accepted, it seems compatible with Jesse Byock's analysis of "proto-democratic tendencies" at work in Icelandic society (Byock 2000, 65). But his claim that "farmers collectively retained control over coercive power" (25) seems to go too far, and so does the reference to a "prototype democracy in action" on the back cover of the book (I do not know whether the latter formulation fully reflects Byock's views). In Nordal's view, the Freestate was not a democracy: it was a half-thwarted oligarchy, a historical stalemate that perpetuated itself for a remarkably long span of time (if it was a "masterpiece" (Ibid., 120), it was an unintentional one). The uneasy combination of typological labels – aristocracy, oligarchy, democracy – reflects the complexity of the phenomenon in question, rather than any inconsistency of the argument. Nordal's difficulties are comparable to those of historians dealing with the early *polis*: its oligarchic character is undeniable, but so is the presence of aristocratic ambitions and networks that often clashed with oligarchic institutions, and it is still a hotly debated issue whether – or to what extent – the early *polis* prefigured democracy. But whatever view we take of parallels and differences at the beginning, there is a massive contrast between later developments of the two political formations. The democratizing dynamic that unfolded in some of the Greek *poleis* – and triumphed in the most important one – has no parallel in the history of the Freestate. Its key institutions underwent some reforms, but there seems to be no reason at all to link them to democratizing trends or pressures. The changes that – in the end – damaged the Freestate beyond repair began much later and were of a very different kind: a new oligarchic offensive upset the institutional balance and created new realities on the ground.

The Althing was the political centre that gave the whole regime the character of a state, albeit a very inchoate one. Nordal analyzes its multiple roles at some length (1942, 142–152, 1993 I, 177–187). But although he does not explicitly dwell on the point, the most telling way to sum up his argument is to stress that the Freestate was an anti-monarchic polity. To grasp the implications of this description, a brief comparative *tour d'horizon* is needed. Monarchy – the embodiment of the separate centre in a single ruler – emerges as the characteristic form of statehood in early civilizations and remains, for a very long time, the dominant type in more advanced ones; sacral rulership – open to structural variations and historical changes form the outset – was, as noted above, the primary pattern of monarchy. On the other hand, the monarchic principle was in practice subject to limitations (social, political and cultural), and its institutional forms incorporated the limiting forces in more or less explicit ways. In some historical situations, the counterweights can develop into alternative models, and state formation then takes an anti-monarchic turn. The legacies of such transformations – and of the cultural developments which they made possible – became key components of the European tradition. As Jan Assmann (2000) has convincingly argued, the invention of monotheism in Ancient Israel belongs in this context, but in a very paradoxical way: the idea of a divine legislator de-values the institution of sacred kingship and changes the relationship between state and community, but does not – apart from a brief phase of hierocracy – translate into a new kind of political order. At the same time, monotheism paves the way for new and more transcendent interpretations of monarchy, but they did not crystallize until after further detours. An epoch-making anti-monarchic turn occurred in the Greek *polis*, and then – in very different circumstances – in the Roman republic. In the long run (i.e. beginning with late antiquity), the legacies of Greek and Roman deviations from monarchy were absorbed into civilizational patterns centring on a new alliance of monotheism and monarchy. From this final synthesis of several traditions, medieval Western Christendom inherited ideas and images of monarchy that in due course developed along three main lines: through efforts to restore imperial authority, evolving models of kingship linked to other cultural backgrounds but adapted to the dominant framework, and the consolidation of the Church as a papal monarchy. Within this unfolding historical context, new anti-monarchic turns could occur, and the Icelandic Freestate may be compared to other cases (see e.g. Borgolte 2002, ch. 2.2: "Freistaaten unter Monarchien: Was Island von den italienischen Kommunen unterscheidet").

There is, however, another side to the question. As the record shows, the rejection of monarchy went hand in hand with continuing concern with it, efforts to make sense of it and evaluate its different forms, and even elaborations of new models for monarchic rule. In this fundamental sense, anti-monarchic turns were ambiguous, sometimes to the point of imaginary self-cancellation. Some recurrent historical reasons for this ambiguity may be noted. There was, in the first place, a general social rationale for strong monarchic rule, never easy to dismiss: the ruler was envisioned as "one before whom the rich and the well-born were as vulnerable as the little man" (Hodgson 1974, I, 282). To put it another way, visions of strong monarchy lent themselves to association with social justice. But they also served to focus the pursuit of power for its own sake. Monarchy represented an eminent, inherently expansive and particularly meaning-laden form of power. Although only a few monarchies could realize imperial ambitions, it can be argued that there is an elective affinity between the ideas of monarchy and empire: "Dans la domination..., il y a, latente, la perspective d'une domination universelle" (Gauchet 1985, 38). At a more modest level, aspirants to power in non-monarchic regimes were prone to monarchic temptations. Finally, the court societies that crystallized around monarchic rulers became cultural centres of a very distinctive kind and with considerable radiating power. Norbert Elias's classic analysis of early modern court society opened up a vast field for comparative study of such cases (Elias 1983).

For all these reasons, the spectre of monarchy haunts the political life and the social imaginary of non-monarchic regimes. The richest evidence for this comes from Ancient Greece (see especially Carlier 1984). To cut a very long story short, the Greeks engaged with monarchy on four different levels. Marginal or strangely transmuted forms of monarchic institutions survived within the context of a political culture centred on non-monarchic patterns. A fundamentally illegitimate form of monarchy, striving for more stable authority, emerged as a response to crises of the *polis*; the Greeks called it tyranny. Efforts to make sense of monarchic orders in the neighbouring Near East brought new perspectives to bear on the indigenous traditions of these civilizations. Finally, and in close connection with the last-mentioned aspect, we can – following Carlier – distinguish between the institution of monarchy and the imaginary signification of kingship; Greek elaborations of the latter, articulated through a variety of cultural genres, had a lasting impact on later ways of theorizing and justifying monarchy.

After this brief comparative excursus, let us return to the Icelandic Freestate. Its deviation from the monarchic mainstream was muted by several factors. The settlers, or at least the most significant part of them, came from a country on which they remained dependent in various respects and with which they continued to identify, in a way that seems to have been compatible with a sense of being a separate community (cf. Kirsten Hastrup's model of a multi-layered Icelandic identity). They had migrated overseas, removed themselves from the orbit of monarchies competing for territorial possessions, and military conflict with a monarchic enemy was never a likely possibility. On the other hand, the resistance to monarchic aspects of the civilizational current coming in from Western Europe was remarkably stubborn. As noted above, the power elite of the Freestate engineered a conversion to Christianity without submission to monarchy. After conversion, the Church was organized in a way that set strict limits to the influence of the rising papal monarchy. Descriptions of the first bishops as kinglike figures should not be taken at face value: they reflect the official self-image of a Church that had more control over textual production in the first stage of literacy than in the closing decades of the Freestate. In this respect Sigurður Nordal's analysis of the early bishops as partners in an oligarchic coalition seems realistic.

If the institutional resistance to monarchy is beyond doubt, what about the cultural and ideological domains? Did the culture of the Freestate articulate the complex attitudes to monarchy mentioned above in connection with other cases? The problem must be posed with proper regard to the cultural genres that come into question. Medieval Icelanders did not theorize about monarchy; they wrote sagas about kings. Images of kingship, including contrasting models of an ideal ruler, figure prominently in these narratives. A certain optical illusion seems inherent in the genre: when kings take centre stage in a story, their presence and their pretensions tend to overshadow other sides of the picture. And in light of the above analysis, the positive aspects and connotations of kingship, as portrayed in the sagas, are unsurprising. There is, nevertheless, solid evidence of a distinctive, detached and to some extent de-mystifying attitude to the ascendant monarchies of the Nordic world. Sverre Bagge argues, to my mind convincingly, that there was a "greater emphasis on politics and explanation in Old Norse historiography" than in the dominant European traditions (Bagge 1997, 428; see also Bagge 1991). The shift towards intelligible political meanings and motives was a major innovation – not a leap beyond the medieval universe of discourse, but a new opening within it. And if *Heimskringla* appears as the paradigmatic example of the political turn, that is also because it tells us more about what Canetti called the "entrails of power" (see the chapter "*Eingeweide der Macht*" in Canetti 1996, 237–263) than did the mainstream Christian historiography of the times. This is particularly clear when it deals with the violent progress of Christianization: the underside of a story that already existed in more hagiographic versions is brought to light (see also von See 1999, 311–344).

Another aspect of Bagge's analysis is worth mentioning; as he sees it, Snorri perceived and portrayed the Norwegian political scene in light of his own political lifeworld, i.e. the conflict-ridden and collapsing Icelandic Freestate (Bagge 1991, 237–240). This approach stands in marked contrast to the emerging self-representation of the Norwegian monarchy, systematized in the *Speculum regale,* and may be seen as a way of cutting the mystique of king, court and sacred order down to size. There are other clues that point to similar conclusions. In recent scholarship (e.g. Sverrir Jakobsson 2005), attention has been drawn to the uniquely eminent position of the Byzantine emperor – not only in the kings' sagas, but also in narratives whose main action takes place in Iceland. It would not seem far-fetched to understand this continuing reverence – *prima facie* surprising in the Western Christian context – as a way to downgrade closer neighbours. The Byzantine summit of kingship was prestigious enough to overshadow lesser figures and remote enough to pose no threat.

There is, of course, still room for controversy on Icelandic visions of and attitudes to monarchy. Ármann Jakobsson's recent works on this subject (Ármann Jakobsson 1997, 2002) contain an unequalled wealth of information drawn from the whole range of the sources, but his conclusion that the kings' sagas "all show kingship in a favourable light" (Ármann

Jakobsson 1997, 318), and that none of them can therefore be regarded as more or less royalist than the others, seems one-sided. In the first place, the abovementioned distinction between kingship as an imaginary signification and monarchy as a historical institution may be relevant to this issue. A cluster of values and virtues associated with kingship represents the enduringly attractive side of monarchy, but the record as a whole does not suggest that its appeal – due to the reasons noted above – led to an unreserved embrace of the monarchic alternative. Moreover, the ability to distinguish between different "images of sovereignty" (Richard Gaskins) and contrasting ideals of rulership reflects a detachment that precluded identification with a given order. The very fact that it has proved difficult to identify clear preferences for one model as against another (does *Heimskringla* favour peasant or warrior kings?) indicates an ongoing confrontation that could only be sustained at a distance from monarchic rule. Last but not least, I find Theodore Andersson's argument about the shift from kings' sagas to Icelanders' sagas persuasive. It was precisely at the moment when absorption into the Norwegian monarchy became an increasingly likely possibility that the Icelanders turned to "a belated redefinition of their own traditions in their native sagas" (Andersson 1999, 934). The same author notes "a vein of anti-monarchism in the sagas of this period, and a will to identify what is peculiar to Icelandic institutions, Icelandic law, and Icelandic character" (Ibid., 933).[3]

---

[3] The interpretation of *Morkinskinna* has emerged as a major issue in the debate on Icelandic attitudes to monarchy. Ármann Jakobsson argues that this text "fuses the loyalty to tradition with the ideal of a new society" (2002, 286; my translation, J.P.A.). The claim could not be phrased more strongly: this "didactic history with an ideological purpose" (337; author's English summary) proposes a return to the monarchic fold, and more precisely to the court society of the Norwegian kingdom at its most ambitious and expansionist. Theodore Andersson reads *Morkinskinna* as a "condemnation of Norwegian expansionism on the part of an Icelandic writer and a forceful recommendation that Norwegian kings should devote themselves to social progress within Norway" (1994, 58). By comparison, Heimskringla can, for all its ambivalence, be seen as a royalist readjustment, and Egils saga as a reminder that one should try to see both sides of the argument. When two uncontested experts disagree in this massive way, a non-expert can only conclude that the message of the text must be very ambiguous indeed. The present writer feels tempted to add that the most accessible sections of *Morkinskinna* (the þættir, which both interpreters see as integral parts of the work) do not – to put it mildly – read like monarchist sermons.

REFERENCES

Andersson, Theodore M. 1994. "The Politics of Snorri Sturluson." *Journal of English and Germanic Philology*, 93(1): 55–78.
Andersson, Theodore. 1999. "The King of Iceland." *Speculum* 74: 923–934.
Ármann Jakobsson. 1997. *Í leit að konungi*. Reykjavík: Háskólaútgáfan.
Ármann Jakobsson. 2002. *Staður í nýjum heimi*. Reykjavík: Háskólaútgáfan.
Arnason, Johann P. 2003. *Civilizations in Dispute. Historical Questions and Theoretical Traditions*. Leiden: Brill.
Assmann, Jan. 2000. *Herrschaft und Heil. Politische Theologie in Altägypten, Israel und Europa*. München: Hanser Verlag.
Bagge, Sverre. 1991. *Society and Politics in Snorri Sturluson's Heimskringla*. Berkeley etc.: University of California Press.
Bagge, Sverre. 1997. "Icelandic Uniqueness or Common European Culture? The Case of the Kings' Sagas." *Scandinavian Studies* 69(4): 418–442.
Borgolte, Michael. 2002. *Europa entdeckt seine Vielfalt, 1050–1250*. Stuttgart: Ulmer.
Byock, Jesse. 2000. *Viking Age Iceland*. London: Penguin Books.
Canetti, Elias. 1996. *Masse und Macht*. Frankfurt/Main. Fischer Verlag [1960].
Carlier, Pierre. 1984. *La royauté en Grèce avant Alexandre*. Strasbourg: De Boccard.
Dawson, Christopher. 1974 [1934]. *The Making of Europe*. New York: New American Library.
Diamond, Jared. 2005. *Collapse. How Societies Choose to Fail or Survive*. London: Allen Lane.
Elias, Norbert. 1983. *The Court Society*. Oxford. Blackwell.
Foote, Peter. 2004. "Conversion moment and conversion period." *Kreddur. Selected Studies in Early Icelandic Law and Literature*. Reykjavík: Hið íslenska bókmenntafélag, 144–153.
Forte, Angelo, Richard Oram, and Frederik Pedersen. 2006. *Viking Empires*. Cambridge: Cambridge University Press.
Gauchet, Marcel. 1985. *Le désenchantement du monde*. Paris: Gallimard.
Gísli Sigurðsson. 1988. *Gaelic Influence in Iceland. Historical and Literary Contacts*. Studia Islandica 46. Reykjavík: Háskólaútgáfan [2.ed. 2000].
Gunnar Karlsson. 2004. *Goðamenning*. Reykjavík: Heimskringla.
Halldór Laxness. 1946. "Minnisgreinar um fornsögur." *Sjálfsagðir hlutir*. Reykjavík: Helgafell, 7–74.
Hastrup, Kirsten. 1985. *Culture and History in Medieval Iceland*. Oxford: Clarendon Press.
Helgi Guðmundsson. 1997. *Um haf innan. Vestrænir menn og íslenzk menning á miðöldum*. Reykjavík: Háskólaútgáfan.

Hodgson, Marshall S. 1974. *The Venture of Islam*, v.1. Chicago: University of Chicago Press.
Meulengracht Sørensen, Preben. 1991. "Om eddedigtenes alder." *Nordisk Hedendom. Et symposium*, ed. Gro Steinsland, Ulf Drobin, Juha Pentikäinen, and Preben Meulengracht Sørensen. Odense: Odense Universitetsforlag, 217–228.
Meulengracht Sørensen, Preben. 1993. *Saga and Society. An Introduction to Old Norse Literature*. Odense: Odense University Press.
Meulengracht Sørensen, Preben. 2000. "Social institutions and belief systems of medieval Iceland (c. 870–1400) and their relations to literary production." *Old Icelandic Literature and Society*, ed. Margaret Clunies Ross. Cambridge: Cambridge University Press, 8–29.
Murray, Oswyn. 1990. "Cities of reason." *The Greek City from Homer to Alexander*, ed. Oswyn Murray and Simon Price. Oxford: Clarendon Press, 1–25.
Olrik, Axel. 1930. *Viking Civilization*. New York: American Scandinavian Foundation.
Pritsak, Omeljan. 1981. *The Origin of Rus'*, vol. 1. Cambridge/MA: Harvard University Press.
See, Klaus von. 1999. *Europa und der Norden im Mittelalter*. Heidelberg: Winter.
Sigurður Nordal. 1942. *Íslenzk menning* I. Reykjavík: Mál og menning.
Sigurður Nordal. 1993. *Fornar menntir* I-III. Kópavogur: Almenna bókafélagið.
Steinsland, Gro. 2000. *Den hellige kongen*. Oslo: Pax.
Sverrir Jakobsson. 2005. "Austurvegsþjóðir og íslensk heimsmynd: uppgjör við sagnfræðilega goðsögn," *Skírnir* 179 (vor): 81–108.
Toynbee, Arnold. 1951. *A Study of History*, vol. 2. Oxford: Oxford University Press.
Vésteinn Ólason. 1998. *Samræður við söguöld*. Reykjavík: Heimskringla.

SUMMARY

This essay discusses the question of civilizational approaches to the medieval Nordic world, and in particular to Icelandic history between the tenth and thirteenth centuries. Attempts to reconstruct the cultural profile of a pre-Christian Scandinavian civilization, achieving its last flowering in Iceland (as argued most forcefully by Arnold Toynbee), have proved unconvincing. But there are also weighty arguments against the "pan-Christian" view that portrays the medieval North as a wholly assimilated part of Western Christendom. The most plausible interpretation stresses the dynamics of marginal regions marked by more or less resilient pre-Christian cultures and integrated into Western Christendom during its expansionist phase. As the case of the Nordic region shows, this process could involve an intercivilizational encounter with a pre-Christian world and an intracivilizational differentiation within the framework of Western Christendom. The result was, particularly in Iceland, a very distinctive variant of Western Christian civilization. This general interpretation must, however, be combined with an account of the main landmarks in medieval Icelandic history: the tenth-century foundation of a non-monarchic political order, Christianization, the thirteenth-century political breakdown, and integration into the Norwegian kingdom.

Jóhann Páll Árnason
La Trobe University, Melbourne
Charles University, Prague
J.Arnason@latrobe.edu.au

SVERRE BAGGE

NORDIC UNIQUENESS IN THE MIDDLE AGES? POLITICAL AND LITERARY ASPECTS

WAS THERE a particular Nordic civilisation in the Middle Ages? There are two possible candidates on which such a characterisation might be based: (1) The unique literary culture of Iceland and (2) "The Scandinavian model", with egalitarianism, democracy, welfare and peace. This latter is a modern phenomenon but may possibly have its origins in earlier periods, even in the Middle Ages. From this point of view, discussion about the Scandinavian model may form part of a wider discussion about the uniqueness of Europe, which has also been traced back to the Middle Ages.

Of course, such claims cannot be based on any deep similarity between medieval and modern society. There is little to suggest that medieval Europe was a better place to live for the majority of its population than other, contemporary civilisations or that it was particularly peaceful, egalitarian or democratic. Claims for a medieval origin of modern, Western civilisation must therefore be based on marginal differences or "cracks" in the generally traditional surface that might eventually lead to major changes. Proto-capitalism, for example, which was stimulated by the existence of free cities, competition between a great number of moderately sized and relatively stable states might be seen as a stimulus to inventions (or at least the spread of them) and the need for the king or ruler to share his power with aristocrats and/or burghers might be seen as the origin of modern democratic theory and practice.[1] While Nordic civilisation can hardly claim to be in the forefront of the development of capitalism or industrialisation, it may have some claims in the field of state formation or possibly democracy.

---

[1] Sverre Bagge, "The Transformation of Europe: the Role of Scandinavia," *Medieval Encounters*, eds. J. Arnason and B. Wittrock, (Leiden: Brill, 2004), 131–65.

Democracy

"Democracy" in a general sense is hardly uniquely European but rather, the normal way of organising small-scale societies; that is, the majority of societies that have existed in the world. "Democracy" in this context need not include formal institutions, elections and so forth, but decisions will often be taken after discussion at meetings of the members of society or a part of them.[2] Some people may emerge as leaders because of greater wealth, charisma or fighting skills ("big men"), but their power will depend on voluntary support from their followers.[3] Formal election or deposition will not be necessary; the leaders may attract a number of adherents who desert them when they are dissatisfied with them. Leadership by big men is contrasted to that of "chiefs" who have a permanent leadership and are able to force people to obey them. However, there is a sliding transition between these kinds of leadership; the leaders may act as chiefs in relationship to some groups and as big men in relationship to others. This seems largely to be the case in medieval Europe, including the Nordic countries. Most people were subordinated to the aristocracy, whereas the relationship between leaders and followers within this group bears some resemblance to that of a big man and his followers.

Monarchy or despotism is a secondary development, the result of greater centralisation, larger political units, greater population density and more intense competition. "Big man" democracy works best in small scale, "face to face" societies. Nevertheless, even states and empires under absolute rule often have some kind of democracy at the local level, as for instance the Roman Empire. A claim for European or Scandinavian uniqueness must therefore be based on evidence that such a structure was preserved even in relatively large political units. This applies to many countries in the Middle Ages. The European state is often regarded as unique in a global context, both the system of independent, relatively stable states in mutual competition and the internal balance of power where the monarch had to rule in co-operation with the leading members of soci-

---

[2] F.G. Bailey, *Stratagems and Spoils. A Social Anthropology of Politics* (New York: Schocken, 1969), 35–71 etc.
[3] Marshall Sahlins, "Poor Man, Rich Man, Big Man, Chief," *Comparative Studies in Society and History* 5 (1963), 285–303.

ety and in accordance with laws or agreements with his subjects. The constitutionalism that emerged in most European countries, particularly from the 13th century onwards, can be regarded partly as a continuation and partly as a modification of the "big man-like" or clientelistic aspects of the relationship between the king and individual aristocrats in the Early Middle Ages. Assemblies or other institutions emerged in order to force the king to share his power with his most prominent subjects and to respect their rights. There is clearly an ideological connection between this medieval constitutionalism and the rise of democracy from the late 18th century onwards,[4] possibly also a practical one, although constitutionalism was replaced with absolutism in most countries of Europe in the Early Modern Period and largely for the same reason as big men succumbed to chiefs: absolute monarchies were more efficient in the fierce military competition between the European states.[5] Only a few wealthy and sheltered states managed to combine efficiency and constitutionalism, the Dutch Republic, England and to some extent Sweden.

Scandinavia did play a part in the formation of the European state system. Although geography and ecology may, to a great extent, serve as the explanation behind this particular feature of European civilisation – the contrast to China is particularly striking – we are also dealing with a historical development. The formation of separate kingdoms on the northern and eastern border of Germany served to prevent a revival of the Carolingian Empire and to establish the multiple state system. The competition between the Scandinavian kingdoms in the Middle Ages and the Early Modern Period also serves as a good illustration of the effects of such a system. With some exceptions, Denmark was the leading country of Scandinavia until the 17th century. Undergoing a revival after a period of decline in the early 14th century, Denmark became the centre of a dynastic union of all three countries which lasted (albeit with intermissions) from 1397 until 1523, by which time Norway had lost its independence, whereas Sweden had broken out of the union. During the 17th century, Sweden

[4] Ideologically, the clearest link is Montesquieu's theory of the division of power, which partly has its background in his own experience as a member of the French aristocracy.
[5] See e.g. Charles Tilly, ed., *The Formation of National States in Western Europe* (Princeton: Princeton University Press, 1975) and idem, *Coercion and Capital, and European States, A.D. 990–1990* (Cambridge, Mass.: Basil Blackwell, 1990); William H. McNeill, *The Pursuit of Power: Technology, Armed Force and Society since A.D. 1000* (Oxford: Blackwell 1983).

overtook Denmark through a thorough modernisation of its military forces and emerged as a European great power, almost conquering Denmark which, however, survived through the introduction of absolutism and by imitating Sweden's military modernisation.

Internally, the two strongest of the Scandinavian kingdoms, Denmark and Sweden, both developed constitutional barriers against the king's power, whereas Norway did not. Norway has been an extremely centralised country from the Middle Ages until the present. The monarchy was stronger and the aristocracy weaker than in the neighbouring countries, in a way that makes Scandinavia resemble two of the kingdoms on the Iberian peninsula: Castile with its strong monarchy and weak aristocracy, and Aragon-Catalonia with its weak monarchy and strong aristocracy.[6] Which of these constitutions was the more democratic is a question that is open to discussion. A country with a strong aristocracy was more likely to develop institutions restricting the king's power but these institutions tended to be dominated by a small elite. The common people might have a greater influence in a country with a strong monarchy, like Norway. In any case, the Icelandic free state, which had no king at all and a relatively weak and divided aristocracy, was clearly the most democratic from this point of view. However, it was also weak and a typical example of a loosely organised small-scale society. It would hardly have survived for as long as it did if it had been located in a more competitive environment. Moreover, despite its distant location, it did succumb to the Norwegian king in 1262–64. The strongest candidate for continuity from medieval to modern democracy in Scandinavia is Sweden, where a constitutional assembly consisting of four estates developed during the Later Middle Ages and survived until it was replaced by a modern parliament in 1866. By contrast, Denmark (which included Norway) became the most absolutist country in Europe in 1660. Although it may still be possible to argue for the importance of the medieval past for the rise of democracy in Europe in the 19th and 20th centuries, there is little to suggest that Scandinavia was very different from the rest of Europe in this respect.

---

[6] Angus McKay, *Spain in the Middle Ages* (Basingstoke: Palgrave 2002 [orig. 1977]), 95–117.

Egalitarianism

A more promising idea seems to be that of Scandinavian egalitarianism: here, Iceland, Norway and Sweden are the candidates, whereas Denmark seems to conform more to the normal European pattern with a strong aristocracy dominating the peasantry. Nevertheless, the current trend is to emphasise the aristocratic character of Nordic society.[7] The "farmers" (bœndr) who play such an important role in the sagas are not the average members of the political community but aristocrats and leaders of local society. Most of the land in all of the Nordic countries (except Iceland) was owned by great lords or ecclesiastical institutions to whom the farmers paid rent, although they mostly had their own personal freedom. Relatively speaking, however, most of the Nordic countries differed from most of Western Europe in the egalitarian direction. The social and economic differences seem to have been less pronounced, although they were increasing during the Middle Ages, and the common people had to be taken into account to a greater extent than in many other countries. The importance of the farmers was reduced from the 12th and 13th century onwards with the development of a royal and ecclesiastical bureaucracy, for instance in Norway with the introduction of permanent royal judges and local officials, and in Iceland after the country submitted to the King of Norway in 1262–64, but the farmers were represented in the Swedish diet that developed during the Later Middle Ages. Moreover, the Swedish farmers played an important military role during the struggles against the Danish king in the 15th and early 16th century. In this respect, Sweden is not unique but conforms to other countries on the periphery, such as Scotland, Switzerland, and parts of Germany and East Central Europe. Furthermore, the farmers continued to play an important part in local government in Norway and Iceland, to some extent also in Denmark, at least until the 17th century.

Here, it may be objected that historians have a natural tendency to imagine the past in the light of the present and Scandinavian historians – particularly Norwegian ones – may well be suspected of making the Middle Ages too egalitarian and "Social Democratic". Medieval society in Scandinavia was very hierarchical and aristocratic but probably less so than

---

[7] Eljas Orrman, „Rural Conditions," *The Cambridge History of Scandinavia* I, ed. Knut Helle, (Cambridge: Cambridge University Press, 2003), 299–306 w. ref.

that of the central regions of Western Christendom. A certain amount of egalitarianism may therefore go back to the Middle Ages but we may also point to significant later changes, such as the reduced importance of the Scandinavian states from the 18th century onwards and their withdrawal from the great power struggles, as well as the growth of towns, trade and a middle class of burghers, wealthy farmers and bureaucrats in the service of the state.

A unique culture? The use of the vernacular

Let us then turn to the cultural aspect, where the strongest claims have been made for Scandinavian or rather Icelandic uniqueness. How unique was this culture? Can it be understood as the expression of a society different to that of the rest of Europe, thus confirming the claims for a greater amount of democracy or egalitarianism in Scandinavia?

One of the claims made for this kind of uniqueness is based on the early and extensive use of the vernacular. This applies only to Norway and Iceland, not to Denmark and Sweden. Moreover, it is less unique than often assumed. The rise of the vernacular was a general trend in most of Western Europe from the late 12th and early 13th century; in other words, from about the same time as the rise of the saga literature.[8] This applies to France, Germany, Spain and Italy. England represents a similar trend, except that the literary language was French rather than English until the mid-14th century. However, this development came considerably later in the "new" countries of Western Christendom, i.e. those countries Christianised from the 9th–10th centuries onwards: Denmark, Sweden and the kingdoms of East Central Europe. Thus Norway and Iceland constitute the exceptions, not in the use of the vernacular as such, but in conforming to the pattern of the "old" rather than to the "new" countries of Western Christendom. This increased use of the vernacular is usually thought to reside in a more extensive degree of lay literacy, or the development of a literature intended for a lay audience, or both.

Whereas the literary use of the vernacular had become quite wide-

---

[8] Erich Auerbach, *Literatursprache und Publikum in der lateinischen Spätantike und Mittelalter* (Bern: Francke, 1958), 205–59.

spread in the central parts of Western Christendom from around 1200, its use for administrative purposes in Norway and Iceland was more exceptional. In Norway, the royal chancery confined its use of Latin almost exclusively to letters to other countries and in a few cases to the Church; ecclesiastical institutions also made extensive use of the vernacular, although less than the royal chancery.[9] This differs clearly from Danish and Swedish practice where Latin was used almost exclusively until the second half of the 14th century, and also from most other European chanceries. The only parallel – except for Iceland which, of course, had no royal chancery – is Anglo-Saxon England which is likely to have influenced Norwegian practice, as Christianity and thereby writing was introduced to Norway mainly from England. Early Norwegian letters seem to have been modelled on the Anglo-Saxon writ.[10] The Anglo-Saxon practice in issuing writs in the vernacular continued for some generations after the Norman Conquest which makes it more likely that it could have influenced the Norwegian one. While in England, a change to Latin took place gradually in the period after the Conquest, the use of the vernacular continued in Norway where there was no comparable revolution. A further reason for the continued use of the vernacular in Norway may be that the less wealthy and exclusive Norwegian aristocrats might not have been as well equipped with clerical expertise as their European counterparts; the importance of propaganda during the troubled period in the second half of the 12th century, which may have stimulated writing in the vernacular, might also be taken into consideration. The extant *Speech against the Bishops* is one example of this and there may have been others, although we have no evidence. Finally, the existence of written laws in the vernacular may have been of some importance as a stimulus to issue the amendments, of which we have some examples from the 12th century, in the same language.

The link to Anglo-Saxon England may possibly explain other aspects of Norwegian-Icelandic culture. Directly or indirectly, Norway and Iceland

---

[9] See the list in Johan Agerholt, *Gamal brevskipnad. Etterrøkjingar og utgreidingar i norsk diplomatik*, (Oslo: Gundersen, 1929–32), 648–57, which includes twenty five letters from the king in Old Norse before 1280. By contrast, there are only four in Latin to Norwegian recipients, all ecclesiastical institutions. During the same period, the bishops are known to have issued eighteen letters in Latin and twenty-seven in Old Norse to Norwegian recipients.

[10] Agerholt, *Brevskipnad*, 646, with reference to Bresslau.

received Christianity from Anglo-Saxon England. The significance of this is not confined to the impulses coming from the English Church but also consists in the fact that Anglo-Saxon rulers, in contrast to their Carolingian and Ottonian counterparts, were not able to introduce Christianity through force or the threat of force. In so far as military or political pressure was used, it came from indigenous kings or magnates who thus played a crucial role in the conversion. This may also serve to explain how so much of the pre-Christian traditions survived in Norway and Iceland, as they also did in Anglo-Saxon England.[11]

A unique culture? The saga literature

The main claim for a unique Icelandic culture is based on the existence of the family sagas, but the kings' sagas show largely the same features and can, in addition, be directly compared with Latin prose. The story of St Óláfr taking the young Hákon Jarl captive may serve as an example; any reader familiar with the sagas may easily find others. The story is told in several sources, the oldest of which is Theodoricus Monachus's work from around 1180.[12] Theodoricus tells how Óláfr, having arrived in Norway, sailed to a place called Saudungsund (in Sunnfjord in Western Norway), where he learned that the young earl was on his way. Óláfr laid a trap for the earl by placing his ships on each side of the narrow sound with a rope between them, lifting the rope at the right moment so that the earl's ship capsized. Hákon was captured, gave up his lordship in Norway and left for England.

Theodoricus writes a simple, matter-of-fact Latin without rhetorical embroidery – Saxo would have made much more out of this passage, had he included it in his work. Theodoricus's account is also relatively detailed. He notes that both Óláfr and Hákon had two ships and even bothers to inform his readers of the size of Hákon's ships, despite the fact that this is of no importance for the message Theodoricus wants to convey. He also adds that the larger of Hákon's ships corresponded to the type the ancients

---

[11] Sverre Bagge, "Christianization and State Formation in Early Medieval Norway," *Scandinavian Journal of History* 30 (2005), 113–16, 123 f.

[12] Theodoricus Monachus, *Historia de antiquitate regum Norwagiensium, Monumenta Historica Norvegiae*, ed. Gustav Storm (Christiania: A.W. Brøgger, 1880), ch. 15, 26 f.

called *liburna* and which Horace mentions in one of his epodes – from which Theodoricus quotes, in accordance with his general tendency to refer to the classics as often as possible, no doubt with the aim of integrating his history of Norway into the mainstream of universal history.[13] Although his exact account of the ruse is not very detailed, he makes it perfectly clear to the reader how the earl was captured. The most characteristic feature in Theodoricus compared to the later sagas is the lack of drama; there is no attempt to describe what happened when the ships capsized or when the earl was brought aboard Óláfr's ship. More important to Theodoricus than such details is the moral aspect. From his point of view, the episode does not portray the saintly king in a very favourable light: Óláfr has attacked the earl without any declaration of war or feud and given him no chance to defend himself. Óláfr may clearly be accused of unchivalrous behaviour but Theodoricus has an excuse ready for him: he wanted to avoid bloodshed.

The two "classical" sagas, *Fagrskinna* and *Heimskringla*,[14] which have almost exactly the same text, tell essentially the same story as Theodoricus, but in a different way. In the first part, they are somewhat more detailed in explaining exactly how the earl's ship capsized. They also add a sentence about how the earl's men dropped into the water, some drowning and some being killed by Óláfr's men. They thus make no point of Óláfr's alleged wish to avoid bloodshed. The main difference comes in the next part. The earl is taken captive and led on board Óláfr's ship. He is seventeen years old and very handsome, with long, beautiful hair like silk, tied up with a golden string:

> He sat down by the mast. Then said King Óláf, "It is certainly true what is said about your kin, that you are of handsome appearance. But luck has deserted you now."
>
> Hákon replied, "It is not that luck has deserted us. It has long been the case that now the one, now the other of two parties have lost out... It may be that we are more successful another time."

---

[13] Sverre Bagge, "Theodoricus Monachus – Clerical Historiography in Twelfth-century Norway," *Scandinavian Journal of History* 14 (1989), 115–17.

[14] *Fagrskinna. Nóregs konunga tal*, ed. Finnur Jónsson (Copenhagen: S.L. Møller, 1902–03), (=*Fsk.*) ch. 26, and *Heimskringla*, ed. F. Jónsson (Copenhagen: S.L. Møller, 1893–1900), II, 38–40.

> Then King Óláf replied, "Has it not entered your mind, earl, that events have taken such a turn that in the future you may have neither victory nor defeat?"
>
> The earl said, "This is in your power, sire, to decide this time."[15]

Suddenly understanding his predicament, the earl asks what he has to do to escape and accepts Óláfr's condition, to leave the country and promise never to return.

W.P. Ker has characterised the difference between Latin and Old Norse historiography in the following way:

> "These two books [Theodoricus and Historia Norwegie] might be picked out of the Middle Ages on purpose to make a contrast of their style with the Icelandic saga. Th[eodoricus]. ... indulges in all the favourite medieval irrelevances, drags in the Roman historians and the Platonic year, digresses from Charybdis to the Huns, and embroiders his texts with quotations from the Latin poets".[16]

A more charitable – and adequate – description is that Theodoricus had a different aim, regarding the external events as signs of some deeper historical meaning which he found in typological parallels to events that had taken place elsewhere.[17] The earl's beauty, the drama of his meeting with Óláfr and the exchange between the two protagonists were of no importance to him, whereas the allusion to Horace links the episode in this distant country to the civilised world, and the statement that Óláfr wanted to avoid bloodshed gives a moral interpretation and serves to protect the saintly king from the accusation that he broke the rules of chivalry by attacking without a formal declaration of war or feud.

---

[15] "settisk hann i fyrrúmit. Þá mælti Óláfr konungr: "eigi er þat logit af yðr frændum, hversu fríðir menn þér eruð sýnum, en farnir eruð þér nú at hamingju." Þá segir Hákon: "ekki er þetta óhamingja, er oss hefir hent; hefir þat lengi verit, at ýmsir hafa sigraðir verit ... kann vera, at oss takisk annat sinn betr til en nú." Þá svarar Óláfr konungr: "grunar þik ekki þat, jarl, at hér hafi svá til borit, at þú mynir hvárki fá heðan í frá sigr né ósigr?" Jarl segir: "þér munuð ráða, konungr, at sinni"", *Heimskringla* II, 39; *Heimskringla. History of the Kings of Norway*, transl. Lee M. Hollander (Austin, University of Texas Press, 1964), 266.

[16] William Paton Ker, "The Early Historians of Norway," *Collected Essays* II (London: Macmillan, 1925), 141 f.

[17] Bagge, "Theodoricus," 113–33.

Fagrskinna's and Heimskringla's version represents classical saga narrative. The accounts are objective, in the sense that the author remains neutral and abstains from comment; visual, in their vivid description of persons and events; and dramatic, in letting the persons confront one another with brief, succinct, intensely meaningful sentences, delivered in a calm tone and often with understatement in a way that heightens the drama, as in Óláfr's words to Hákon. The sagas generally prefer direct speech, in contrast to classical Latin prose, which prefers indirect. In this way, the actors in the drama are presented on the stage without interference from the author. Irony is often used. King Sverrir's speeches and sayings are particularly famous for this,[18] but irony is also found in other sagas, as in Heimskringla's story of Ásbjǫrn selsbani's fatal expedition from Northern Norway to Sola in the south to buy grain from his uncle Erlingr Skjálgsson. When Ásbjǫrn returns empty-handed, having been humiliated by King Óláfr's ármaðr Selþórir, and declines his other uncle Þórir hundr's invitation to spend Christmas with him, Þórir comments:

> There is ... a great difference between us kinsmen of Ásbjorn in the honor he does us ... seeing the effort he put forth this summer to visit Erling and his kin; whereas now he disdains to come to me who lives next door to him! I don't know but he fears that Seal-Thórir be there on every islet.[19]

The saga style also seems to suggest a closer connection to the material, visible world, than the learned, Latin tradition. Not that the sagas excel in description for its own sake; there are few descriptions of nature, and when descriptions do occur, there is always a practical reason, depicting a battleground or showing the difficulty in crossing a certain area, for example. When necessary, however, such descriptions can be very precise, as for instance Snorri's description of how Þórir hundr and the brothers Karli

---

[18] Sverre Bagge, *From Gang Leader to the Lord's Anointed. Kingship in Sverris saga and Hákonar saga Hákonarsonar*. The Viking Collection 8 (Odense: Odense University Press, 1996), 27–29.

[19] "bæði er ... at mikill er virðinga-munr vár frænda Ásbjarnar, enda gerir hann svá, slíkt starf sem hann lagði á í sumar, at sœkja kynnit til Erlings á Jaðar, en hann vill eigi hér fara í næsta hús til mín; veit ek eigi, hvárt hann hyggr, at Selþórir myni í hverjum hólma fyrir vera" (*Heimskringla* II, 249; Hollander, 381).

and Gunnsteinn raided a burial site and destroyed a statue of the pagan god Jómali in Bjarmaland.[20] The story has a vividness that might suggest that Snorri had been an eyewitness to the episode or at least had visited the site, which of course was not the case. Nor are the details so specific that it is necessary to assume any local knowledge; most probably, Snorri has invented them himself. Nevertheless, his need for visualising is striking. We are presented almost with a map of the site and are told details such as that Þórir used his axe to climb the wall and that mud stuck to the gold and silver taken out of the burial mound, which seems obvious enough but which increases the vividness of the story. The attack on the statue plays a major part in the story and is also described in dramatic detail. Snorri does not confine himself to merely noting that its head dropped off, but describes exactly where Karli aimed his axe so as to loosen the costly necklace the statue was wearing in the easiest way possible. The detailed description of this attack, from Þórir's warning against touching the statue to Karli's chopping off its head, might look like a story of greed leading to disaster. Admittedly, the sound of the dropping head alerts the guards that are on their way – Snorri tells us that the raiders exploited an interval during the change of guards – but Þórir's magic saves the Norwegians. Instead, the attack on the god serves as an anticipation of the later conflict between Þórir and the brothers. Þórir's warning seems to have served as a pretext to keep the others away from the main booty, as he fails to heed it himself, snatching a bowl full of silver from the statue, which results in Karli's attack on the statue. On their return from the expedition, Þórir and Karli quarrel about the booty and Þórir kills Karli, partly because of this and partly as revenge for Karli's having killed Þórir's nephew Ásbjǫrn; he pierces him with the spear with which Ásbjǫrn had been killed, which he had received from Ásbjǫrn's mother and with which he later pierced King Óláfr. In this way, the raiding expedition in Bjarmaland enters into the main story of Óláfs saga (below p. 61).

Representation and argument

The visual character of the sagas and the contrast here between the sagas and classical and medieval Latin prose is reminiscent of Auerbach's com-

[20] *Heimskringla* II, 292–99.

parison between the latter and Gregory of Tours's "barbarous" prose – a contrast that Mark Phillips has characterised with the terms "representation" and "argument". According to Auerbach, Gregory's Latin is primitive and unclassical; he has no idea of composition and his detailed narrative is so obscure as to be almost incomprehensible. On the other hand, Gregory's prose has a freshness and immediacy, derived from popular narrative, which represent a renewal of the ancient tradition. In a similar way, Phillips distinguishes between the vivid but chaotic Italian chronicles of the 14th century and the classicising, abstract, well-ordered and intellectual histories in Latin from the Renaissance of the 15th century, which aimed at reviving the classical tradition.[21]

This contrast catches an important feature of the Old Norse sagas but does not give a complete picture. The sagas are not chaotic; the visual details serve to underline important points in the narrative. Nor is there a necessary conflict between representation and argument. Some of the classical sagas, notably *Heimskringla* and *Sverris saga*, contain argument as well as representation; visualisation is not l'art pour l'art, but has an intellectual purpose. In *Heimskringla*, the story of Óláfr and Hákon is followed by a series of others which explain how Óláfr managed to defeat his enemies and become king of Norway in half a year.[22] By capturing Hákon, Óláfr eliminates an important rival, while at the same time demonstrating his luck, which – together with the wealth he has brought from England – gains him the support of his relatives, the petty kings of Eastern Norway. This in turn enables him to defeat his other rival, Sveinn jarl, in the battle of Nesjar. After this victory, the rest of his enemies, including Einarr Þambarskelfir in Trøndelag and Erlingr Skjálgsson in Sola, find it necessary to come to terms.

The story of Óláfr and Hákon also plays a crucial role in the saga of Óláfr as a whole. Readers of the saga can hardly avoid comparing this episode with another episode towards the end, namely the last meeting between Óláfr and Erlingr Skjálgsson which takes place at a time when Óláfr is about to lose the country. Starting with the story of Ásbjǫrn

[21] Erich Auerbach, *Mimesis. Dargestellte Wirklichkeit in der abendländischen Literatur* (Bern: Francke, 1946), 81–97; Mark Phillips, "Representation and Argument in Florentine Historiography," *Storia della storiografia*, 10 (1986), 48–63.

[22] Sverre Bagge, *Society and Politics in Snorri Sturluson's Heimskringla* (Berkeley etc.: University of California Press, 1991), 90–92.

selsbani's fatal expedition to the south, Snorri has described how Óláfr runs into conflict with one after another of the mightiest men in the country, a narrative in which the Bjarmaland episode also plays a part (above p. 60). Óláfr's adversaries rally around King Cnut the Great who arrives in Norway and is accepted as king over most of the country. After Cnut's return, Óláfr, who has remained passive in his stronghold in the east during Cnut's expedition, tries a raid along the coast of Western Norway. He is pursued by Erlingr, who has a largely superior force, but Óláfr nonetheless manages to lay an ambush for Erlingr's ship which is much faster than the rest of his fleet. Erlingr fights until all his men have been killed, after which Óláfr offers him quarter. Erlingr lays down his arms but is killed by one of Óláfr's men, to whom Óláfr says: "With that blow you struck Norway out of my hands".[23] Shortly afterwards, Óláfr is forced to leave the country and finds refuge in Russia.

Thus, the lesson is that clemency brings Óláfr success, whereas killing an enemy who surrenders leads to disaster. In accordance with what seems to be Snorri's general way of thinking, this conclusion is based on political rather than moral considerations. On both occasions, Óláfr is in a weak position; he is in desperate need of friends. In a society of feuds and revenge, killing an enemy makes it more difficult to come to terms with his clients and relatives. Killing Hákon might easily have led to a dangerous alliance of his friends and relatives against Óláfr. Killing Erlingr did lead to Erlingr's whole network uniting against Óláfr and chasing him out of the country. Admittedly, Óláfr is not responsible for Erlingr's death in Snorri's account, although he most probably is in the stanza by Sighvatr, which Snorri quotes.[24] Snorri's conclusion therefore may be that Óláfr wanted to do the same to Erlingr as to Hákon, but that luck, which had so emphatically favoured him in his early career, had now deserted him. More generally, however, both episodes show the importance of support. No king can rule only by force; he needs the support of the majority of the leading men in the country. Towards the end of his reign, Óláfr loses this support, largely through his own fault, in antagonising a number of the

---

[23] "nú hjóttu Nóreg ór hendi mér" (*Heimskringla* II, 406; Hollander, 467).
[24] "Erlingr fell, en olli/ allríkr skipat slíku/ ...bragna konr með gagni"/ "Erling fell; that outcome/ Óláf caused ... and gained the victory", *Den norsk-islandske Skjaldedigtning*, ed. Finnur Jónsson (Copenhagen: Rosenkilde og Bagger, 1908–14), B I, 230; cf. Hollander, 468.

greatest magnates by insisting on his rights down to the smallest detail.[25] Had Óláfr succeeded in reaching a settlement with Erlingr, he might possibly have turned the tables. However, a detail in Snorri's account might suggest that Óláfr would have been unlikely to achieve this. After Erlingr's surrender, Óláfr gives him a wound on his cheek, saying: "A mark he shall bear, the betrayer of his king".[26] This remark may actually have provoked Áslákr, Erlingr's second cousin and enemy, to kill Óláfr; Áslákr would hardly have dared if Óláfr instead had embraced Erlingr or in some other ways expressed his wish for Erlingr's friendship.

More importantly, Óláfr's act shows that he would never have gained Erlingr's friendship which was what he needed to be able to remain in the country. In the long run, Óláfr needed Erlingr more than Erlingr needed Óláfr, despite the situation at the time. Forcing Erlingr to a similar agreement as Hákon's would hardly help Óláfr; his other enemies were too strong and numerous. What Óláfr needed was Erlingr's genuine friendship, which would make him and his network Óláfr's allies. In order to achieve this, Óláfr had to show more generosity than marking Erlingr as a traitor. It would therefore seem that Snorri, despite acquitting Óláfr of Erlingr's death, does use this scene as a contrast to the one between Óláfr and Hákon and intends it as another example of Óláfr's political blunders towards the end of his reign.

Icelandic and European narrative

Snorri's combination of representation and argument thus shows a clear difference from the dominating Latin-clerical culture of contemporary Europe. On the other hand, we are not dealing with two diametrically opposed traditions; there are individual variations within both as well as similarities between the two, and influence from one tradition to the other. Stylistically, there is a considerable difference between the two Norwegian examples of historical narrative in Latin, Theodoricus Monachus and *Historia Norwegie*. While the narrative in the former is simple and direct, the latter contains more rhetorical embroidery, particularly through a rich

---

[25] Bagge, *Society and Politics*, 66–70.
[26] "merkja skal dróttinsvikann" (*Heimskringla* II, 406; Hollander, 467).

and varied vocabulary and extensive use of synonyms.[27] Moreover, although both authors have a religious attitude, theological thought is more explicit in Theodoricus, whose digressions serve to relate the history of Norway to the universal history of salvation.[28] Theodoricus also includes considerably more factual information, whereas the author of *Historia Norwegie* shows a greater interest in political explanation,[29] and seems to have used classical Latin historiography as his model to a greater extent. In this respect, he resembles the greatest Latin writer in Scandinavia, Saxo Grammaticus, who was one of the most accomplished Latin writers of the Middle Ages, and who developed a highly complex and rhetorical style modelled particularly on Valerius Maximus. Comparable differences can also be found throughout the rest of Europe, for instance in Germany, where Widukind of Corvey (c. 960) and Lampert of Hersfeld (c. 1080) represent the classical style, with a greater emphasis on secular matters, whereas Wipo (c. 1040) and above all Otto of Freising (1140s, 1157/58) are more explicitly theological.[30] However, there is no exact correspondence between style and contents: there are many intermediate forms and it is probably too early to attempt a complete categorisation of twelfth-century Latin historiography.[31] If we compare the sagas to the two Norwegian representatives of Latin historiography, they are closer in style to Theodoricus and closer in content to *Historia Norwegie*. Of the German authors, Widukind is the one who has most in common with Snorri, in his occasionally very vivid accounts of individual episodes, his understanding of political conflicts as mainly the result of individuals competing for power and defending their own interests, and in his depictions of leadership as based on charismatic qualities rather than a holding of office on

---

[27] Eiliv Skard, *Målet i Historia Norwegiae, Skrifter utgitt av Det Norske Videnskapsakademi i Oslo, Hist.-fil. klasse* 1930.5 (Oslo: J. Dybwad, 1930); Lars Boje Mortensen, "Introduction," *Historia Norwegie*, 24–28.

[28] Bagge, "Theodoricus Monachus", 117–23.

[29] Thus, the author explains why the Danish King Sveinn attacked Óláfr Tryggvason, whereas Theodoricus only mentions the fact (Mortensen, "Introduction," *Historia Norwegie*, eds. Inger Ekrem and Lars Boje Mortensen (Copenhagen: Museum Tusculanum Press, 2003), 27 f.).

[30] Sverre Bagge, *Kings, Politics, and the Right Order of the World in German Historiography c. 950–1150. Studies in the History of Christian Thought* 103 (Leiden: Brill, 2002), 88–94, 98–107, 215–30, 277–96, 376–88.

[31] Mortensen, *Historia Norwegie*, 27.

NORDIC UNIQUENESS IN THE MIDDLE AGES?   65

God's behalf. There is thus not a total gap between the sagas and European historiography but nevertheless, there is quite a strong difference in emphasis.[32]

Secular literature and secular audiences were also to be found in other countries at the same time; vernacular literature that developed from the 12th century onwards was largely intended for the laity and dealt with war, heroic deeds and love. This literature demonstrates some of the same features as the Old Norse sagas but also some differences. Descriptions of kings, heroes and beautiful women are panegyric in tone in both genres, but those in the sagas are closer to descriptions of missing persons in police announcements, to draw a modern analogy: height, colours, special characteristics.[33] In contrast, European chivalric literature shows greater subtlety in the rendering of emotions, particularly when dealing with love.[34] Characteristically, such passages are omitted or abbreviated in the Old Norse translations. Is this because of less understanding for such phenomena or because of the tendency, very pronounced in the mature sagas, to describe emotions through external signs ("red like blood" etc.) and to leave the interpretation to the reader? Secondly, this European vernacular literature is more concerned with norms, chivalry and so forth, although it also contains strategic-political features similar to those in the saga literature. William Brandt's characterisation, that this literature "seeks to celebrate, not to explain",[35] catches a characteristic difference compared to the saga literature, but is not entirely just. There is a considerable amount of strat-

[32] Sverre Bagge, "Icelandic Uniqueness or a Common European Culture. The Case of the Kings' Sagas," *Scandinavian Studies* 69,4 (1997), 418–42 and "Medieval Societies and Historiography," in Michael Borgolte, ed., *Das europäische Mittelalter im Spannungsbogen des Vergleichs. Zwanzig internationale Beiträge zu Praxis, Problemen und Perspektiven der historischen Komparatistik* (Berlin: Akademie Verlag, 2001), 223–47.

[33] Lars Lönnroth, "Det litterära porträttet i latinsk historiografi och isländsk sagaskrivning. En komparativ studie," *Acta Philologica Scandinavica* 27 (1965), 85 ff. and Bagge, *Society and Politics*, 146–48. Cf. also the comparison between chivalric and a saga description in Bjarne Fidjestøl, *Selected Papers* (Odense: Odense University Press, 1997), 363 f.

[34] See e.g. Jonna Kjær, "Censure Morale et Transformations Idéologiques dans Deux Traductions de Chrétien de Troyes: *Ívens saga* et *Erex saga*," *The Eighth International Saga Conference. The Audience of the Sagas* (Gothenburg 1991), 287–96; Liliane Reynaud, "Når en roman av Chrétien de Troyes blir til en norrøn saga. Fra Yvain ou Le Chevalier au Lion til Ívens saga," *Historisk tidsskrift* 83 (2004), 245–59.

[35] William J. Brandt, *The Shape of Medieval History* (New Haven: Yale University Press, 1996), 88.

egy and political manoeuvring in works like *L'Histoire du Guillaume le Maréchal* and *Froissart's Chroniques*.[36] The actual "game of politics" need not have been fundamentally different; similar conflicts and manoeuvring can be detected in European vernacular as well as Latin historiography, although it is less prominent there.

Narrative and society

The saga style has been increasingly admired in modern times and has made a great impact on European literature from the mid-19th century onwards. There is no doubt about its difference to the style current in intellectual circles in most of Europe in the Middle Ages, but its origin and development are open to discussion[37] and deserve further examination. Are we dealing with a genuinely popular style, based on oral narrative, or with some kind of development from Latin prose?

We are certainly not dealing with a culture completely isolated from the rest of Europe, a kind of medieval Galapagos.[38] Both Iceland and Norway had early and regular contact with the rest of Europe, and some of the earliest texts, such as Sæmundr's lost history of the Norwegian kings and Oddr Snorrason's life of Óláfr Tryggvason, were in Latin. The Latin *sermo humilis*, as used in the Bible, in saints' lives and other religious texts,[39] is also a possible model for saga prose. Writing was, after all, introduced from abroad through the conversion, and it seems likely that imported texts may have had some influence on what was eventually written down. Moreover, the classical saga style seems to be a late development,[40] which

[36] John Gillingham, *Richard Coeur de Lion. Kingship, Chivalry and War in the Twelfth Century* (London: The Hambledon Press, 1994), 227–41, with criticism of Georges Duby, *Guillaume le Maréchal ou Le meilleur chevalier du monde* (Paris: Fayard, 1984); Kristel Skorge, *Ideals and values in Jean Froissart's Chroniques* (Doctoral thesis, Bergen, 2006), 68–123.

[37] Frederic Amory, "Saga Style in some Kings' Sagas, and Early Medieval Latin Narrative," *Acta Philologica Scandinavica* 32 (1979), 67–86; Þórir Óskarsson, „Rhetoric and Style," *A Companion to Old Norse-Icelandic Literature and Culture*, ed. by Rory McTurk (Oxford: Blackwell, 2005), 354–71.

[38] Gunnar Karlsson, "Was Iceland the Galapagos of Germanic Political Culture," here, 77.

[39] Auerbach, *Literatursprache und Publikum*, 25–53.

[40] On the development of the saga literature, see most recently Theodore M. Andersson, *The Growth of the Medieval Icelandic Sagas (1180–1280)* (Ithaca: Cornell University Press, 2006), 1–101.

can also be illustrated by the story of Óláfr taking Hákon captive. The description of the earl as well as the dialogue between him and Óláfr is also found in the *Legendary Saga* from around 1200 but with a number of additions that are omitted in the two later sagas.[41] The earl's vanity is emphasised; he wants to sail between Óláfr's two ships – which he believes are merchant ships – in order to impress the spectators as much as possible, and he and his men drink heavily while sailing. Both pieces of information serve to place the earl in bad light and may thus have a moralistic aim similar to Theodericus's comment about Óláfr's wish to avoid bloodshed. Most importantly, after his words to the earl that he may have neither victory nor defeat any more, Óláfr goes on to tell the earl that he may be killed and gives him an alternative option that the earl turns down. Finally, the two agree on the same solution as in the two later sagas. To modern readers, these additions weaken the drama of the story. The two later authors seem to have thought in the same way and omitted them.[42] Thus, whatever the origin of the story, its classical version appears as a late and refined product of various versions produced over a period of around forty years. Nor does Snorri confine himself just to narrating good stories; he combines them in a way that gives them considerable explanatory force. His departure from the Latin intellectual and rhetorical tradition is the result of deliberate choice.

Nevertheless, the saga style probably has some basis in popular narrative or is at least closer to such narrative than classical Latin prose. Some of its features, such as irony, understatement, silence and acute observation of the external world, fit well in with a relatively egalitarian or at least non-hierarchical society of farmers, and resemble the culture of rural society many places in contemporary Scandinavia.[43] Moreover, there is some resemblance between the saga style and the so-called *prófbref* in Norway,

---

41 *Leg. saga* ch. 19–21.
42 This of course implies that the two authors knew the *Legendary saga*, which is by no means certain. However, the two sagas show enough similarities with the *Legendary saga* that we can conclude that they must either have used the saga itself or some of its sources, such as *The Oldest Saga*. Only fragments survive of this saga, none of which deal with the early part of Óláfr's reign. See Theodore M. Andersson, "Kings' Sagas," in Carol Clover and John Lindow, eds., *Old Norse-Icelandic Literature. A Critical Guide*. Islandica 45 (Ithaca: Cornell UP, 1985), pp. 204 f., 212 f.
43 Eva Österberg, *Mentalities and Other Realities. Essays in Medieval and Early Modern Scandinavian History* (Lund: Lund University Press, 1991), 9–30.

testimony about the circumstances around cases of homicide, recorded by local officials and sent to the king: the exact description of details, the paratactic style and the frequent use of direct speech, often with striking formulations, invite direct comparison.[44] As these letters primarily contain the testimony of witnesses, often apparently directly quoted, they are likely to stand relatively close to oral discourse.

Although, as we have seen, the egalitarian character of medieval Icelandic society should not be exaggerated, it was certainly more pronounced than in most other places at the same time. As Icelandic society was without a clear hierarchy, status depended more on personal qualities than on inherited or bureaucratic positions, with intense competition and with a great risk for the loser to be the subject of ridicule. It was also a society where a man's success depended more on his ability to form alliances, persuade people to join him and to outmanoeuvre his opponents than on courage and skills at arms. Above all, the saga literature differs from contemporary European historiography in the less exclusively aristocratic character of the players which made the chieftains more dependent on broader support and increased the importance of the personal qualities of the players, in the form of intelligence, eloquence, generosity and the ability to handle various kinds of people. *Heimskringla* consistently points out that the farmers are helpless without their leaders and generally attributes most important decisions to the latter. The farmers are thus in a subordinate position, but they are always there, in contrast to what is found in European historiography.[45] The importance of oratory in the sagas serves to illustrate this point. The frequent references to regal eloquence in the characterisations of kings, as well as the many speeches attributed to them, notably in *Sverris saga* and *Heimskringla*, show the importance of persuading people to do what the leader wants.[46]

Might some of the features of the saga literature also be explained by

---

[44] Trygve Knudsen, *Skrift, tradisjon og litteraturmål* (Oslo: Universitetsforlaget, 1967), 81–83; cf. Olav Solberg, *Forteljingar om drap: kriminalhistorier frå seinmellomalderen* (Bergen: Fagbokforlaget, 2003), 40–64 etc.

[45] Bagge, *Society and Politics*, 138 f.

[46] Ibid., 149, and Sverre Bagge, "Oratory and Politics in the Sagas," L'Histoire et les nouveaux publics dans l'Europe médiévale (XIIIe–XVe siècles), Actes du colloque international organisé par la Fondation Européenne de la Science à la Casa de Vélasquez, Madrid, 23–24 Avril 1993, ed. Jean-Philippe Genet, Publications de la Sorbonne, Paris 1997, 215–28.

the more secular character of Nordic and particularly Icelandic society? It seems at least that the laity — in Iceland the chieftains and their followers, in Norway the royal court — was a very important literary audience. Nor is there any doubt that the Icelandic church was weaker than its counterparts in most other areas of Europe. The episcopal sees were poor, there were no cathedral chapters and the church was largely under the control of lay chieftains until the end of the 13th century. By contrast, the Norwegian church seems to have been relatively — but of course not absolutely — wealthier than the European average and had a considerable amount of independence from the king. [47] In accordance with this, Norwegian literature is also less secular than the Icelandic one. Nevertheless, the distinctly secular character of the Old Norse literature should not be exaggerated. The great majority of texts in Old Norse are actually religious: sermons, saints' lives and other devotional literature, and there was also a considerable secular literature in other countries at the time. The most characteristic feature of the literature of Iceland and Norway — as far as we can judge from what is extant — is the absence of scholasticism and theological — as opposed to devotional — writing. From this point of view, the main weakness of the Icelandic and Norwegian churches, in contrast to their Danish and Swedish counterparts, was that they had very limited contact with the expanding European universities and thus only developed a specifically clerical elite culture to a limited extent.

The classical saga is, to a considerable extent, the product of the pre-state Icelandic society and expresses this society's values. The writing of the kings' saga reached its peak during the intense struggles in Iceland in the 1220s and -30s and declined with the formation of a strong monarchy in Norway and the Icelanders' submission to the king of Norway in 1262–64. The writing of the family sagas continued, probably for the rest of the century, but whether they were composed before or after 1262–64

---

[47] Halvard Bjørkvik, "Nyare forskning i norsk seinmellomalder", *Norsk lektorlags faglig-pedagogiske skrifter. Nytt fra norsk middelalder* II (Oslo: Cappelen, 1970), p. 88, suggests that the Church owned around 40% of the land incomes around 1300, whereas the European average is unlikely to have been more than 20–30%. Although this calculation is uncertain and has been criticised, most recently by Jo Rune Ugulen,"*alle the knaber ther inde och sædescwenne...*" *Ei undersøking i den sosiale samansetninga av den jordeigande eliten på Vestlandet i mellomalderen* (Doctoral thesis, Bergen 2007), pp. 521–77, there are indications that the Norwegian Church at the time was very wealthy.

they mostly represent the norms and values of the old society. However, the kings' sagas also show connections with Norway. Although most saga authors were Icelanders, the Norwegian court was an important audience. Some sagas were directly commissioned by the king of Norway, such as *Sverris saga*, *Hákonar saga* and most probably *Fagrskinna*. King Sverrir is even said to have supervised the writing of the first part of his saga. As the kings' sagas have the Norwegian dynasty as their subject and frequently express Norwegian patriotism in describing the Norwegian kings' conflicts with neighbouring peoples, there can hardly be any doubt of the Norwegian influence on their composition, although it is more difficult to distinguish between Norwegian and Icelandic elements.

The contrast or even conflict between Norway and Iceland is often emphasised in modern scholarship, and the end of the so-called free state in 1262–64 is regarded as a kind of conquest. There are also hints at such an opposition in the saga literature. One example is the famous episode of Snorri's return to Iceland from Norway in 1220, when the high rank and rich gifts bestowed on him by the Norwegian king and earl are met with envy and ridicule;[48] another example is the explanation of the emigration to Iceland as the result of Haraldr hárfagri's "tyranny", most clearly expressed in *Egils saga's* account of the conflict between King Haraldr and Skallagrímr and his family.[49] The latter, as well as some other saga episodes, contrasts the simple, straightforward, egalitarian manners of the Icelanders – in accordance with the description above – with the refined, haughty, courtly manners of those in Norway. However, the extent to which Egill and his father represent an Icelandic ideal is an open question, and even more is the extent to which this ideal was still valid later in the 13th century. Nor is the account of Haraldr hárfagri consistently negative, not even in *Egils saga*.[50] Taken together, the Icelandic family sagas are more likely to express ambivalence towards the Norwegian king: on the one hand, the wealth and honour that might be gained from his service, on the other the loss of independence. The actual behaviour of the Icelandic

---

[48] *Sturlunga saga*, eds. Jón Jóhannesson, Magnús Finnbogason and Kristján Eldjárn I–II (Reykjavík: Sturlunguútgáfan, 1946) I, 278 f.; Preben Meulengracht Sørensen, *Fortælling og ære* (Århus: Aarhus Universitetsforlag, 1993), 121–23.

[49] Meulengracht Sørensen, *Fortælling og ære*, 127–47.

[50] Slavica Rancović, "Golden Ages and Fishing Grounds: The Emergent Past in the *Íslendingasögur*," *Saga-Book* 30 (2006), 56–59.

chieftains in the 13th century seems to indicate that the former consideration outweighed the latter, or perhaps more correctly, that the chieftains tried to retain as much independence as possible without losing the king's favour.[51]

If we move to the middle of the 13th century, we also find Norwegian courtliness and authoritarian monarchy described in a highly rhetorical style, the very opposite of that of the sagas, in *Konungs skuggsiá* (The Kings Mirror, c. 1255). In many ways, however, this work forms the best evidence for the similarity rather than the difference between Norwegian and Icelandic norms and manners, through its violent polemics against the bad manners of the courtiers, the lack of respect for the king, the courts of law and the royal officials and its condemnation of feuds and competition. The strength and amount of detail in these attacks, plus the Son's evident surprise at many of the Father's lessons in this dialogue, form clear evidence of the distance between doctrine and practice. At least ideologically, to some extent also in practice, great changes took place with the firm establishment of the royal power in Norway after the end of the so-called civil wars in 1240. These changes are also expressed in the last of the kings' sagas, that of Hákon Hákonarson, but we cannot use the ideals of the 1250s and -60s as evidence for practice in the 1220s and -30s.[52]

The connection between narrative and society would also seem to be confirmed by the parallel between north and south, "republican Iceland" and the Italian city republics. In one sense, these two parts of Europe are the most different of all, the wealthy, densely populated and urbanised Northern and Central Italy, with proto-capitalism, extensive trade routes and highly developed political institutions, versus the poor island in the north, with no towns at all, depending on foreign merchants for import and export and with no real government until the submission under the Norwegian king in 1262–64. There are, however, similarities. Both societies were less hierarchical and more competitive than the kingdoms and principalities in the zone between them, such as England, France and the Empire, and secular values were stronger in both. Politically, the Church had a weak position in Italy, and the main focus of learning in Italian uni-

---

51 Jón Viðar Sigurðsson, *Chieftains and Power in the Icelandic Commonwealth* (Odense: Odense University Press, 1999), 71–83.
52 Bagge, *From Gang Leader*, 147–60.

versities and elsewhere was on secular disciplines, law and medicine. Although we can hardly claim any detailed similarity, the Italian urban chronicles, for instance the works of the Florentines Villani and Compagni, share some of the characteristics of the sagas, in their vivid representations of men and actions and their relatively secular outlook. These authors also serve as some of the main examples of representation in Phillips's study of representation and argument mentioned above.[53] While these authors do refer to divine intervention and miracles, and lament the struggles they narrate to a greater extent than the saga writers, the main topic of their narratives is the external world, human actions, success and failure, political alliances, family and other networks, and competition. Like the sagas, these chronicles are composed by men of action for men of action, and their authors as well as their audience are people engaged in the external, material world rather than the spiritual and supernatural one, merchants in Italy, combined farmers and politicians in Iceland.

Conclusion

While taking medieval Scandinavia and particularly Iceland as models of later European democracy seems to be methodologically doubtful, there is a more solid basis for identifying a distinct cultural tradition expressed in the saga literature, which in turn is related to the character of Icelandic society, and to some extent also the other Scandinavian countries, notably Norway. Taken as a whole, the kings' sagas clearly differ from the main European tradition in narrative style, composition and in their attitude to politics and society. The retreat of the author, the use of irony and understatement, dramatic "representation", the emphasis on political manoeuvring and the kings' and leaders' need for popular support are all characteristic features. To some extent, these features can be understood against the background of a competitive society without a clear hierarchy and a literary audience dominated by practical men of action, a hypothesis that seems to be confirmed by the comparison with the contemporary Italian towns.

---

53 Phillips, "Representation and Argument," 51–55; Sverre Bagge, "Medieval and Renaissance Historiography: Break or Continuity?" *The Individual in European Culture, The European Legacy*, vol. 2 no. 8, ed. Sverre Bagge (1997): 1336–1371.

Admittedly, literature cannot be explained sociologically in the sense that a certain kind of society will inevitably produce a certain kind of literature. Individual creativity also plays a part; we are dealing with connections and probabilities, not with exact correlation.

REFERENCES

Agerholt, Johan. *Gamal brevskipnad. Etterrøkjingar og utgreidingar i norsk diplomatikk*, I–II. Oslo: Gundersen, 1929–32.
Amory, Frederic. "Saga Style in some Kings' Sagas, and Early Medieval Latin Narrative." *Acta Philologica Scandinavica* 32 (1979): 67–86.
Andersson, Theodore M. "Kings' Sagas." *Old Norse-Icelandic Literature. A Critical Guide*, ed. by Carol Clover and John Lindow. Islandica 45. Ithaca: Cornell UP, 1985, 197–238.
Andersson, Theodore M. *The Growth of the Medieval Icelandic Sagas (1180–1280)*. Ithaca: Cornell University Press, 2006.
Auerbach, Erich. *Mimesis. Dargestellte Wirklichkeit in der abendländischen Literatur*. Bern: Francke, 1946.
Auerbach, Erich. *Literatursprache und Publikum in der lateinischen Spätantike und Mittelalter*. Bern: Francke, 1958, 205–59.
Bagge, Sverre. "Theodoricus Monachus – Clerical Historiography in Twelfth-century Norway." *Scandinavian Journal of History* 14 (1989): 113–33.
Bagge, Sverre. *Society and Politics in Snorri Sturluson's Heimskringla*. Berkeley etc.: University of California Press, 1991.
Bagge, Sverre. *From Gang Leader to the Lord's Anointed. Kingship in Sverris saga and Hákonar saga Hákonarsonar*. The Viking Collection 8. Odense: Odense University Press, 1996.
Bagge, Sverre. "Icelandic Uniqueness or a Common European Culture? The Case of the Kings' Sagas." *Scandinavian Studies* 69 (4, 1997): 418–42.
Bagge, Sverre. "Oratory and Politics in the Sagas." *L'Histoire et les nouveaux publics dans l'Europe médiévale (XIIIe–XVe siècles), Actes du colloque international organisé par la Fondation Européenne de la Science à la Casa de Vélasquez, Madrid, 23–24 Avril 1993*, ed. by Jean-Philippe Genet. Paris: Publications de la Sorbonne, 1997, 215–28.
Bagge, Sverre. "Medieval and Renaissance Historiography: Break or Continuity?" *The Individual in European Culture, The European Legacy*, vol. 2 no. 8, ed. by Sverre Bagge (1997): 1336–1371.
Bagge, Sverre. "Medieval Societies and Historiography." in Michael Borgolte (ed.), *Das europäische Mittelalter im Spannungsbogen des Vergleichs. Zwanzig internationale Beiträge zu Praxis, Problemen und Perspektiven der historischen Komparatistik.* Berlin: Akademie Verlag, 2001, 223–47.

Bagge, Sverre. *Kings, Politics, and the Right Order of the World in German Historiography c. 950–1150.* Studies in the History of Christian Thought 103. Leiden: Brill, 2002.

Bagge, Sverre. "The Transformation of Europe: the Role of Scandinavia." *Medieval Encounters*, ed. by J. Arnason and B. Wittrock. Leiden: Brill, 2004, 131–65.

Bagge, Sverre. "Christianization and State Formation in Early Medieval Norway." *Scandinavian Journal of History* 30 (2005): 113–16, 123 f.

Bailey, F.G. *Stratagems and Spoils. A Social Anthropology of Politics.* New York: Schocken, 1969.

Bjørkvik, Halvard. "Nyare forskning i norsk seinmellomalder." *Norsk lektorlags faglig-pedagogiske skrifter. Nytt fra norsk middelalder* II. Oslo: Cappelen, 1970, 70–105.

Brandt, William J. *The Shape of Medieval History.* New Haven: Yale University Press, 1996.

Duby, Georges. *Guillaume le maréchal ou Le meilleur chevalier du monde.* Paris: Fayard, 1984.

Fagrskinna. Nóregs kononga tal, ed. by Finnur Jónsson. Copenhagen: S.L. Møller, 1902–03.

Fidjestøl, Bjarne. *Selected Papers.* Odense: Odense University Press, 1997.

Gillingham, John. *Richard Coeur de Lion. Kingship, Chivalry and War in the Twelfth Century.* London: The Hambledon Press, 1994.

Heimskringla. History of the Kings of Norway, transl. by Lee M. Hollander. Austin: University of Texas Press, 1964.

Historia Norwegie, ed. by Inger Ekrem and Lars Boje Mortensen. Copenhagen: Museum Tusculanum Press, 2003.

Hkr. = *Heimskringla* I-IV ed. by F. Jónsson. Copenhagen: S.L. Møller, 1893–1900.

Jón Viðar Sigurðsson. *Chieftains and Power in the Icelandic Commonwealth.* The Viking Collection 12. Odense: Odense University Press, 1999.

Ker, William Paton. "The Early Historians of Norway." *Collected Essays* II. London: Macmillan, 1925, 131–51.

Kjær, Jonna. "Censure Morale et Transformations Idéologiques dans Deux Traductions de Chrétien de Troyes: *Ívens saga* et *Erex saga*," The *Eighth International Saga Conference. The Audience of the Sagas.* Gothenburg 1991, 287–96.

Knudsen, Trygve. *Skrift, tradisjon og litteraturmål.* Oslo: Universitetsforlaget, 1967.

Lönnroth, Lars. "Det litterära porträttet i latinsk historiografi och isländsk sagaskrivning – en komparativ studie." *Acta Philologica Scandinavica* 27 (1965), 68–117.

McKay, Angus. *Spain in the Middle Ages.* Basingstoke: Palgrave, 2002 [orig. 1977].

McNeill, William H. *The Pursuit of Power: Technology, Armed Force and Society since A.D. 1000*. Oxford: Blackwell, 1983.
Meulengracht Sørensen, Preben. *Fortælling og ære*. Århus: Aarhus Universitetsforlag, 1993.
Mortensen, Lars Boje. "Introduction." *Historia Norwegie*, 2003, 8–48.
Den norsk-islandske Skjaldedigtning, ed. by Finnur Jónsson, A1–B2. Copenhagen: Rosenkilde & Bagger, 1908–1914.
Orrman, Eljas. "Rural Conditions." *The Cambridge History of Scandinavia* I, ed. by Knut Helle. Cambridge: Cambridge University Press, 2003, 250–311.
Phillips, Mark. "Representation and Argument in Florentine Historiography." *Storia della storiografia* 10 (1986): 48–63.
Rancović, Slavica. "Golden Ages and Fishing Grounds: The Emergent Past in the *Íslendingasögur*." *Saga-Book* 30 (2006): 39–64.
Reynaud, Liliane. "Når en roman av Chrétien de Troyes blir til en norrøn saga. Fra Yvain ou Le Chevalier au Lion til Ívens saga." *Historisk tidsskrift* 83 (2004): 245–59.
Sahlins, Marshall. "Poor Man, Rich Man, Big Man, Chief." *Comparative Studies in Society and History* 5 (1963): 285–303.
Skard, Eiliv. *Målet i Historia Norwegiae*. Skrifter utgitt av Det Norske Videnskapsakademi i Oslo, Hist.-fil. klasse 1930.5. Oslo: J. Dybwad, 1930.
Skorge, Kristel. *Ideals and values in Jean Froissart's Chroniques*. Doctoral thesis, Bergen, 2006.
Solberg, Olav. *Forteljingar om drap: kriminalhistorier frå seinmellomalderen*. Bergen: Fagbokforlaget, 2003.
Sturlunga saga, ed. by Jón Jóhannesson, Magnús Finnbogason and Kristján Eldjárn I–II. Reykjavík: Sturlunguútgáfan, 1946.
Theodoricus Monachus. *Historia de antiquitate regum Norwagiensium, Monumenta Historica Norvegiæ*, ed. by Gustav Storm. Kristiania: A.W. Brøgger, 1880, 1–68.
Tilly, Charles, ed. *The Formation of National States in Western Europe*. Princeton: Princeton University Press, 1975.
Tilly, Charles. *Coercion, Capital, and European States, A.D. 990–1990*. Cambridge, Mass.: Basil Blackwell, 1990.
Ugulen, Jo Rune. *"alle the knaber ther inde och sædescwenne..." Ei undersøking i den sosiale samansetninga av den jordeigande eliten på Vestlandet i mellomalderen*. Doctoral thesis, Bergen 2007.
Österberg, Eva. *Mentalities and Other Realities. Essays in Medieval and Early Modern Scandinavian History*. Lund: Lund University Press, 1991.
Þórir Óskarsson, „Rhetoric and Style." *A Companion to Old Norse-Icelandic Literature and Culture*, ed. by Rory McTurk. Oxford: Blackwell, 2005, 354–71.

SUMMARY

The article addresses the question of Nordic uniqueness in the Middle Ages in the political and social fields, as well as in the literary field. With regard to the political dimension, there is not much evidence to support the notion that countries like Iceland and Norway were any more democratic than the rest of Europe in that they had more developed constitutional arrangements. They may, however, be regarded as more democratic in the sense that the social and economic differences between the elite and the common people were not as pronounced as they seem to have been in most other European countries. The main evidence for Nordic – i.e. Icelandic and to some extent Norwegian – uniqueness comes from the literary field. The sagas differ significantly from Latin historiography in not only being written in the vernacular but also because of their distinctive style, the aim of which was to convey a concrete representation of external reality and a political explanation for this reality. By contrast, Latin historiography tended to regard external events as the expression of a spiritual reality and to comment on the significance of these events from an ethical or typological point of view. Finally, the relationship between the literary features of the Icelandic sagas and Icelandic/Norwegian society is discussed. Does the sagas' literary style reflect a more egalitarian Icelandic/Norwegian/Nordic society than any contemporary European society, as well as a society less dominated by ecclesiastical culture and ideals?

Sverre Bagge,
Centre for Medieval Studies,
The University of Bergen.
Sverre.Bagge@cms.uib.no

GUNNAR KARLSSON

WAS ICELAND THE GALAPAGOS OF GERMANIC POLITICAL CULTURE?

I

BEHIND the presumptuous title of my talk is an attempt to deal with the question of whether the political system of medieval Iceland, before its submission to the Norwegian kingdom in the 13th century, should be considered as being of its own special kind, rather than just a variant of a medieval European political system. First of all, though, I should draw attention to three limitations. Firstly, I work on the assumption that there once existed something which could be called *a* Germanic political culture although our knowledge about what it was really like is of course very limited. I will only go as far as searching for traces of such a culture in early Iceland. Secondly, I must inevitably work with a drastically simplified model of *the* medieval European political system. I am aware that there were immense local variations in European politics in the middle ages, and Iceland was far from being the only society practically without royal power. I am not going to treat it as unique in a strict sense, but as anomalous to the most usual and best-known model. For obvious reasons I shall particularly view Iceland in comparison with Norway, and within Norway, particularly with the law district of Gulaþingslög. My third reservation is that the comparison in the title of my paper between Iceland and the Galapagos is of course an exaggeration. Whether or not any considerable amount of exclusively Germanic political culture existed in Iceland, obviously, I do not argue that it lived there in a perfect isolation as the tortoises or lizards of the famous archipelago do.

II

Running the risk of being too basic and stating the obvious, I will begin by describing explicitly the political system of Iceland which is the subject of my discussion.

First and foremost I am thinking about the formal ruling system as it is set out in the law-code *Grágás*, described in Ari's *Book of the Icelanders* and referred to in the sagas. At the bottom of this system were the local chieftains, *goðar*, somewhere around 40 in number, all roughly and formally equal in power. The term *goði* seems to derive from *goð/guð*: "god", and in the sagas one can see that their authors took it for granted that the *goðar* served as priests of some kind in pagan times. All farmers' households belonged to the domain of a *goði*, a *goðorð* as it was called, but were legally free to change allegiance from one *goði* to another. The *goðar* in turn were free to expel farmers from their *goðorð*. The *goðar* were supposed to hold a spring assembly each year, three *goðar* together. Then there was the central *alþing*, the general assembly at Þingvellir, where the *goðar* sat in the *lögrétta* or law council, decreed what was the right law on specific issues, and passed new laws. Furthermore, at the *alþing* there were five separate courts of justice, nominated by the *goðar*: Four were quarter courts, *fjórðungsdómar*, each of them dealing with cases from one of the quarters of the country, and the fifth court, the *fimmtardómr*, was a kind of appeal court which dealt with cases that had not been settled in a satisfactory way in the quarter courts.

Alongside this system of formal courts there was a complicated informal system for settling disputes by arbitration and reconciliation. Space here does not allow me to take this into consideration; I must concentrate on the formal system of government, and even within that I can only deal with a few important points.

Many scholars have had their doubts about the real existence and functionality of this system. But I would like to state categorically that I do not see any strong reason to doubt that it existed and worked roughly in the way it is described in the law-code. The lawbook *Grágás* is not a single piece of text: it is a huge collection of legal provisions which have been organized in different ways in different books. It is difficult to imagine that this collection could have emerged in any other way than in the form of actual law.[1] In many cases, episodes related in the sagas confirm the evidence of the law. In some cases, the sagas seem to contradict individual prescriptions of laws, and some scholars have made much of such cases,

---

[1] Gunnar Karlsson, *Goðamenning. Staða og áhrif goðorðsmanna í þjóðveldi Íslendinga* (Reykjavík: Heimskringla, 2004), 28–59.

but during my study of the ruling system which is published in my book *Goðamenning*, I became convinced that in all major points, the saga literature supports the evidence of the law. The question that then arises is how this system originated.

III

For a long time, the colonization of Iceland was seen as a deliberate quest for freedom from the oppression of royal power in Norway. It is easy to read this interpretation from the Icelandic sagas. The *Book of Settlements* recounts that some 30 original settlers in Iceland, i.e., around 7% of the total number of all settlers, fled to Iceland to escape the oppression of King Harald Fairhair, or left the country after some kind of conflict with him. Only four settlers are said to have emigrated to Iceland after consultation with the king.[2] This indicates strongly that in the 13th century, when the extant versions of the *Book of Settlements* were written, it was a well-known theory that the unification of royal power in Norway in the 9th century, attributed to King Harald, was an important cause of the colonization of Iceland. This text was written at the time when the king of Norway was attempting to gain control of Iceland, and his ambitions no doubt met some resistance in Iceland although we cannot discern any clear pro- or anti-royalist parties among the Icelandic elite. It seems at least possible, perhaps likely, that the stories of settlers fleeing the oppression of King Harald were intended to comment in some way on the undesirability of belonging to a kingdom.

The theory of King Harald's oppression is expressed even more clearly in *Egil's saga*:

> In each province King Harald took over all the estates and all the land, habited or uninhabited, and even the sea and lakes. All the farmers were made his tenants, and everyone who worked the forests and dried salt, or hunted on land or at sea, was made to pay tribute to him.
>
> Many people fled the country to escape this tyranny and settled various uninhabited parts of many places, to the east in Jamtland

---

[2] Gunnar Karlsson, *Drög að fræðilegri námsbók í íslenskri miðaldasögu I. Landnám, stjórnkerfi og trú* (Reykjavík: Háskóli Íslands, 1997), 55.

and Halsingland, and to the west in the Hebrides, the shire of Dublin, Ireland, Normandy in France, Caithness in Scotland, the Orkney Isles and Shetland Isles, and the Faroe Islands. And at this time, Iceland was discovered.[3]

This evidence can easily be read in such a way that Iceland was chosen as an abode of freedom at a time when oppressive royal power was gaining strength in the Nordic world. A trace of such a reading can also be found in the first published history of Iceland, Arngrímur Jónsson's *Crymogæa*, printed in 1609. According to this account many settlers of Iceland went there in order to seek freedom.[4] This statement contains two elements which are of major importance here. One is that the emigration took place for a deliberate political purpose; the other that this purpose was freedom.

After the emergence of liberal, democratic ideas in Europe and North America in the 18th and 19th centuries, the understanding of these elements developed and they acquired an increased and partly new significance. It came to be considered normal, which had been extremely rare earlier, for new ruling systems to be established purposefully and formally, usually in the form of written constitutions. And the most important element of these constitutions was normally freedom, which consisted of formal equality and democracy. This was to have immense influence on how scholars interpreted the medieval Icelandic commonwealth. I am not saying, however, that the liberalist development of European culture necessarily led scholars astray about the commonwealth. The possibility that some kind of liberalism, search for equality and democracy occurred in individual societies before the 18th century cannot be excluded. If it did, it is more than likely that the development of these ideals in the 18th and

---

[3] *The Complete Sagas of Icelanders including 49 tales*. General editor: Viðar Hreinsson. I (Reykjavík: Leifur Eiríksson Publishing, 1997), 36 (ch. 4). "Haraldr konungr eignaðisk í hverju fylki óðul ǫll ok allt land, byggt ok óbyggt, ok jafnvel sjóinn ok vǫtnin, ok skyldu allir búendr vera hans leiglendingar, svá þeir, er á mǫrkina ortu, ok saltkarlarnir ok allir veiðimenn, bæði á sjó ok landi, þá váru allir þeir honum lýðskyldir. En af þessi áþján flýðu margir menn af landi á brott, ok byggðusk þá margar auðnir víða, bæði austr í Jamtaland ok Helsingjaland ok Vestrlǫnd, Suðreyjar, Dyflinnar skíði, Írland, Norðmandí á Vallandi, Katanes á Skotlandi, Orkneyjar ok Hjaltland, Færeyjar. Ok í þann tíma fannsk Ísland." *Egils saga*. Ed. Sigurður Nordal. Íslenzk fornrit II (Reykjavík: Hið íslenzka fornritafélag, 1933), 11–12.

[4] Arngrímur Jónsson, *Crymogæa. Þættir úr sögu Íslands*, translated by Jakob Benediktsson (Reykjavík: Sögufélag, 1985), 95 (ch. II).

19th centuries opened the eyes of scholars to these traits in earlier history. Nothing is more likely to hinder understanding of remote times than the common tendency among scholars to attribute definite characteristics to historical periods and to refuse to see anything that does not fit with those characteristics. Nevertheless, we should be certain to remember that deliberate state-building, equality and democracy were especially the ideals of the times that I am coming to now in my survey of the history of the research of this topic.

In the 19th century, two scholars dominated research on the constitutional history of medieval Iceland, the German Konrad Maurer and the Icelander Vilhjálmur Finsen, who spent most of his working lifetime in Denmark. Maurer wrote his first extensive work on the political system of the Icelandic commonwealth, *Die Entstehung des isländischen Staats und seiner Verfaßung*, in 1852. There, of course, he discussed the stipulation of the law on the freedom of farmers to leave one *goðorð* and enter another one, but he added the important reservation, obviously based on evidence from sagas, that this right could in practice never be much more than a dead letter because no powerful chieftain would accept his followers leaving him to enter the *goðorð* of another chieftain.[5] Without saying so directly, Maurer obviously doubted that the right to choose a *goðorð* could bring the farmers any real democracy when there was no state power in the country to protect them against encroachment and to secure their rights.

Vilhjálmur Finsen, on the other hand, described without reservation the stipulation of the law regarding the free choice of *goðorð*,[6] and on the whole he was clearly more apt to see the commonwealth as a purposefully established institution. Thus he thought that the *alþing* had been established in the early 10th century with a definite number of *goðorð*, namely 36, while Maurer doubted that the number of *goðorð* had been decided until the country was divided into quarters, some three or four decades later. Maurer was of the opinion, which had been put forward earlier, that *Grágás* largely comprised customary rights, rather than law which had been passed formally, while Finsen denied this, maintaining that customary

5 Konrad Maurer, *Die Entstehung des isländischen Staats und seiner Verfaßung* (München: Christian Kaiser, 1852), 109. – Konrad Maurer, *Upphaf allsherjarríkis á Íslandi og stjórnarskipunarþess*, translated by Sigurður Sigurðarson (Reykjavík: Bókmenntafélag, 1882), 96.
6 Vilhjálmur Finsen, "Om de islandske Love i Fristatstiden," *Aarbøger for nordisk Oldkyndighed og Historie* 1873 (1873): 202.

rights were mainly valid in the infancy of peoples, "i Folkenes Barndom" as he expressed it in Danish, but in his opinion that obviously did not apply to Iceland.[7]

One does not find much discussion about this in Icelandic in the 19th century. But after the turn of the 20th century, especially after the establishment of the University of Iceland in 1911, Icelandic scholars who were working in Iceland and mostly writing in Icelandic, took the lead in studies of the commonwealth age. The early 20th century was a period of ardent nationalism in Iceland; successful steps were made towards state formation in the country and economic progress was rapid. Of course Icelandic scholars of this time adopted the views of Vilhjálmur Finsen rather than Konrad Maurer, and portrayed the commonwealth rather incautiously as mirroring the democratic society that they were building in Iceland, an egalitarian polity where the choice of *goðorð* by farmers could be equated with elections in a representative democracy. Among these scholars were the legal historian and professor of law Ólafur Lárusson, the literary historians Sigurður Nordal and Einar Ólafur Sveinsson, and the historian and Marxist politician Einar Olgeirsson.[8] The last of these, Einar Olgeirsson, even suggested that the *goðar* had been elected to their posts when the *alþing* was established. This was not entirely unsupported by the evidence, because in a 13th-century text it is said that the *goðar* were originally *chosen* ("valdir") to be responsible for the pagan temples.[9] Even as careful and down-to-earth a scholar as the history professor Jón Jóhannesson said, in the English translation of his *History of the Old Icelandic Commonwealth*, that "the leaders of the country held to the idea of carefully maintaining a balance of authority between various chieftaincies, a principle which had already developed at the time of the founding of the Althing." In the Icelandic original Jón used even a stronger word than 'idea'; he talked about 'hugsjón' which could be translated more exactly as 'ideal' or 'vision'.[10]

Jón Jóhannesson published this study in 1956, but soon after, in the late

[7] Gunnar Karlsson, *Goðamenning*, 30, 66.
[8] Ibid., 181–184.
[9] Einar Olgeirsson, *Ættasamfélag og ríkisvald í þjóðveldi Íslendinga* (Reykjavík: Heimskringla, 1954), 93–97.
[10] Jón Jóhannesson, *A History of the Old Icelandic Commonwealth. Íslendinga saga*, translated by Haraldur Bessason ([S.l.]: University of Manitoba Press, 1974), 226. – Jón Jóhannesson, *Íslendinga saga* I. *Þjóðveldisöld* (Reykjavík: Almenna bókafélagið, 1956), 270.

1960s and 1970s, scholars seriously began to doubt this general picture of the commonwealth. Although little had been published which presented a new view on this issue, I followed the trend of the time faithfully in 1972, when I published an article on the relationship between *goðar* and the farmers and criticized the idea of seeing the choice of *goðorð* as an election of a kind.[11] In the first volume of *Saga Íslands* (The History of Iceland) two years later, Jakob Benediktsson wrote about the establishment of the commonwealth. He mentions, of course, the right of farmers to change their allegiance to a *goði*, but he does not mention any similarity to the modern franchise. On the contrary, he stresses the fact that farmers inevitably had to live in the neighbourhood of the *goði* they belonged to in order to enjoy his protection and to be able to support him in providing protection for other members of the *goðorð*.[12]

I have not yet mentioned the historian Björn Þorsteinsson, although he had written two books about the Icelandic commonwealth before 1970.[13] This is because he never expressed himself very clearly about those characteristics of the political system that I have been discussing. But in his third book on the subject, *Íslensk miðaldasaga* (History of Medieval Iceland), which was published in 1978, he turned strongly against the view of the commonwealth as a democracy which had dominated in the first half of the 20th century. His chapter about *goðar* now carries the title "Forréttindastétt" (A Privileged Class). He does not even mention the farmers' free choice of *goði*, but states that farmers seem to have been able to live without belonging to any *goðorð*, whatever the evidence for that may be. On the other hand, Björn mentions the right of *goðar* to refuse to accept a farmer into their *goðorð* and states, correctly, that there are examples of *goðar* who ousted farmers from their neighbourhood if they did not like them.[14]

The emphasis on opposition to the Norwegian king among commonwealth-era Icelanders has also diminished since the mid-20th century. In the first volume of *Saga Íslands* in 1974, Sigurður Líndal, a professor of law and a historian, wrote a chapter about Iceland and the neighbouring world.

[11] Gunnar Karlsson, "Goðar og bændur," *Saga* 10 (1972): 27–34.
[12] Jakob Benediktsson, "Landnám og upphaf allsherjarríkis," *Saga Íslands* I, ed. by Sigurður Líndal (Reykjavík: Bókmenntafélag, 1974), 173–174.
[13] Björn Þorsteinsson, *Íslenzka þjóðveldið* (Reykjavík: Heimskringla, 1953). – Björn Þorsteinsson, *Ný Íslandssaga. Þjóðveldisöld* (Reykjavík: Heimskringla, 1966).
[14] Björn Þorsteinsson, *Íslensk miðaldasaga* (Reykjavík: Sögufélag, 1978), 52–53.

He points out that written sources make a clear distinction between Norwegians and Icelanders, but thinks that this distinction was more based on a feeling of region than of a nation state. Further, Sigurður points out two examples from medieval sources where Icelanders living in the commonwealth period are said to have talked about Norway and Iceland as one kingdom and about themselves as the "men" of the Norwegian king.[15] To mention one last example of the new view, in 1997 a young Icelandic scholar, Ármann Jakobsson, published a book called *Í leit að konungi* (In Search of a King). There he argued that the writing of the sagas of kings in Iceland reflected the Icelanders' consideration of the idea of belonging to a kingdom, or even their wish to do so, in the century before they entered the kingdom of Norway.[16]

One can discern here two basically opposite views of the Icelandic commonwealth. One of them, which could be called romantic, sees it as a deliberately founded egalitarian and democratic society, albeit with its inherent weaknesses. The other one is a bleaker view which sees the commonwealth as having been shaped by external necessity, without much thought or initiative, mostly ruled by an oppressive upper class and longing for royal power some time before it submitted to it. As I mentioned, I participated in setting out this bleak view in the 1970s, but when I returned to the subject in the late 1990s and began to write my book *Goðamenning*, I felt that the revision of the romantic view had perhaps come far enough and that it was now time to establish a more balanced view. I will use the remainder of the present article to give a brief survey of my conclusions, some of them set out directly in *Goðamenning*, others more or less implied there.

IV

I do not find any pressing need to assume that the Icelandic commonwealth was founded on an idea of creating something new or original. It is well known of course that Germanic people used to come together at

---

[15] Sigurður Líndal, "Ísland og umheimurinn," *Saga Íslands* I, ed. by Sigurður Líndal (Reykjavík: Bókmenntafélag, 1974) 215–217.
[16] Ármann Jakobsson, *Í leit að konungi. Konungsmynd íslenskra konungasagna* (Reykjavík: Háskólaútgáfan, 1997).

assemblies to make decisions about their societies, like many other people, and had done so for centuries. As far as we know, there were three *þing*-districts in Norway when Iceland was discovered and settled. Judging mainly on the basis of place-names, *þing*s were established in most or all of the Norse Viking Age colonies in the North Atlantic: the Faroes, Shetland, the Orkneys, the Isle of Man, districts in Ireland, Scotland, England, the Greenland colony.[17] There is no reason to think that the Icelandic *alþing* differed initially from other such assemblies.

What about the *goðar* then, the central figures of the Icelandic *þing* system? Nowhere outside Iceland are there chieftains with this title in Christian times. The term *goði* seems to occur attached to personal names in three runic inscriptions in Denmark. It may occur in a few Swedish place-names, although it seems difficult to determine whether the places are named after the gods themselves or their servants, the *goðar*. Other instances to which attention has been drawn by scholars seem to be even more doubtful.[18] I believe that the explanation why the *goði* institution was preserved in Iceland lies in the way Christianity was introduced in the country. To put it simply, among Germanic people in pagan times there were probably two kinds of chieftains with special relationship to the divinities of the time, namely kings and *goðar*. I see no reason to believe that the kings were less attached to religion than the *goðar*, and this attachment can be seen in Christian times where the first local saints were kings, such as King Olaf Haraldsson in Norway and King Knut Sveinsson in Denmark. In most European countries, amongst them the Scandinavian ones, conversion to Christianity was instigated by kings who decided to switch their allegiance from pagan gods to Christ and who used the change to consolidate the countries under their rule. In this process, the kings eradicated the *goðar* so completely that we hardly find any trace of them in written sources.

In Iceland, exactly the opposite took place. According to Ari the Learned's account of the conversion, the *goðar* decided at the *alþing* to

---

[17] Michael Barnes, "Tingsted. Vesterhavsøyene for øvrig," *Kulturhistorisk leksikon for nordisk middelalder* XVIII (Reykjavík: Bókaverzlun Ísafoldar, 1974), 382–387. – Gillian Fellows-Jensen, "Tingwall, Dingwall and Thingwall," *Twenty–Eight Papers Presented to Hans Bekker-Nielsen on the Occasion of his Sixtieth Birthday 28 April 1993* (Odense: Odense University Press, 1993), 53–63.

[18] Gunnar Karlsson, *Goðamenning*, 374–379.

change their allegiance to Christ, probably not least in order to free themselves from the interference of the king of Norway, Olaf Tryggvason, who had been forcing his subjects to accept Christianity for four or five years. The Icelanders were not able to eradicate royalty in the same way as Scandinavian kings probably eradicated the *goðar* in their countries, because no king was present in Iceland. We can speculate, though, that the reason why the Icelanders were usually so sure that they did not belong to the Norwegian kingdom was an elimination of royalty of a kind, comparable to the elimination of the *goðar* in Scandinavia.

This is of course not meant to be an exhaustive description of the process of conversion. I am also well aware that I have little evidence for my interpretation. What I am suggesting is only that it is possible to explain the special characteristics of the political system of Iceland, with the *goðar* as central figures and devoid of royal authority, without assuming that it was established purposefully and intended to represent something entirely new.

It is not my role here to talk about literary culture. Nevertheless I might add that the uniqueness of medieval Icelandic literature can be explained by the theory that Iceland kept its class of priests through the conversion. At the same time, the status of literature supports the theory of a unique process of conversion. My suggestion is not least intended to explain how Icelandic skalds seem to have monopolized Norwegian and even Danish court poetry after the conversion, how Icelanders gained their reputation as experts on history of Scandinavian kings in the late 12th century, as testified by the Scandinavian authors Theodoricus and Saxo, and how 13th- and 14th-century Iceland managed to produce classical literature.

V

One characteristic of the political system of Iceland is its apparent elaborateness. To mention one measurable variable, the law code of Iceland is about three times longer than the longest law-books of Scandinavia.[19] I suggest that the excessive growth of the legal text in Iceland can be explained by the absence of executive power in the country. In a society

---

[19] Ibid., 434–435.

where no one single party or system of officials had the role of keeping law and order, feud and minor warfare must have been a constant nuisance. It seems likely that people tried to restrict this nuisance by setting down rules about as many possible moot points as they could possibly think of.

When we come to the content of the laws, the most distinctive feature of the Icelandic ruling system is the separation of legislative and judicial power, which is said to have been all but unknown in Europe until the 18th century. In Norway, the *lögrétta* was predominantly a court of justice, although the name of the institution, *lög-rétta*, "law-corrector" indicates that its original role was to ensure that the law of the district was kept correctly at all times. Because of this and other differences that scholars find between Norwegian and Icelandic law, it has sometimes even been doubted that Ari's statement in his *Book of the Icelanders*, that the Icelanders based their law on the Norwegian Gulaþingslög, can be correct.[20] On this question Icelandic scholars have followed the lead of Vilhjálmur Finsen, who stated that the Norwegian system was "primitive and imperfect" compared to the Icelandic one.[21]

It appears to me that this difference between Norwegian and Icelandic law has been greatly exaggerated. The hierarchy of courts is even more complicated in Gulaþingslög than in *Grágás*; in Gulaþingslög cases are supposed to start in *ad hoc* courts nominated by the litigants and they can go through *skiladómr, fjórðungsþing, fylkisþing* and finally to *lögrétta* at Gulaþing itself.[22] This makes five successive instances, whereas in Iceland the instances are three at most: *vorþing, fjórðungsdómr* and *fimmtardómr*. It is true that the distinction between the legislative role of the *lögrétta* and the judicial role of the courts in Iceland appears to be remarkably modern. But I do not find anything that makes it likely that this was done in order to secure the impartiality of the courts, as was the purpose of independent courts in 18th-century Europe. The *goðar*, the holders of legislative power, nominated all judges to all courts from the farmers in their following, and there are no stipulations in the law to secure the independence of judges

---

[20] Ólafur Lárusson, *Lög og saga*, ed. by Lögfræðingafélag Íslands (Reykjavík: Hlaðbúð, 1958), 120.
[21] Vilhjálmur Finsen, "Om de islandske Love i Fristatstiden," 206n ("den primitive, mindre fuldkomne Character, som viser sig i den norske Ordning").
[22] *Den eldre Gulatingslova*, ed. by Bjørn Eithun, Magnus Rindal,Tor Ulset (Oslo: Riksarkivet, 1994), 146–148 (ch. 266).

vis-à-vis *goðar*. The peculiar development of the Icelandic court system seems to be a consequence of a short-lived attempt to establish quarter *þing*s, one in each quarter of the country. Thereby, the judicial power of the *alþing* was moved away from it, and when the quarter *þing*s were abandoned, perhaps because they did not prove practical, they were succeeded by quarter courts at the *alþing*. This is my interpretation of the process, admittedly based on rather little evidence, but that is the best I can offer.[23]

VI

The last point I wish to discuss here is the question of democracy. Is it true that the Icelandic commonwealth was a democratic society? And, if so, was this democracy invented in Iceland? It is easy to give a negative answer: the commonwealth was of course not what we call a democracy nowadays. Only a limited group of men could inherit a *goðorð*. The right of farmers to choose between *goðar* was seriously restricted. Only male farmers had this right, no women and no male farmhands had any formal say in the choice. But it seems to me more fruitful to look at the question of democracy in a different way. Long ago, the Austrian-English historian Walter Ullmann wrote that the history of political ideas in the Middle Ages was to a large extent about two conflicting theories of government: the ascending one, which maintained that original power was located in the people, and the descending one, which saw the original power as located in a supreme being. The ascending theory is the earlier one according to Ullmann.[24] It seems to me fruitful to look at the question of democracy in the light of this distinction and to call all ascending power an indication of democracy, however small and imperfect. Seen in that way, there is no doubt that there were conflicting forces of democratic and anti-democratic traits operative in the Icelandic commonwealth. It seems tempting to believe that there was somewhat more freedom in Iceland than in Europe in general, when royal power gained increased control in European kingdoms, although there too, royal power differed greatly from one district and one time to another. Anyway, if there was more democracy in Iceland there is no rea-

[23] Gunnar Karlsson, *Goðamenning*, 121–128.
[24] Walter Ullmann, *Medieval Political Thought* (Harmondsworth: Penguin, 1975), 12–13.

son to believe that it was created by the Icelanders; it was most likely a tradition which the original settlers brought with them to the country.[25]

VII

In general, it is my conclusion that medieval Iceland enjoyed, in many ways, an interestingly distinctive political culture. But there is little reason to think that this was due to the inventiveness or ideals of the people of Iceland. It was above all due to the distance from royal power. It was the Atlantic Ocean with its high waves and predominant westerly winds which kept the arms of kings away from the country for more than three centuries after human habitation began there.

REFERENCES

Arngrímur Jónsson. *Crymogæa. Þættir úr sögu Íslands*, translated by Jakob Benediktsson. Reykjavík: Sögufélag, 1985.

Ármann Jakobsson. *Í leit að konungi. Konungsmynd íslenskra konungasagna*. Reykjavík: Háskólaútgáfan, 1997.

Barnes, Michael. "Tingsted. Vesterhavsøyene for øvrig." *Kulturhistorisk leksikon for nordisk middelalder* XVIII. Reykjavík: Bókaverzlun Ísafoldar, 1974, 382–387.

Björn Þorsteinsson. *Íslensk miðaldasaga*. Reykjavík: Sögufélag, 1978.

Björn Þorsteinsson. *Íslenzka þjóðveldið*. Reykjavík: Heimskringla, 1953.

Björn Þorsteinsson. *Ný Íslandssaga. Þjóðveldisöld*. Reykjavík: Heimskringla, 1966.

The Complete Sagas of Icelanders including 49 tales. General editor: Viðar Hreinsson. I. Reykjavík: Leifur Eiríksson Publishing, 1997.

Egils saga Skalla-Grímssonar, ed. by Sigurður Nordal. Reykjavík: Hið íslenzka fornritafélag, 1933.

Einar Olgeirsson. *Ættasamfélag og ríkisvald í þjóðveldi Íslendinga*. Reykjavík: Heimskringla, 1954.

Den eldre Gulatingslova, ed. by Bjørn Eithun, Magnus Rindal, Tor Ulset. Oslo: Riksarkivet, 1994.

Fellows-Jensen, Gillian. "Tingwall, Dingwall and Thingwall." *Twenty-Eight Papers Presented to Hans Bekker-Nielsen on the Occasion of his Sixtieth Birthday 28 April 1993*. Odense: Odense University Press, 1993, 53–67.

[25] Gunnar Karlsson, *Goðamenning*, 199–202.

Grágás. Lagasafn íslenska þjóðveldisins, ed. by Gunnar Karlsson, Kristján Sveinsson and Mörður Árnason. Reykjavík: Mál og menning, 1992.

Gunnar Karlsson. *Drög að fræðilegri námsbók í íslenskri miðaldasögu* I. *Landnám, stjórnkerfi og trú*. Reykjavík: Háskóli Íslands, 1997.

Gunnar Karlsson. *Goðamenning. Staða og áhrif goðorðsmanna í þjóðveldi Íslendinga*. Reykjavík: Heimskringla, 2004.

Gunnar Karlsson. "Goðar og bændur." *Saga* 10 (1972): 5–57.

Jakob Benediktsson. "Landnám og upphaf allsherjarríkis." *Saga Íslands* I, ed. by Sigurður Líndal. Reykjavík: Bókmenntafélag, 1974, 153–196.

Jón Jóhannesson. *A History of the Old Icelandic Commonwealth. Íslendinga saga*, translated by Haraldur Bessason. [S.l.]: University of Manitoba Press, 1974.

Jón Jóhannesson. *Íslendinga saga* I. *Þjóðveldisöld*. Reykjavík: Almenna bókafélagið, 1956.

Maurer, Konrad. *Die Entstehung des isländischen Staats und seiner Verfaßung*. München: Christian Kaiser, 1852.

Maurer, Konrad. *Upphaf allsherjarríkis á Íslandi og stjórnarskipunar þess*, translated by Sigurður Sigurðarson. Reykjavík: Bókmenntafélag, 1882.

Ólafur Lárusson. *Lög og saga*, ed. by Lögfræðingafélag Íslands. Reykjavík: Hlaðbúð, 1958.

Sigurður Líndal. "Ísland og umheimurinn." *Saga Íslands* I, ed. by Sigurður Líndal. Reykjavík: Bókmenntafélag, 1974, 197–223.

Ullmann, Walter. *Medieval Political Thought*. Harmondsworth: Penguin, 1975.

Vilhjálmur Finsen. "Om de islandske Love i Fristatstiden." *Aarbøger for nordisk Oldkyndighed og Historie* 1873 (1873): 101–250.

SUMMARY

The political system of the Icelandic commonwealth has been described in two different ways. Some scholars, especially those from the early and mid-twentieth century, regarded it as the product of a conscious attempt to create a new kind of democracy, unparalleled anywhere else at the time. Other scholars, especially towards the end of the same century, tended to view the Icelandic commonwealth as a variation on the kind of political organisation found elsewhere in medieval Europe, dominated by a small ruling elite for several centuries while the nation was without a monarchy, because of its geographical isolation from mainland Europe. This paper offers a third possible characterisation, whereby the Icelandic commonwealth may be seen, in essence, as a remnant of an older Germanic political culture in which general assemblies (*þing*) played a key role. The unique nature of the Icelanders' conversion to Christianity exercised a decisive influence on their subsequent system of government. Most Germanic nations were converted to Christianity when individual kings decided to abandon their heathen deities in favour of the Christian God, thereby compelling their followers to adopt Christianity. So total was the disappearance of heathen priests that evidence of their title, *goði*, was scarcely to be found anywhere thereafter. In Iceland, on the other hand, the *goðar* decided to accept Christianity; they therefore retained secular power, and royal power did not reach the country for another two and a half centuries. Because of this the Icelandic political system developed several distinctive features. There were attempts to compensate for the lack of specific holders of executive powers through the development of comprehensive legislation and a system of law courts. Evidence for an element of democracy could certainly be found in the sense that the power of the rulers was dependent on the power of their subordinates, but, in all probability, this was a remnant of an ancient Germanic peasant community, and had survived in the absence of a king. There is scant evidence to support the notion that the political system of the Icelandic commonwealth was consciously innovative. Nevertheless, it is likely that this system of government did play a part in the creation of one of the greatest innovations of European medieval culture, Icelandic literature.

Gunnar Karlsson
Faculty of History and Philosophy
School of Humanities
University of Iceland
gunnark@hi.is

RICHARD GASKINS

CREATING AT THE MARGINS: CULTURAL DYNAMICS IN EARLY ICELAND

> *"Every society embodies conflicting factors, simply because it has gradually emerged from a past form and is tending toward a future one."*
>
> Émile Durkheim (1960, 59)

Introduction

The study of *civilizations* is an emerging scholarly pursuit that revives some venerable traditions of social history (Jóhann Páll Árnason 2003). Its proponents investigate patterns of cultural development in widely dispersed times and places. From a range of such examples, they hope to weave broader comparative theories. It comes as no surprise that "civilizational" theory has begun to consider early Icelandic society and sagas. With its literary heritage and accompanying historical data, the Icelandic cultural record may provide a rich laboratory for testing new interpretations of cultural development. The encounter between civilization theorists and scholars of early Iceland should produce benefits for both sides. For broad theorists, civilizational concepts need to find concrete applications, especially through a range of textual sources, historical periods, and geographic locations. If this approach should bear fruit, it may provoke new questions and lend new resources to Icelandic literary and historical scholarship.

This recent concern with civilizations reflects contemporary interests and is not a regression to older styles (Wittrock 2006). We no longer share the gloomy prospects of Spengler's *Untergang* (1918–22) or the eschatology of Toynbee's mythic vitalism (1934–61), both of which belong to the last century. In the new millennium, as nations and cultures become increasingly focused on global connections and diverse conflicts, social historians search for patterns of cultural growth and decay. The study of civilizations is part of the self-commentary of our own age, providing us with critical distance on our basic notions of modernity. Given the special dominance of the West, we are curious about tensions and conflicts that were likely present when our modern institutions first emerged in transitional societies. As a pre-modern cultural episode on the periphery of Christianizing Europe, the dynamic society portrayed in sagas and contemporary histories offers an unusually rich source of self-reflection. It responds fully to sociologist Jóhann Páll Árnason's interest in finding "connections between the internal pluralism of modernity and the civilizational pluralism of its prehistory" (2003, 13). A civilizational perspective on early Iceland invites us to roam with unusual freedom across normal scholarly boundaries of history, politics, philosophy, the arts, and literature.

The 2007 Skálholt symposium provided a multidisciplinary response to the challenge laid down by Jóhann, one of the leading exponents of the civilizational approach. The symposium was an occasion for scholars of medieval Iceland to revisit standard findings and controversies, including some that were assumed to have been safely settled (Gunnar Karlsson 2007). At its core, Jóhann's framework encourages a retrospective search for cultural tensions, contrasts, variations, and novelty within the cultural epoch of the Icelandic commonwealth [*þjóðveldi*]. His framework casts suspicion on static interpretive models, norms, and structures as tools for understanding what was plainly a changing society, evolving over four centuries. It asks skeptically whether we can reduce that distant culture to its legal codes, social functions, systematic ideologies, historical data sets, narrative structures, religious doctrines, artistic symbols. Indeed, the new framework suggests that standard disciplinary categories may need to be recast as more fluid and dynamic. Alongside the fixed rule, one must also look for the exception, the deviation, and the underlying creative force that blurs the boundaries of academic specialties. Some interpretations of early Iceland are content to presume monolithic world views, mentalités, or closed value systems, and to enforce strict boundaries between historical and literary modes of understanding. Jóhann's framework questions these standard interpretive categories and boundaries. His civilizational perspective leads to a more subversive, iconoclastic spirit of inquiry, accompanied by the scent of risk and danger. When it comes down to what we really know about the Icelandic commonwealth, one is tempted to quote, with mild irony, the dictum that "all that is solid melts into air."

Dynamics of Political Expansion

Taking up Jóhann's challenge to think more experimentally, this paper describes some possible scholarly paths for civilizational theory. The paper focuses on an important theme suggested by Jóhann (Gunnar Karlsson 2007, abstracts), concerning the "mechanisms of political expansion" during the commonwealth period. Current historical scholarship provides a solid foundation for analyzing political structures in Iceland from the time of early settlement until the collapse of the commonwealth in 1262. Perhaps the most comprehensive treatment is Gunnar Karlsson's *Goðamenning* (2004), which Gunnar admirably summarized for the discussants at Skálholt. Based on careful analysis of historical data and legal texts, Gunnar has described a coherent system of political organization, one that famously lacked any true executive function. The most distinctive political role within this system was that of the *goði*, a leader of sometimes charismatic dimensions around whom public duties and power struggles seemed to revolve. Gunnar has reconstructed the complex system of *goðar*, testing the structural rules against what we know about historical realities across the space of several centuries. His work seeks to establish the date when the number of *goðar* became stable, and when presumably the system functioned something like the model described in *Grágás* and in at least some saga texts.

Gunnar's emphasis on formal structures leaves room for further questions, however, since political practices were manifestly changing over the course of four centuries. During the final century of the commonwealth, as we know from reading *Sturlunga*, Iceland experienced a series of civil struggles centered on family-dominated regions or domains (*ríki*). Gunnar outlines this subsequent structure in his book, cataloguing the seven *ríki* that were eventually whittled down to even smaller numbers, until the system imploded in 1262–64. By formulating these two distinct formal structures separated by time, Gunnar's work points to the very questions that hold special interest for civilizational theorists. These questions concern the dynamics of development, beginning with how and why the system of *goðar* underwent its particular shift. What forces guided the evolution and eclipse of the "*goðamenning*," and what propelled the consolidation (and then competition) of domains? Gunnar is fully aware that formal political structures leave unsettled these key dynamic questions. He reminds us of the truism that political power has an inherent tendency toward consolidation, but acknowledges that such general assumptions fail to specify the particular mechanisms through which the competitive struggle played out across the commonwealth period, with its destructive outcome (Gunnar Karlsson 2004, 314). He is also properly skeptical about some conventional dynamic explanations, including imputed belief systems or ideologies attributed to Icelandic settlers (e.g. the desire to be free of Norwegian precedents, the desire to establish "democratic" associations) (Gunnar Karlsson 2009). And it is likewise problematic to personalize complex political trends by attributing historical agency to saga protagonists featured in the *Sturlunga* compilation. For the historian, these saga-mediated personalities explain both more and less than we would like to know. In short, even with the most prodigious historical research on political structures, we are left with an intriguing set of questions about underlying dynamic forces of development.

A similar set of questions arise from the work of historian Jón Viðar Sigurðsson, who posits a series of structural shifts in the political order during the commonwealth era (1999). In contrast to Gunnar's analysis, Jón believes that an "unstable" *goðar* system probably never conformed in fact to the formal prescriptions found in *Grágás*. He outlines multiple stages in which political power could have evolved from early decentralized alliances, soon after settlement, to the consolidation of power in family domains, and ultimately to fatal competition. The evidence for this more fluid pattern remains speculative, and it requires bolder assumptions about how the historian might weave saga texts into the scholarly tapestry. And the civilizational theorist can still ask what particular forces drove these multiple structural shifts. Jón suggests a wider range of explanations for his structural shifts: population density, the consolidation of wealth within families, increasing scale of landholding, new ideologies of power imported from Norway, control over church properties. But historians everywhere face the common difficulty of showing how such broad causes can serve as "mechanisms" of development in concrete situations. The dynamic orientation of civilizational theory points to a new kind of approach, and in doing so pushes interpretation further in the direction of the sagas.

Like Gunnar, Jón is willing to supplement the historical record with references to events described in sagas, and not just to those events contemporary with *Sturlunga*. He notes patterns of alliance-building found in tales of the *söguöld*, and he mentions numerous sagas in which law serves as a strategic tool for gaming the prevailing authority structure. By accepting the sagas as supplementary evidence for historical generalizations, Jón seeks some greater leverage for Icelandic historical studies. His approach is compatible with recent European historiography, which has accepted more porous boundaries between historical "fact" and narrative "fiction" (Iggers 1997, 144). But important questions remain about exactly how to unlock the cultural meaning that is presumed to reside within the sagas. Although Jón subscribes to a relatively dynamic view of history and politics, paradoxically, when it comes to sagas he assigns them a monolithic cultural outlook or world view. Despite his eagerness to explore the fluidity of political development, Jón treats the broader culture as frozen into a constant value system. He seems to need that normative stability (or "high degree of continuity") in cultural values as a guarantee of fixed reference for the whole field of saga evidence—as a condition for bringing saga examples into his historical work (1999, 28).

At this point the civilizational theorist will push the dynamic impulse still farther. Why should we accept the postulate of a single, unified value system standing behind the society portrayed in the sagas? It seems more likely that cultural values themselves evolved over the period of four centuries, and may thus have been riven with internal tensions. In the same way that Gunnar allows a second formal model into his political scheme, Jón suggests that the Icelandic commonwealth may have held two successive coherent value schemes, identified respectively with the *söguöld* and with the final century of the *samtíðarsögur* (1999, 31). With this approach, Jón follows standard historical conventions, hoping to explain the evolution of political forms in terms of an implied normative consensus in the broader culture (and hence reflected in saga writing). But the civilizational perspective asks whether it is in fact necessary to assume that value structures meet this requirement of coherence and stability. Values may rather be dynamic and fluid—perhaps even the central engine for evolution within a particular culture. Is it possible to integrate saga evidence into historical studies without falling back on this static model of culture? If cultural meaning is integral to the expansion of institutional structures (Jóhann Páll

Árnason 2003, 202), a dynamic value system may reveal the key pressure points. We may require a different approach that admits value tensions and variations as part of the cultural texture of early Iceland.

Dynamic undercurrents (a brief interruption)

All attention turns therefore to values. But before shifting to that topic, let us step back and review the particular concerns that have emerged about "mechanisms of political expansion" during the commonwealth period, using the civilizational perspective. Here we confront a problem that haunts all historical scholarship, in that the *outcomes* of political dynamics over time are always more complex than the mere historical *conditions* from which they evolve. Even when we master the whole gamut of data about laws, norms, individual ambitions, local feuds and battles, church initiatives, and foreign interventions, the synergistic process of political development transforms these baseline data into qualitatively new results. These results are like the emergent properties of complex systems: they are path-dependent mutations of individual motives and social structures, where the whole is always greater than the sum of its parts. We confront a critical gap between "input data" (such as structural patterns and micro-motives of individual actors) and transformative "outputs," (the resulting macro-effects that emerge over time, jointly produced out of complex behavioral and cultural environments). As I have proposed elsewhere, one way to bridge this gap is to apply techniques of "network analysis," which mediates between historical/social data and transformative social outcomes (Gaskins 2005). Network analysis operates on the assumption that historical outcomes are always richer than the sum of all inputs. By augmenting the study of social structures and personal motives, networks look for dynamic forces in transactional patterns, firmly embedded in alliance-building activities that reveal how and why new structures develop. In the case of Icelandic political development, we can take this dynamic step only by integrating the textual resources of the sagas – with all the subtlety and difficulty entailed by crossing disciplinary boundaries. In taking this step, it is important to state clearly what we hope to learn from sagas, and how to go about the task – a project that leans heavily on the humanistic content of Iceland's vast literary heritage.

A civilizational perspective helps push us across this narrow bridge between historical studies and literary interpretation, while encouraging frequent return trips in both directions (Jóhann Páll Árnason 2003, 5, 52, 217). If the mediating path crosses through the field of moral values, we need a more dynamic conception of how those values enter into the flow of history and saga narrative. Taking values as a cultural pivot, we may come to understand the transformative powers embedded in historical causes. By way of contrast, we know of two scholarly strategies that fail to perform this connection between sagas and standard history, both of which make the fatal assumption that the secret of development lies entirely within individual agency. One such strategy uses exchange models, rational actors, and efficiency concepts to intensify the strength imputed to individual actors in charting their own historical destiny. (Some of these approaches have been critically examined by Sverre Bagge, including the mantra that "nothing succeeds like success" [1991, 96].) Such methods invariably downplay the complex social environments in which individuals assert their presumed power. Stories from the *Sturlunga* compilation provide us with tempting portraits of just such powerful personalities, and it seems plausible enough that increasingly large political domains (*ríki*) allowed their powerful masters to become more "effective" or "efficient" in 12th-century Iceland. But unless one reads the sagas solely for the plot, this line of interpretation has serious limits. Whether powerful individuals earn success or defeat depends also on the horizons of possibility available to them under actual circumstances (possibilities alluded to in the subtle framing qualities of saga narrative). Even the strongest agents must take their chances in ambiguous action arenas, where limits are not fully specified, where outcomes are field-contingent, and where cultural ironies abound. In using saga evidence, we need to attend both to agents and to the more elusive cultural fields in which their actions play out.

A second flawed method for supplementing history projects back onto individual actors a set of intentions or ideologies that are presumed to be sufficiently powerful to produce historical change. For example, in order to rescue the agency of Icelanders at various stages of political development, it is tempting to assign them a prior belief system that devalues kingship. (It is also possible, according to Ármann Jakobsson [1997], to posit the opposite belief.) But such projections tend to reduce cultural forces to static ideologies, rather than treating values and beliefs as part of an evolving cultural field. Gunnar Karlsson seems properly skeptical that implied belief systems of this sort can tell us very much about why history turns out the way it does (Gunnar Karlsson 2009). As conflicts unfolded in the thirteenth century on a very broad canvas, certain underlying forces favored actors with one or another set of strong beliefs. The beliefs alone can never explain the results. Unless the eventual outcomes of those heightened struggles are treated as simply inevitable, we need to identify the contingencies favoring their success. A civilizational approach pursues these matters into the field of values.

Evolving moral structures

Over the space of four centuries, a newly settled land passes through a succession of political forms, culminating in an expanding series of regional conflicts. The historical evidence, separated from us by nearly a thousand years, provides structural snapshots of that development, but the process itself must have been continuous, fluid, oblique, complex. Social scientists may look for supplementary theories to codify these hidden dynamics, anything from Marxism to rational choice; but the choice of such theories is itself a matter of scholarly taste, if not a leap of faith.

Historians like Gunnar and Jón Viðar bring saga texts into their analyses – although with considerable circumspection, in light of the traditional divide between historical and literary modes of interpretation. And yet the most distinctive quality of the Icelandic commonwealth must surely be its singular capacity for self-commentary in the sagas, which continued even as the political order ceded autonomy to the Norwegian crown. Such creative expression at the periphery of Europe, flourishing at the margins of kingly power and Christianizing forces, may point to dynamic undercurrents that elude traditional history. If civilizational theory hopes to gain from its experimental tour through early Iceland, its path must pass through the sagas.

The notion that sagas may reveal the deeper cultural fabric of commonwealth Iceland has its own history of caution and excess. In recent decades, scholars have sought detours around the old dichotomy of interpreting sagas as either historical fact or literary fiction (Gísli Pálsson 1992). The most common route has been to treat sagas as repositories of cultural values contemporary with their time of composition. According to this approach, even if we reject their historical references as literal truth, the sagas remain undiminished as cultural artifacts, and thus as normative evidence of some kind. But this approach does not require us to regard the sagas as embracing a fixed scheme of values, any more than we accept timeless structures in historical or sociological studies. If Icelandic social history evolved over a period of four centuries, we would expect to find comparable movement at the level of norms, impelled by parallel forces. The pattern of evolution amid conflict should apply just as well to cultural values.

This dynamic perspective is often missing from social scientific studies of norms. Some anthropologists, for example, have tried to import the sagas into their professional domain as a type of alien "culture" ripe for antiquarian field studies. But their efforts have achieved mixed results. Anthropologists may overstate the coherence of value systems, in the same way that static models flourish in studies of Icelandic law, politics, and social structures. In their zeal to bring their discipline to bear on saga texts, social scientists have managed to distort the narrative complexities of saga writing (Gaskins 1997). They may also be captives of their own cultural assumptions, which oscillate between treating value systems as either consensus-based or conflict-based. Consensus theories led to the reductive arguments of structural/functionalism, while conflict theories impose a contrived disorder on the texture of moral life.

A promising approach to exploring values in Icelandic sagas and society has been presented by philosopher Vilhjálmur Árnason, starting with his seminal essay (1985). Reviewing past efforts to find moral content in the sagas, Vilhjálmur notes the tendency of interpreters to reduce the contents of saga texts to one or more moral ideologies. It is common enough, for example, for interpreters to find a finished set of Christian moral beliefs in various sagas, either replacing or in serious conflict with an opposing "pagan" moral system. Vilhjálmur questions whether we should read sagas as advocating (or contesting) such monolithic belief systems, especially when these systems have been defined centuries later by critics with their own cultural agendas. Following Hermann Pálson's terminology, Vilhjálmur also explores (1985, 23) a contrast between "romantic" and "humanistic" interpretations of saga morality: the romantic mode focusing on the intrinsic qualities of singular individuals (notably the "heroic" individuals), and the humanistic mode (following Hermann himself) on the moral qualities of deeds in these action-packed tales. Both methods of moral interpretation present difficulties, according to Vilhjálmur. I think he would be especially dubious about reducing saga culture to a mere "clash of civilizations," where distinct pagan and Christian ideologies are locked in single combat. To be sure, there is plenty of combat to be found in these pages; but the protagonists are best not confused with static, abstract belief systems.

Vilhjálmur explains why we should understand values in the sagas as complex and evolutionary – no less so than the political, legal, and social systems in which they are embedded. He warns against reducing moral actions to either abstract belief systems or mere sociological functions. To be sure, the sagas are deeply concerned with moral issues, and these issues cannot be isolated from the social structures in which they develop. But moral actions portrayed in the sagas occur within a specific horizon of social possibilities, the contours of which stand outside the control of moral choice. Moral actions and social structures are thus distinct but mutually interacting features of a common culture (Vilhjálmur Árnason 1991). The actions of saga characters acquire moral significance within the boundaries of social possibilities, which are often implied or tacitly invoked in the delicate balancing of saga narrative. Vilhjálmur calls for a different kind of moral reading from the romantic or humanistic scholars of earlier generations. His approach treats sagas as a mode of self-reflection on tensions between situational moral choices and the social or political order under which moral problems arise. One can say that morality is present in, but distinct from, a field of social possibilities – a condition Vilhjálmur appropriately compares to the Hegelian concept of *Sittlichkeit* (1991, 163). As this self-reflective culture passes through four centuries of development, we can assume that moral possibilities appear within a constantly changing horizon. And as sagas flourish during the final century of the commonwealth era, they scrutinize the virtues of prior centuries under the inevitable strain of an ever-present "law of unintended consequences." Examples of how saga narratives convey this form of commentary can be found in Vilhjálmur's contribution to this current symposium (here, 217–240).

Civilization as self-reflection: the importance of sagas

Early Iceland was a society in transition, filled with conflicting tensions and dynamic forces. But where was it all coming from, and where was it going? So far I have used the civilizational perspective as a methodological guide, but have withheld specific historical labels. Was the Icelandic commonwealth late pagan? Early Christian? Some combination of the two? These are very broad categories created retrospectively by modern scholars, and subject to styles of scholarly consensus. It is certainly possible to explicate sagas as a competition of world views, but it is more useful to look for qualities of self-reflection in the elusive forms of narrative practice (Sigurður Nordal 1942). If we want to find deeper undercurrents and subtle dynamics that have eluded both the social scientist and the moralist, we must pursue this conjunction of narration and representation (Vésteinn Ólason 1998, 191–205).

This direction seems entirely consistent with the aims of civilizational theorists. Sociologist S.N. Eisenstadt finds the core interest in civilizations in the specific reflective capacities of "transitional" societies (2006). For Eisenstadt the "civilizational turn" looks to the emergence of transcending ideas, symbols, utopias, technologies and alternative realities, held up against a background of prior stability. This notion of transcendence marks a culture that encompasses a plurality of standpoints, where mere realities are continually contrasted with alternative possibilities. According to Eisenstadt, societies where pluralistic conceptions are integral to the culture are dynamic in ways that contrast sharply with static empires, frozen in their monotonic cultural landscapes. The dynamic civilization displays epistemological complexities, generating fruitful and fractious tensions, while serving also as an engine of development for law, politics, morality, and cultural expression. (Long before Eisenstadt, the philosopher Hegel [1993–95] described civilizations as dynamic by virtue of such divided visions.) According to Eisenstadt, the notable civilizations of the "axial age" were the loci of profound theological insights, including the bifurcated vision of the early Christian culture with its dichotomous realms of God and man. The emergence of a competing, transcendent order opens the way for revolutions, radical discoveries, new social institutions, but also constant strife. When the distance between dichotomous realms reaches into infinity, the most stringent battles are waged by the supreme authority assigned to that transcendent realm, as it casts perpetual suspicion on the mundane features of the temporal realm.

In summarizing Eisenstadt's general model, Jóhann emphasizes the connections between cognitive transcendence and the dynamics of political development:

> The axial visions give rise to more ambitious and elaborate ways of legitimating more complex and expansive power structures...; the axial transformation broadens the cognitive horizon and therefore the strategic scope of power centres and elites, but the growing quantity and diversity of cognitive resources is at the same time an obstacle to the monopolization of power... (Jóhann Páll Árnason 2003, 47).

Questions about authority and legitimacy thus shift from the strategic realm of mundane competition and acquire a new horizon and potentially a new conceptual vocabulary, importing values from a newly accessible normative realm.

In applying this model to early Iceland, Jóhann seems to identify that new realm as already belonging to transcendent religion. For him, the turning point is the emergence of sacred kingship, often a pivotal transition for the civilizations of the axial age (2003, 42). And surely this emphasis on the sacred deserves to be developed further. But there is another possibility, if one regards this transitional period in Iceland from the vantage point of its own past, and especially from the perspective of "the only European people who remember their beginnings" (Sigurður Nordal 1942, 1). Saga writing presents us with a muted or inchoate form of transcendence – one that retains a distinctly human or pragmatic dimension, where the distance between realms falls short of the infinite distance found in Plato, St. Augustine, and other visionaries of the axial age. Elsewhere I have suggested that a work like *Heimskringla* offers a fundamentally secular vision of concepts that later periods would eventually label "legitimacy" and "authority," a vision that holds great interest for us because of its pre-conceptual richness (Gaskins 1998). That elusive saga voice may resound strongly for a post-Enlightenment age like our own, where we struggle with paradoxes of political authority, but without the consolation of theological certainties. (For more on the secular perspective of diverse saga types and periods, see Vésteinn Ólason 1998, 49).

In this less canonical form of transcendence, the dynamic tensions of a transitional society are nonetheless on display. The heroic moral virtues of earlier days appear as socially problematic; the conciliatory spirit (seen as weak in an earlier context) may be superior in meeting new political demands for social peace. A cultural system based on kinship loyalties reveals its dysfunctions as the young society advances multiple generations past the time of first settlement. Alliances created outside the bonds of kinship open up new but yet unknown political possibilities—revealed in future disorder, as disparate layers of loyalty come into open conflict. Lawfulness can build up a new nation, as trust and friendship flower in a system of decentralized authority; but that same nation may soon be laid waste with lawlessness, amid the diffusion of authority and lack of a unifying center. The charismatic individuals who build large domains of power cannot ultimately sustain competion against comparably sized units, especially when power must learn to survive transitions across generations. Societies with kings may be understood to have strengths and weaknesses, and the very idea of a single highest form of authority (whether secular or sacred), must be carefully weighed in secular terms.

Precisely how does saga narrative address these puzzles and paradoxes? This is a question that cannot be adequately addressed in a conclusion; and there are obviously diverse types of sagas and poetry that may capture different sides of this emerging capacity for self-reflection. Along with multiple styles, one finds a comparable variety of rhetorical effects directed toward transcending notions. Vésteinn Ólason has provided a broad overview of these effects, showing how narrative displays of balance and judiciousness project their own sense of authority and reason (Vésteinn Ólason 1998, 59, 101). Elsewhere I have offered brief examples of how some standard conventions of saga writing may capture cultural undercurrents (Gaskins 2005). In the present essay my goal has been to connect this self-reflective activity to the special concerns of civilizational theory. For some Iceland scholars the civilizational approach may seem tangential, grandiose, or both. But Jóhann and his colleagues have laid down an intriguing challenge, which holds great promise for future scholarly experimentation.

It is often said that "heroic societies" are static places where reflection has no place—where social structure and morality are one and the same, as in Eisenstadt's definition of the stable empire (Vilhjálmur Árnason 1991, 164, citing Alasdair MacIntyre). Perhaps early Iceland can be seen as an exceptional case study: a heroic society in the process of emerging from that static condition, spreading out over four centuries, and recorded in singular fashion by a contemporary literature of self-reflection. As Sigurður Nordal pointed out long ago, the retrospective orientation of later sagas can be seen as an occasion for cultural renewal, as has been the pattern in other cultures (1942, Part III). In Icelandic prose and poetry, the distinctive quality of this reflection may reside in its restraint in embracing a stricter, theological form of transcendence, in favor of a more humanistic, immanent form (Vésteinn Ólason 1998, 137). This evolutionary phase may have lasted for a brilliant moment, before its visions of authority adapted more fully to the Christian dichotomy of sacred and temporal.

As suggested earlier, our own post-Enlightenment concerns with authority and legitimacy may find special resonance in the early Icelandic experience, if we see it as preoccupied less by theological imperatives than by humanistic interests in peace and honor. A recent study by intellectual historian Mark Lilla notes that most civilizations in history have been organized on the more extreme premises of "political theology," which bases the correct order of society on transcendent revelation. Our own liberal culture, according to Lilla, has struggled to reconcile our continuing need for authority with the demise of its theological underpinnings, starting with Hobbes. We honor our liberation from sacred transcendence, but we yearn for stories and myths that reconcile us to the rigors of that freedom:

> We are still like children when it comes to thinking about modern political life, whose experimental nature we prefer not to contemplate. Instead, we tell ourselves stories about how our big world came to be and why it is destined to persist. These are legends about the course of history, full of grand terms to describe the process supposedly at work—modernization, secularization, democratization, the 'disenchantment of the world,' 'history as the

story of liberty,' and countless others. These are the fairy tales of our time. Whether they are recounted in epic mode by those satisfied with the present, or in tragic mode by those nostalgic for Eden, they serve the same function in our intellectual culture that tales of witches and wizards do in our children's imaginations: they make the world legible, they reassure us of its irrevocability, and they relieve us of responsibility for maintaining it (Lilla 2007, 6).

We may find it useful to contrast these modern legends to the sagas told by Icelanders, which serve as the prelude to the rise of "political theology," and not its postlude. A self-commentary on our own age draws us into such distant times and places, and civilizational theory should be especially grateful for its encounter with commonwealth Iceland.

REFERENCES

Ármann Jakobsson. 1997. *Í leit að konungi*. Reykjavík: Háskólaútgáfan.
Bagge, Sverre. 1991. *Society and Politics in Snorri Sturluson's* Heimskringla. Berkeley: University of California Press.
Durkheim, Émile. 1960. *Montesquieu and Rousseau*. Ann Arbor: University of Michigan Press [originally published 1953 based on Durkheim's 1892 Latin dissertation].
Eisenstadt, S.N. 2006. The *Great Revolutions and the Civilizations of Modernity*. Leiden: Brill.
Gaskins, Richard. 1997. "Félagsvísindamanna saga." *Skírnir* 171:185–207.
Gaskins, Richard. 1998. "Visions of Sovereignty in Snorri Sturluson's *Heimskringla*." *Scandinavian Journal of History* 23:173–88.
Gaskins, Richard. 2005. "Network Dynamics in Saga and Society." *Scandinavian Studies* 77: 201–16.
Gísli Pálsson, ed. 1992. *From Sagas to Society*. Enfield Lock: Hisarlik Press.
Gunnar Karlsson. 2004. *Goðamenning: Staða og áhrif goðorðsmanna í þjóðveldi Íslendinga*. Reykjavík: Heimskringla.
Gunnar Karlsson. 2009. "Was Iceland the Galapagos of Germanic Political Culture." This volume, 77–91.
Hegel, G.W.F. 1993–95. *Vorlesungen über die Philosophie der Religion*, ed. Walter Jaeschke [material from Hegel's lectures 1824–1831]. Hamburg: Felix Meiner Verlag.
Iggers, Georg G. 1997. *Historiography in the Twentieth Century*. Hanover NH: Wesleyan/University Press of New England.

Jóhann Páll Árnason. 2003. *Civilizations in Dispute: Historical Questions and Theoretical Traditions*. Leiden: Brill.
Jóhann Páll Árnason, Eisenstadt, S.N. and Wittrock, Björn. 2005. *Axial Civilizations and World History*. Leiden: Brill.
Jón Viðar Sigurðsson. 1999. *Chieftains and Power in the Icelandic Commonwealth*. Odense: Odense University Press.
Lilla, Mark. 2007. *The Stillborn God: Religion, Politics and the Modern West*. New York: Knopf.
Sigurður Nordal. 1942. *Íslenzk menning* I. Reykjavík: Mál og menning.
Spengler, Oswald. 1918–22. *Der Untergang des Abendlandes*. München: C.H. Beck'sche Verlagsbuchhandlung.
Toynbee, Arnold. 1934–61. *A Study of History*. Oxford: Oxford University Press.
Vésteinn Ólason. 1998. *Dialogues with the Viking Age: Narration and Representation in the Sagas of the Icelanders*. Reykjavík: Heimskringla.
Vilhjálmur Árnason. 1985. "Saga og siðferði." *Tímarit Máls og menningar* 46:21–37.
Vilhjálmur Árnason. 1991. "Morality and Social Structure in the Icelandic Sagas." *Journal of English and Germanic Philology* 90:157–74.
Wittrock, Björn. 2006. "Civilizations in Dispute" [Review]. *European Journal of Sociology* 47: 407–416.

SUMMARY

The Icelandic þjóðveldi was a society in transition, filled with conflicting tensions and dynamic forces. The civilizational perspective advanced by Jóhann Páll Árnason and others provides a useful approach to understanding Icelandic cultural development over four centuries, including the development of political forms. That approach casts suspicion on static interpretive models, stable norms and ideologies, and fixed legal structures in favor of more dynamic analysis. It also prompts us to use creatively the rich materials contained in saga narratives, written near the end of this period. For it is here, in the self-reflection of a culture, that the fault-lines within ethical forms are revealed, along with the subtle mechanisms of legal and political development. Civilizational analysis overplays its hand by applying standard categories of paganism or sacred kingship to the Icelandic case. Rather the sagas display a more fundamentally secular vision of authority and legitimacy, imbued with a humanism and immanence that marks the cultural temper of the Icelandic þjóðveldi.

Richard Gaskins
Brandeis University (USA)
gaskins@brandeis.edu

KIRSTEN HASTRUP

NORTHERN BARBARIANS:
ICELANDIC CANONS OF CIVILISATION

THE NOTION of civilisation implies its own negation – that which is not civilised. For civilisation to register, a negative mirror image must be invoked, located either in another time or in another place. Whether the opposition is constructed temporally or spatially, and whether it is symbolic or real, images of otherness may provide fresh insights into the constitution of the declared civilisation.

In the case of Iceland, literary and other written sources provide rich material for reflecting on the Icelanders' perceived position in the world; by defining and redefining 'the others' they constantly sought to distinguish themselves and redraw the relevant boundaries of their own civilisation. This paper starts by exposing some of the classical ideas of civilisation and otherness, by which the Icelandic singularities may be measured. Having themselves once been perceived as Barbarians of the North, the Icelanders were particularly explicit in redrawing the boundaries of proper culture. Through their literary efforts they provided canons of a civilisation that is recognisably 'European', yet also quite distinct.

In my reassessment of the Icelandic canons of civilisation, I shall not waste much time on problems of definition. I shall simply say that my starting point is a view of civilisation as a comprehensive whole, which stands out from a general and more amorphous backdrop of an un-civilised world in the mind of the civilised people themselves. Civilisation is thus a matter of self-perception, and – of course – of some degree of self-objectification. This will be substantiated in more detail in the course of my article. The implicit argument is that while a culture or a society is simply one of a kind, civilisation is unique and absolute. There can only be one. My aim here is to focus on the implicit contrast between the self-declared civilisation and its Other, a non-discrete category of barbarians. Neither civilisation nor barbarians were native terms in medieval Iceland, but I shall use them to sum up the perceived contrast between self and others at the time.

Antique civilisation: The prototype effect

In starting my discussion with a brief look on the antique origins of perceived civilisation as against perceived barbarism, I do not pretend to cover the ground so well researched by classical scholars. My aim is solely to establish a few salient points that have a bearing on the Icelandic case, on the general principle that the classical world came to be seen as the cradle of European civilisation itself and the beginnings of a distinctly European way of thinking. While it is hard to tell what the Icelanders thought about the yet indistinct 'Europe', we do know that learned Icelanders were versed in classical readings. To give just one example at this stage, the author of the remarkable *First Grammatical Treatise* wrote (c. 1140): "Because languages differ from each other – which previously parted or branched off from one and the same tongue – different letters are needed in each, and not the same in all, just as the Greeks do not write Greek with Latin letters, and Latinists (do) not (write) Latin with Greek letters, nor (do) the Hebrews (write) Hebrew with Greek or Latin letters, but each nation writes its language with letters of its own" (*The First Grammatical Treatise* 1972, 206–207).[1] The distinction between languages here is made on the basis of a sense of original (linguistic) unity. Already at this stage, learned Icelanders saw themselves in the mirror of a larger and *literate* world. There were many known languages – and cultures – but they were united in civilisation through writing. In the vernacular, writing implicitly reflected an extensive Norse and pre-Christian tradition, while Latin carried the load of a long European tradition, a tradition that was not simply borne by Christendom and the Latin alphabet but went beyond it to Greek legend and myth (Bagge 2004; Eldevik 2004). This is where the barbarians first appeared.

[1] "En af því at tungurnar eru úlíkar hver annarri, þær þegar er ór einni ok hinni sǫmu tungu hafa gengiz eða greinz, þá þarf úlíka stafi í at hafa, en eigi ena sǫmu alla í ǫllum, sem eigi ríta Grikkir latínu stǫfum girzkuna ok eigi latínumenn girzkum stǫfum latínu, né enn heldr ebreskir menn ebreskuna hvárki girzkum stǫfum né latínu, heldr rítar sínum stǫfum hver þióð sína tungu." [Spelling normalized by editor]

In ancient Greece, the word 'barbarian' was used in the *Iliad* (l. 2,867), where it figures as an adjective to the unintelligible language of a named group of people. Barbarians were inarticulate within the ethnocentric framework of the Greeks. It was Herodotus, however, who in the 5th century B.C. was to launch an absolute distinction between the Hellenes and the barbarians, the latter simply being people who were *not* Hellenes (Lund 1993: 10ff). In the process, Herodotus inadvertently defines a Greek 'nation', when he – in *The Histories* – renders the Athenians' reasons for not submitting to Xerxes, the Persian king:

> No doubt it was natural that the Lacedaemonians should dread the possibility of our making terms with Persia; none the less it shows a poor estimate of the spirit of Athens. There is not so much gold in the world nor land so fair that we would take it for pay to join the common enemy and bring Greece into subjection. There are many compelling reasons against our doing so, even if we wished: the first and greatest is the burning of the temples and images of our gods – now ashes and rubble. It is our bounden duty to avenge this desecration with all our might. Again, there is the Greek nation – the community of blood and language, temples and ritual; our common way of life; if Athens were to betray all this, it would not be well done (Herodotus, 1972, 574–575).

What transpires is a sense of distinction relating to descent, language and religion that had to be protected, not only against the Persians, but against all barbarians, who by the same token could not take part in the Athenian sports and games. Interestingly, The First Grammarian also speaks of nations (*þjóðir*), each with their own language. Possibly as significant in relation to the Icelandic case is Herodotus' overarching notion of history being a well researched story about what had happened; where true historical sources are lacking, Herodotus draws on (sometimes conflicting) oral traditions (Burn 1972, 9–10). We know a similar feature from Ari's *Íslendingabók* ('The Book of the Icelanders'), written sometime between 1122 and 1130 (*Íslendingabók. Landnámabók* 1968).

At the present stage of my argument my main point is that within the classical scheme of thought, barbarians were not an ethnic group as were the Hellenes; they were a category of people beyond the intelligible world. At various points in time, different people were depicted as 'standard-barbarians'. In Greek pottery-art the Scythians were singled out as prototypical barbarians, being a nomadic people of horsemen and bow-fighters who in their life-style contrasted starkly with people of the Greek *polis*, the city-state (Hastrup, H 1997). This is a first significant observation of an asymmetrical relationship between the civilised and the un-civilised, the former providing the yardstick of civilisation itself.

This skewed relationship was to become cemented in the third century BC, when political thinking developed further with Plato and his pupil Aristotle, who dealt with the nature of the state – that is the *polis* itself. In Book One of his *Politics*, Ch. 2, Aristotle frames his position by referring to a natural order of things in which some are born to rule, others to be ruled; among the latter are women and slaves, internally distinguished by nature by their different functions. He continues: "But among barbarians no distinction is made between women and slaves, because there is no natural ruler among them: they are a community of slaves, male and female. Wherefore the poets say – "It is meet that Hellenes should rule over barbarians"; as if they thought that the barbarian and the slave were by nature one" (Aristotle 1943, 52). Interestingly, the will (and capacity) for distinction here becomes a mark of civilisation itself, along with a recognition of born rulers.

Being the highest mark of human achievement and the natural goal of development, "it is evident that the state is a creation of nature, and that man is by nature a political animal. And he who by nature and not by mere accident is without a state, is either a bad man or above humanity; he is like the "Tribeless, lawless, heartless one", whom Homer denounces – the natural outcast is forthwith a lover of war" (Ibid., 54). In the political domain, lacking a state is a token of homelessness on a comprehensive scale. The counterpoint to civilisation is a free-roaming outcast, tribeless, lawless, heartless – and stateless. Already we detect the Icelandic sequel.

I shall refer to only one more example from Aristotle, namely his discussion of slavery. In *Politics*, Book One, Ch. 6, he maintains that "there is a slave or slavery by law as well as nature" (Ibid. 1943, 60). The former refers to the Hellenic order, within which slavery is simply a practical convention, while the natural slaves are found elsewhere.

> Wherefore Hellenes do not like to call Hellenes slaves, but confine the term to barbarians. Yet, in using this language, they really mean the natural slave of whom we spoke at first; for it must be admitted that some are slaves everywhere, others nowhere. The same principle applies to nobility. Hellenes regard themselves as noble everywhere, and not only in their own country, but they deem barbarians noble only when at home, thereby implying that there are two sorts of nobility and freedom, the one absolute, the other relative (Ibid., 61).

This is a stunning declaration to the effect that the Hellenes stands out as unique; only they are measurable on an absolute scale of nobility and freedom, applicable exclusively to themselves, not to humanity at large. While on the surface, learned Greeks from Homer to Aristotle saw humankind as *one* biological species, and the barbarians as merely babblers within it, the distinction between Hellenes and others went deeper. The inability to speak Greek was in effect much more than a linguistic shortcoming; people who were devoid of both *logos* and *polis* were by definition outside of the *oikumene* (Pagden 1982, 16). The babblers may have been of the same species, but they were certainly of a different kind not having been taught the virtues of the *polis*. The state is a precondition for virtue and the proper use of human intelligence. Says Aristotle in *Politics*, Book One, Ch. 2:

> But he who is unable to live in society, or who has no need because he is sufficient for himself, must be either a beast or a god: he is no part of a state. A social instinct is implanted in all men by nature, and yet he who first founded the state was the greatest of benefactors. For man, when perfected, is the best of animals, but, when separated from law and justice, he is the worst of all; since armed injustice is the more dangerous, and he is equipped at birth with arms, meant to be used by intelligence and virtue, which he may use for the worst ends. Wherefore, if he have not virtue, he is most unholy and the most savage of animals, and the most full of lust and gluttony (Ibid., 54).

The barbarians are no longer simply incomprehensible; they are uncivilised by all tokens of civilisation that are now seen to form an integrated whole.

When the Romans inherited the word barbarian from the Greeks, the shift of emphasis from language to culture was explicit (Lund 1993, 16). In the first century BC, Cicero wrote his treatise *The Republic*, in which he answers the question of whether Romulus' subjects were barbarians in the following manner: "If, as the Greeks say, all people other than Greeks are barbarians, I'm afraid his subjects *were* barbarians. But if the name should be applied to character rather than language, then the Romans, in my view, were no more barbarous than the Greeks" (Cicero 1998, 26). In contrast to the notion of Hellenes as an exclusive ethnic category, the notion of Romans was inclusive and comprised different groups within the empire. Gradually, some became more Roman than others, and the classification of the (ideal) Romans as barbarians that had been accepted by way of the Greek gaze subsided to a new alignment between Greeks and Romans as equally civilised – they were humans of the same kind in contrast to the Germanic tribes on the northern frontier, for instance (Lund 1993, 18ff).

These preliminary observations serve to highlight the so-called prototype effect inherent in classification which greatly complicates the viewpoint held by semanticists that all members of a particular category are equal (Rosch 1978; see also Hastrup 1995: 26ff). In practice, including linguistic practice, some members are always 'better' examples of the category than others; when 'birds' are mentioned, for Danes, little songbirds spring to mind more easily than ostriches, for instance. Prototypes reflect clusters of experience and socially embedded semantic densities that incorporate experience into the category system (Ardener 1989, 169).

This insight into the nature of categories has important implications for our understanding of social stereotypes, where the prototype effect often results in a metonymic replacement of the entire category by only parts of it (Lakoff 1987, 79ff). It seems to be particularly pertinent in relation to identity categories – such as Hellenes or Icelanders – where all members are not equally good examples; slaves for instance cannot be said to represent the category in either case. When it comes to the identity of civilised or even human, clearly 'we' are always a more likely prototype than the 'others'; the others are less representative of the category to which we ourselves belong. In this way, the eccentric nature of words intervenes in the experience of worlds. When the perspective chosen is from within a self-declared civilisation, the others are by definition less human than us;

this was the case with the ancient Greeks but I shall argue that it is a general feature of the definition of a civilisation is that it marginalises and often dehumanises others, the barbarians, and lumps them together in a single image of alterity in relation to humanity proper.

This was a model that was easily transposed into the early perception of the Christian world, based upon a myth of a single progenitor of humanity but also on a clear demarcation between insiders and outsiders. The Christian congregation was set apart from the rest of the world, but in contrast to the Greek *oikumene* it was open to others who could enter by way of conversion. The barbarians could – and for their own good, should – convert to proper society. As a term for the ultimate others, the barbarians remained a mirror for civilisation proper until modern times. The mirror, of course, was held up by the self-professed civilisation – as first defined in the classical world, where the North was as yet in the mists.

Ultima Thule: Maps and metaphors

When the far North was first brought to the attention of the classical world of Southern Europe, it was encapsulated in the notion of *Ultima Thule*. Tracing Thule as a concept for the ultimate North means engaging with particular horizons, notably the boundary between known and unknown worlds. As recently discussed by Vincent Crapanzano, people are constantly concerned with both openness and closure in their construction of horizons that determine what we experience and how we interpret what we experience. "When a horizon and whatever lies beyond it are given articulate form, they freeze our view of the reality that immediately confronts us – fatally I'd say, were it not for the fact that once the beyond is articulated, a new horizon emerges and with it a new beyond" (Crapanzano 2004, 2). This process of the shifting of horizons is a key issue in the understanding of any image of the North.

Since classical times, Thule marked the imaginative horizon of the unknown North, and for some it inspired a distinct call. Among the pioneers was Pytheas of Massalia who in the 3rd century B.C. went further north than any other from the classical world. Pytheas visited the British Isles, "but the bold and hardy explorer does not seem to have stopped here.

He continued his course northward over the ocean, and came to the uttermost region, "Thule", which was the land of the midnight sun, "where the tropic coincides with the Arctic Circle"'" (Nansen 1911, 53). Pytheas was an astronomer and the most important observation he brought back was the length of the day during summer in this place, which was 'six days' sail north of the Orcades. The actual location of Pytheas's Thule remains uncertain because most of Pytheas's own observations have been lost, and are known only through slightly later, and highly critical renditions (by Pliny and Strabo, among others), who were sceptical about the possibility of life that far north.

In the early twentieth century, the Danish geographer H.P. Steensby used geographical evidence to assert that Pytheas's Thule would have been located in western Norway, and probably in the region of present day Bergen (Steensby 1917, 17). Steensby was further inclined to suggest that Pytheas himself had actually only come as far north as the western coast of Jutland (of present day Denmark), where he would have gathered information about this place even further north that he then named Thule. This would fit the mythical portent of the name.

Whatever the actual geographical turning point for Pytheas, the notion of *Thule* soon took on a life of its own and was to refer to a moving and imaginary horizon between an inhabitable and civilised South, and a barely inhabitable land of barbarians in the far North. Perhaps the most influential source for this particular image of the North was found in Virgil's vision of Augustus's resurrection of the Roman Empire to which even Ultima Thule would surrender (Harbsmeier 2002, 37). In Seneca's *Medea* (1st century), the Chorus comments on the future possibilities of the Argonauts, and says that when the world grows older the ocean will open and new continents will be disclosed, and Thule will no longer be the farthest of lands (*nec sit terris ultima Thule* (Seneca. *Medea*, 1927, 267–279).

Thus it is fair to say that in antiquity, Thule belonged to the imaginary horizon of human life, on the edge of which an unknown people lived in strange ways. Space does not permit me to go further into this, and I shall leave antiquity by giving the final word to Fridtjof Nansen, whose image of the misty relationship between the antique south and the far north is evocative of Thule itself:

Thus at the close of antiquity the lands and seas of the North still lie in the mists of the unknown. Many indications point to constant communication with the North, and now and again vague pieces of information have reached the learned world. Occasionally, indeed, the clouds lift a little, and we get a glimpse of great countries, a whole new world in the North, but then they sink again and the vision fades like a dream of fairyland (Nansen 1911, 124).

There is an oscillation between the openness and closure of horizons in this image that was to find a new balance in the Middle Ages. With the extensive travels of the Vikings and Norsemen, communications between North and South became more regular, and with the Viking expansion on the North Atlantic, new horizons opened. People from the British Isles and Scandinavia moved out – to Iceland and beyond. Meanwhile, the various geographies that had been produced in the first millennium maintained the idea of the 'outer sea', and the island of Thule on the edge of the world; interestingly, in quite a number of medieval texts, the Scythians are now living in the North, and more precisely in Sweden (Hemmingsen 2000).

In 825 A.D., Thule appears in a work by the Irish monk Dicuil (*Liber de Mensura Orbis Terrae*) and given the context, there is no doubt that it refers to Iceland – as it would for Adam of Bremen and Saxo Grammaticus a little later. Some authors have wanted to project this back onto Pytheas's Thule (e.g. Stefánsson 1942), but this is highly unlikely, given that Pytheas (allegedly) speaks of a people threshing and eating oats, among other things. So far, there is no archaeological evidence of human presence in Iceland at Pytheas' time.

In *Landnámabók* (*Sturlubók*, Ch. 1), the identification of Thule with Iceland is taken for granted. Sturla refers to Beda, who had mentioned the island of Thile six days' sailing north of Britain, where the sun shines all night when the days are longest but is not seen at all when the nights are longest. The echo from Pytheas is still audible across all of these centuries, and Sturla readily embraces the name of Thile for his island, whose history of settlement he then proceeds to describe. Again, there is a strong feeling that the Icelanders knew their classical texts.

From the outside, the position of the Icelanders in the larger scheme of things is not entirely clear. For Adam of Bremen (1968), writing in the late eleventh century, the inhabitants of Thule were somewhat anomalous: The Icelanders treated their bishop as king, and took his words for law. It has been suggested that Adam mistook the Lawspeaker for a bishop, but the implication is clear: the Icelanders had no proper king, as had otherwise become the mark of civilised government (Hastrup 1985). This state of affairs was correlated with another apparent paradox in Iceland. According to Adam, the inhabitants were exceedingly primitive (as befalls the inhabitants of legendary Thule!) and lived in a state of nature; yet they were Christians. From the perspective of Bremen, the Icelanders mediated between the truly wild peoples such as the Finns – who had been identified by Procopius as the last barbarians of the northern countries – and the civilised world of Christians and kingdoms. Implicitly, this observation echoes Brink's point that Christianisation is not 'an event', or an abrupt ideological shift; it is rather a gradual change in mentality (Brink 2004).

The history of Thule – first as a metaphor for a distant land in the mysterious North and later as a distinct island in the North Atlantic – is a revealing case of the interpenetration of maps and metaphors. In this case the metaphor preceded the map; or, in a different phrasing, the illusion of an unknown land drove the explorers to the limit and urged them to map the blank spaces; later, the maps themselves became new metaphors as happened to Vancouver's chartings of the Pacific coast of America (Fisher and Johnston 1993). The result of mapping is as much a continuation of metaphor as it is a new map. Even when Thule was finally situated in northern Greenland, when in 1910 Knud Rasmussen established his Thule station (Hastrup 2009), the result was still a 'cartographic illusion' (Ingold 2000, 234). The map never simply represents the world, because in the process of representation, two important processes are bracketed: first, the process by which the explorers had arrived there in the first place – including the process by which they came to imagine Thule as their goal; and, second, the process by which they inadvertently came to represent it in particular terms. The actual way-finding across the sea, the experience of drift-ice and unreliable climes corroborated the classical image of Thule that again filtered into the final map through the process of (mentally) mapping the experience in comprehensible terms.

The illusion of Thule reminds us that both maps and histories are matters of perspective and of available imagery. In the process of the vision and revision of the image of Thule, the mental map turned into a tenacious metaphor that was itself remapped every time the horizon shifted. The horizon moved but metaphors still informed the maps by which people oriented themselves in space. Thule remained on the edge of the world – as Adam of Bremen articulated so well. For a long time, Iceland fitted this image very neatly.

In a general way, the Scandinavians of the Middle Ages accepted that they were, indeed, peripheral. They lived 'on the far edge of the dry land' (Bagge 2004); as testified to by *Konungs skuggsjá*, the learned Scandinavians knew that their lands bordered on the outer sea. Yet at the time, these lands were increasingly affected by the literary impulses reaching them from the centre in the shape of translations or adaptations of European books; and within the northern world a new elite emerged, defined as such because of their having incorporated the literate culture of the larger Christian civilisation. As Sverre Bagge has it, the very position as elite depended on the definition of Scandinavia as peripheral; Bagge continues:

> In this situation, two strategies were possible: (1) [to] try to become as similar as possible to what was understood as the 'common European culture', or (2) [to] cultivate one's own originality and show that one's own traditions were equal to those of the rest of Europe. Both strategies are found all over Scandinavia, but generally the first approach is more common in Denmark and Sweden, and the second in Iceland, with Norway in an intermediate position (Bagge 2004, 356–357).

Thus while Saxo Grammaticus – writing in Latin in compliance with the Danish view of what should be done to match European Christendom – complains that the Danes have only a poor knowledge of Latin, clearly implying that they were still rather uncivilised, the Icelanders take great pride in devising a vernacular literature that is both singular and on a par with southern traditions. By means of both strategies the northern lands gradually became integrated into European civilisation (Adams and Holman 2004).

For Iceland (and for the Norse tradition in general), it has been suggested that writing in the vernacular may not simply have been a matter of pleasing the public, but a more profound issue of the use of older skaldic sources for the new historical literature – sources that were not easily transported into Latin (Mundal 2000). At yet another level, we might also see this as an expression of an ideology of civilisation based on a distinct – and sacred – spirit of 'Norseness', in no way inferior to the spirit of Athens invoked by Herodotus.

Iceland on its own: Textualisation

When Thule was first located in Iceland in the early Middle Ages, it was not yet permanently populated, but this was soon to happen. The process is well described in early Icelandic sources, as is the constitutional moment of the Icelandic commonwealth – when the Alþing was inaugurated and Icelandic law was formalised in 930. At the time, law was synonymous with society in Scandinavia, as explicated in the proverbial statement *með lögum skal land byggja*. The highest office in Iceland was held by the Lawspeaker, who had to recite all the laws over a period of three successive meetings at the Alþing; constitutional matters had to be spoken every year, however. We recall how law was diacritical also for the classical notion of civilisation.

In the mind of the Icelanders, law was a precondition for proper society – as it was for the classical scholars. Conversely, if people did not abide by the law, they were outlawed. Outlaws and other outsiders played an important part in the self-perception of Icelandic society, as can be seen from some of the most popular sagas like *Grettis saga Ásmundarsonar* (Hastrup 1986). The outsiders were convenient 'others' against which the insiders could see themselves; on the whole the inside-outside dichotomy persisted in Icelandic cosmology as a conceptual scheme for distinguishing between the familiar and the alien, the known and the unknown, at many levels of social life (Hastrup 1981). The law itself was a main factor in closing off a civilised space against the untamed wild. While the actual legal practice was peculiar to Iceland, the general idea of defining society by way of law was also part of the Aristotelian tradition.

Vár lög ('our law') was the only comprehensive term for Icelandic society in the early middle ages, and it goes without saying that any settler could become part of it by abiding to the law. Icelandic society was inclusive, as Roman society had been. At the dawn of Icelandic history there are no specific claims to a distinct Icelandic culture, only to a shared law. In those few contexts where a distinct 'we' is pertinent, the diacritical feature is one of language. Thus, to be a member of any court, a person had to be a native speaker of *dönsk tunga* (*Grágás* Ia, 38). This is well known of course, but we may reassess its significance in view of the civilising project; the law cannot be spoken in barbarian babble.

The first notion of the Icelanders as a distinct people is owed to Ari *inn fróði*, whose *Íslendingabók* launches an idea of historical continuity from the settlements until the time of writing, between 1122 and 1130. 'The Icelanders' emerged as an ethnic category – with retrospective application from the settlements (Hastrup 1990b). A shared history is what connects them; the formal legal entity is supplemented by a substantial, if implicit reference to what Herodotus said about 'the common ways' of the Greek. This was further substantiated with the advent of the *First Grammatical Treatise* (c. 1140), which is singular in its being the only known grammatical work in a vernacular language of the period. The author states that he was prompted to write the treatise because reading and writing had become common by then, and he wanted to facilitate the reading and writing of "laws, genealogies, religious works, and the learned historical works, which Ari has written with great acumen" (Hreinn Benediktsson, ed. 1972, 208–209).[2] Demonstrating the inadequacy of Latin letters for expressing the sounds of Icelandic, he subsequently suggested an alphabet for 'us, the Icelanders' (Ibid., 21). The distinctiveness of the Icelandic language is fully recognised – even if it was not until c. 1400 that the deep affinity to west Norwegian seems to have dissolved, judging from the fact that the export of Icelandic books to Norway had come to a complete stop by then (Stefán Karlsson 1979).

The first civilising move had occurred with the *landnám* itself, however much it was only retrospectively identified as made by 'Icelanders'. The tradition established by *Íslendingabók*, *Landnámabók* and the Icelandic sagas provides a detailed and vivid history of the settlements as personal-

---

[2] "... lǫg ok áttvísi eða þýðingar helgar eða svá þau hin spaklegu fræði, er Ari Þorgilsson hefir á bœkr sett af skynsamlegu viti." [Spelling normalized by editor]

ised in freedom-loving farmers of predominantly Norwegian origin. This could be seen as an expression of the predominant local self-perception. From the outside, the picture was less clear. In *Historia Norwegiæ*, a twelfth-century history composed by a Norwegian, the first settlers Ingólfr and Hjǫrleifr are said to have left their native Norway because they were killers (Storm, ed. 1880, 92–93). The inferiority of the (would-be) Icelanders is thus beyond question. By fleeing to Thule they have turned their back on civilisation and whatever safe haven they may have found, they remain criminals – barbarians.

Possibly, this allegation is the reason why the writer of the *Melabók*-version of *Landnámabók* is so articulate about his wish to get history right: "It is important to be able to tell outlanders, who believe that we descend form thralls or criminals, about our true ancestry ... it is mark of all civilised peoples that they themselves want to know about the origin of their country's habitation" (*Landnámabók. Melabók* 1921, 143).[3] As against the Norwegian claim to superiority, the Icelandic retort is clear: We, the Icelanders, descend from men of honour as appropriate historical knowledge ascertains.

In some ways this is also the key to the Icelandic sagas written in the same period. In the sagas, tenth-century Iceland is depicted as a time of legal and social integrity, of manly honour and of kin loyalty. There were deviants, scoundrels and outlaws, but the social dramas were played out on a scene of original nobility – a nobility that depended on the scoundrels for their own distinction. Through this literary rehabilitation of the past, and of the tenth century in particular, an idea of a pre-Christian era of freedom and statesmanship was established. This is what Gerd Weber called the *Freiheitsmythos* of the Icelanders (Weber 1981). Law, literature and freedom merge in the tradition of the Icelandic settlers fleeing from the tyranny of King Harald Fairhair that is but another way of distinguishing oneself from past compatriots. The literature itself bears witness to what seems like an 'auto-civilising' process – with new claims to distinction in terms of language, law and descent.

The literary mediation of the dilemma related to the pagan beginnings

---

[3] "En vér þykkjumst heldr svara kunna útlendum mönnum, þá er þeir bregða oss því at vér séum komnir af þrælum eða illmennum, ef vér vitum víst vorar kynferðir sannar ... eru svo allar vitrar þjóðir at vita vilja upphaf sinna landsbyggða ...". [Normalised by editor]

of Icelandic civilisation had an interesting counterpart in the actual conversion of the Icelanders c. 1000. The story has been told and retold a number of times, and I shall only relate the most salient points within the present context. Following missionary activities and a general shift towards Christianity in the rest of Scandinavia (along with the establishment of kingdoms), the *goðar*, that is the lesser local chieftains who had both religious and secular functions and who played a main role also at the annual Alþing, had started to convert. This transformed Christianity from a private to a political matter and accelerated the process of Christianisation considerably. At the opening of the Alþing in the year 1000, the people were divided in two camps, heathen and Christian. Some suggested that the two groups declare themselves 'out of law with one another' (*Íslendingabók* Ch.7), thus effectively establishing two societions within the same space. Others, and among them the Lawspeaker, the heathen Þorgeirr, felt that to rend asunder law was to rend asunder peace, and he suggested a compromise within one law that he then 'spoke': the Icelanders would accept Christianity with some provisos; the exposure of newborn children, the consumption of horsemeat, and sacrificing to heathen gods were still to be permitted on the condition that these activities took place in secrecy.

Within the context of contemporary European views of the world, the shift from heathenism to Christianity marks a shift from barbarism to civilisation, albeit a hesitating one in this case. One element in this is the advent of writing as a corollary to mission and conversion. The more important element, however, is the paving of the way for kingship and a new sense of the state – thus realising what Aristotle saw as the primary element in civilisation. Although the conversion occurred at one point in time in Iceland, we need not believe that there is a distinct before and after in the actual social life of the Icelanders. It is simply a way of thematising a historical process that had begun long before and which was to continue for a long period yet. We should also remember that 'heathenism' itself emerged simultaneously with Christianity, for which it provided an apt counterpoint – which could be annulled through conversion. It was insufferable that the Icelanders were to remain barbarians in the eyes of the bearers of Christian civilisation, even if they had to suffer peculiarly unfortunate material disadvantages on their far northern island.

There is another sense in which the literary activity makes up for something awkward in Icelandic history, namely the descent from pagans. If, as suggested by Kurt Schier (1981), the entire literary activity of the thirteenth century may be read as a more or less explicit wish to raise and maintain a consciousness of the Icelandic prestations in *terra nova*, it also sets the stage for the Icelandic love of freedom and for their noble activities. In other words, the stage was one upon which 'the noble heathen' played an important part (Lönnroth 1969) – a strange precursor to Rousseau's noble savage. In a thoroughly Christianised period – if such is possible – such as the thirteenth century, the literary motif of the noble heathen was a way of solving the dilemma between a pagan past and the teachings of the Church – a dilemma that Adam of Bremen had puzzled over in the eleventh century. Within Iceland itself, the dilemma was solved in writing – the literature mediating the awkward descent from pagans and present nobility.

It is no accident, therefore, that the central and most elaborate chapter of *Íslendingabók* concerns the introduction of Christianity in Iceland; it is supplemented by the accounts of the three last chapters which deal with the early history of the Church. No doubt this was seen as a major civilising move, a move that definitely signalled a turning away from heathenism – and by consequence from barbarism. *Landnámabók* too testifies to a civilising process on the Icelanders' own account. By naming and historicising nameless tracts, the authors of *Landnámabók* definitively claimed Thule for civilisation. The categorical others of the learned classical world now defined themselves, and reclaimed a degree of nobility. Additionally, *The First Grammatical Treatise* measured vernacular Icelandic against Latin and found the latter did not entirely match the sounds of Icelandic. These three texts are among the oldest literary pieces in Icelandic, and together they testify to a local self-consciousness as a civilised society within a larger order of civilisation. The texts offer their own solutions to the paradox of having a kingdom without a king, a law without ruler, a written language without religious imperatives.

In this connection it is worth mentioning Saxo Grammaticus who, in his prologue to the *Danish Chronicle*, writes about the nature of Iceland being so savage that one should hardly expect people to live there; he thereby echoes the general opinion held in 'the South' that Thule is on the margins of human habitation. It is well established that Saxo was influenced by classical authors, and among them Virgil who spoke so elaborately about Thule (Friis-Jensen 1975). What is more significant in the present context is Saxo's reverence for the Icelanders' historical writings, which are important sources for his own work. The Icelanders, so to speak, fast all the year round because of natural scarcities, but they use their days to collect and expand knowledge of their own and other people's ways of life; "they make up for their privations by means of their art" (Saxo 1941, 34). Saxo gives a hint of another measure of civilisation here: artistic expression may compensate for material wants. The irony is that all the time that they were (re-)claiming European civilisation for themselves, the Viking descendants had to live with increasingly pointed European literature, which derided their achievements and once again portrayed them as the true villains of Europe, merging them with Saracens and other 'others' who were presented as waiting (in vain, as it happened) to destroy the virtue of Christendom (Levy 2004).

Looking back at Icelandic literary activity from a broad perspective, however, there is no doubt that it contributed to an accelerating process of self-objectification through writing. It is not a simple matter of technology and I am not making a universal statement of writing in itself being civilisational; studies of literacy have made us aware that it is not so simple (e.g. Bloch 1989). Even in ancient Greece, writing itself was not liberating (Andersen 1989). I am more concerned with *textualisation*, understood as a "double process which consists in a society's adopting writing as a social usage, and, as a consequence of that, understanding and construing social life, and society considered as a whole, as a text" (Meulengracht Sørensen 2001, 309). This was what made it possible for the Icelanders to write themselves (and their fellow Norsemen) into European history and – in the same move – to do so from a peculiar Icelandic perspective. The Icelanders' artistic activities did not simply make up for material wants, they placed Iceland solidly within European civilisation on the basis of an autonomous canon.

Relocating the Barbarians: Canonicity

The creation of a distinct textual canon of (a Northern) civilisation almost immediately co-produced a new counterpoint. In Iceland itself, heathens had been converted, slaves freed, and criminals outlawed according to the canon; and in the colonising of Greenland (and the voyages to Vineland and Markland), the Icelanders expanded Northern civilisation into a new and apparently empty territory that had to be textualised accordingly. As intimated by the author of *Konungs skuggsjá*, it was now Greenland that was located on the absolute edge of the land (*Konungs skuggsjá* ch. xix; cf. Bagge 2004). With the discovery of new territories, the unknown was translated into the known, and the canon was stretched to incorporate new knowledge (cf. Paine 1994:2). The horizon shifted but the canon remained in place.

However, in these new lands, the Icelanders met with people who defied every notion of civilisation, namely the *skrælingar*. The others by law (the Icelandic converts and outlaws) once again were measurable against the Other by nature. The civilised Self was further cemented with the new-found knowledge of a truly savage people. In a paradoxical way these savage people confirmed the canon of civilisation; by definition, a canon is exclusive and impregnable to the possibility of critique (Paine 1994:5). This is in contrast to — say — modern scholarship, which was founded on a principle of doubt in the Enlightenment and an idea of referentiality, rather than canonicity. In canon-governed circumstances, the unknown is closely linked to the known, either by incorporation or by refutation. The *skrælingar* are an example of the latter.

The etymology of *skrælingar* is not entirely clear, but probably it is related to *skræla*, 'skrante', and to *skrælna*, 'to shrink' (KLNM XV, 715; de Vries 1977). The general bearing of the term is a small person, and a weakling. Others have suggested that it refers to a howling creature, reminding us of the original use of the word barbarian as an adjective, denoting an incomprehensible speech.

The earliest source for the Skrælings is, again, Ari's *Íslendingabók*: Eiríkr and the first settlers in both east and west found remains of skinboats and stone-smithies '... from which we may understand that the people who built Vineland and whom the Greenlanders called skrælingar had gone there.' (*Íslendingabók. Landnámabók* 1968, 13–14).[4] Interestingly, here it is suggested that the people of Vineland had originally populated

---

4 '... af því má skilja, at þar hafði þess konar þjóð farit, es Vínland hefir byggt ok Grænlendingar kalla Skrælinga.' — Where no translated edition is referred to, the translations are the author's own.

Greenland, and on the whole it is impossible at this stage to say definitively whether the *skrælingar* were Indians or Eskimos; the distinction certainly was immaterial at the time, when the people that met the Norsemen were truly 'new'.

In *Eiríks saga rauða* ('The Saga of Eric the Red') itself, the *skrælingar* are described thus: 'They were black and ferocious men, who had wiry hair on their heads; they had big eyes and broad cheeks' (*Eyrbyggja saga* 1935, 227).[5] The Norse observers were none too pleased by what they saw; in other stray references to the native Greenlanders, the *skrælingar* were described as trolls (e.g. *Flóamanna saga* 1932, 43). Seen from the Icelandic centre, the Eskimos were definitely not human. They could in fact be anything but.

In slightly later sources, where actual meetings between the settlers and native inhabitants of Greenland are related, the references are still slightly mythical. When the (Greenlandic) Norsemen went hunting for seal and walrus at Norðrseta (their northernmost hunting grounds on the western coast of Greenland) they would see traces of settlements and also meet the 'small people' of *skrælingar*. An early source is *Historia Norwegiae* (c. 1200) in which it is said that "further north, hunters have found a small people, whom they call *skrælingar*. Hit by weapons when alive, their wounds turn white and do not bleed, but when they die their blood does not stop flowing" (*Historia Norwegiae* 1880, 75ff). The encounter probably was not entirely peaceful but that notwithstanding, a picture is given of a people of hunters, totally lacking iron but with a remarkable craft in using walrus bone and stone. These people would have been members of what was later to be known as the Thule-culture among archaeologists (Hastrup 2008); from the detailed description of their weapons and skin-boats, there is no doubt that the references in both *Eiríks saga rauða* and *Grænlendinga saga* are to members of this (archaeologically defined) early Eskimo culture – in so many ways the 'Scythians of the North' by their hunting and nomadic ways. Most encounters between the Greenlanders (of Icelandic descent) and the *skrælingar*, are depicted as a meeting between a farming and a hunting people that are driven towards each other by equal amounts of curiosity, enmity, a wish to exchange goods and a wish to remain untouched (e.g. *Eyrbyggja saga* 1935, 261f).

5 'Þeir váru svartir menn ok illiligir ok hǫfðu illt hár á hǫfði; þeir váru mjǫk eygðir ok breiðir í kinnum.'

The Norse colonies in Greenland were Christianised like Iceland, and even had their own bishop after 1126; they established their own Alþing, shared by the two settlements (Vestribyggð and Eystribyggð), and eventually they pledged allegiance to the Norwegian king in 1261, a year before Iceland. The story thus far is parallel to that of Iceland, but it took its own turn with the disappearance of the settlements. Characteristically, the lingering explanation for this is the enmity of the *skrælingar*. It is very likely, however, that changes of climate and a decline in commercial and other forms of exchange with Iceland proper, as well as countries further away, were the main factors. We know how in Iceland, similar developments account for a remarkable demographic and social decline (Hastrup 1990a).

The settlers died out, the story goes, and quite likely they had trouble in reproducing themselves. However, with a stock of c. 5000 people at their height (KLNM XIII, 654), the settlements would not have died out over night, without leaving a solid trace of human remains. We therefore may have to think in different terms; instead of dying out, possibly the Norsemen in Greenland were 'defined out'; they no longer knew themselves as before. By no longer adhering to old farming and herding ways, and having out of necessity adopted local 'Thule' ways, the Norsemen – as they knew themselves until then – ceased to exist. (The Hellenes had merged with the Scythians, so to speak.) In Iceland, we know how the farmers at the Alþing recurrently sought to counterbalance the demographic decline by introducing various restrictions on fishing (Hastrup 1990a, 67ff). As a kind of hunting, it could not take centre stage in a population of *soi-disant* farmers, even when farming was seriously hampered by climatic and other developments.

Farmers and hunters were not on a par; the former were civilised, the latter were barbarians. By becoming one with the Other, the Norsemen in Greenland could no longer be distinguished. They had 'died out'. The Norse colonies simply fell out of the civilisational range, and the metaphor of Thule took on a new life. Thus, when the Spanish King Charles V set out to conquer the New World, he took Virgil's *Tibi serviat ultima Thule* as his motto (Harbsmeier 2002, 37). His quest did not take him North, but others went there and warned their compatriots. Jean Malaurie, who went to the northernmost part of Greenland in the 1950s, quotes a certain Pierre Bertius, cosmographer of the Roy Trés-Chrestien, Louis XIV, who wrote in 1618:

The cold is indomitable ... and ... it kills in number. Winter lasts nine months without rain ... The richest protect themselves ... by fire; others by rubbing their feet and others by the warmth of the caves in this earth ... All this land is full of cruel bears with which the inhabitants wage continual war. There are also ... if what they say is true – unicorns. They hold that there are men called pygmies .. Pygmies have, it appears, a human form, hairy to the tips of the fingers, bearded to the knees, but brutish, without speech or reason, hissing in the manner of geese" (Quoted by Malaurie 1956, 30).

The little people, the trolls, the *skrælingar* or whatever the prototypical others had been named so far, are here joined by the Pygmies. They are located in a mythical nature, populated also by 'unicorns' (probably narwhals that had become larger-than-life). Whatever trace – genetic and otherwise – the Norsemen had left, they were no longer visible. Civilised life in Greenland had proved too far out.

The general point of this section is that once a true canon of civilisation is established, other ways of life cannot find a place within it – as 'other' that is. Canonicity turns thought into ideology, and either 'the other' is incorporated into the known as 'same' or must remain homeless and lawless within the civilised world as perceived. The others, however, remain necessary as accessories to self-perception and to ward off doubt about the canon by their very otherness.

Shifting horizons of civilisation: Urtexts

As is well-known, Icelandic civilisation declined after the Black Death in 1402–04. This is not simply an external, pejorative observation, it was also a decline by Iceland's own canonical standards (Hastrup 1990a), even if the foreigners were more outspoken. Internally, there were endless battles against fishermen refusing to take up residence as farm labourers, against *flakkarar* (vagrants), *útilegumenn* ('outliers') and others who did not fit the scheme of proper sedentary life. Even the humble practice of distant herding on *sel* (shielings) was given up, in the interest of keeping the shepherdesses at home. While before, the boundary had been drawn between lawful and lawless people, in the centuries following the Black Death which were gradually more marked by decline in many ways, the boundary was redrawn: people who did not fit the local standards, as set by the farmers, were simply deemed inhuman – *ómennskir*. They abounded in the sixteenth and seventeenth centuries.

For 16th- and 17th-century travellers from other parts of Europe, Iceland had (once again) turned barbarian. Gories Peerse, a German observer, left no doubt about the savage nature of the Icelanders. Thus: "Ten or more of them sleep together in one bed, and both women and men lie together. They turn heads and feet towards each other, and snore and fart like pigs under the homespun" (Sigurður Grímsson, ed. 1946, 27); Peerse also noted how "many priests and clerics make only two sermons a year" (Ibid., 25). So, beastly habits were accompanied by a notable laxity towards matters of religion. The latter is testified to in other contemporary sources; thus the critical observer Dithmar Blefken noted about the Icelanders that they "are all prone to superstition and have demons and spirits in their service. Some of the men with luck in fishing are woken up at night by the devil to go fishing" (Sigurður Grímsson 1946, 37). In a different manner, this is also the implication of the *stóridómur* of 1564, in which heresy of all kinds is banned (*Lovsamling for Island* I, 84–90). Probably, Iceland was hardly faring any worse than other European peasant communities, but when measured against the medieval self-perception as embodied in the literature, the one-time flourishing part of, and contributor to, European civilisation had certainly come down in the world.

The allegation of barbarism once again spurred a textual response. Just like the author of *Melabók* had once sought to redress the external assumption of Icelandic descent from scoundrels, so Arngrímur Jónsson now sought to improve the image of Icelandic society as essentially savage. In his *Brevis Commentarius* (1593, 1968) Arngrímur explicitly wanted to redress the negative image that had been bestowed upon Iceland, notably by Münster's cosmography. He wanted learned European contemporaries to know about Iceland's true geographical position (that the island is not as far off as assumed), and to convince them that if Thule was once seen as barbarian and inhabited by 'Skriðfinns', this has no bearing on the Icelanders who are Christians and live in proper houses. A significant feature in the present context is his wide use of classical points of reference, and his explicit position as a spokesman for Iceland as civilised. In his *Crymogæa* (1609, 1985), Arngrímur further describes the initiatives taken by the Danish kings after the reformation to improve the standards of the Icelanders. Significantly – with a view to the wave of European humanism in the wake of the renaissance, Arngrímur wrote in Latin – this was now the means to re-inscribe Iceland into European learning. No autonomous canon would now serve this end. Latin was instrumental to emphasizing the oneness of European civilisation. In the case of *Crymogæa*, it was further burdened by bearing the Greek name for Iceland.

I shall not continue this story, only use it to note how the horizons of civilisation shift, even if some of the parameters remain the same. The boundaries between selves and others are constantly redrawn, but it is only in the process of textualisation that a definite boundary towards an absolute Other – the radically different, or the barbarian – can be drawn. The power of literature in the process of civilisation – which is also a process of canonisation – is to provide a means of self-objectification; Cicero was well aware of that when he hailed poetry as the true means to eternal knowledge.

What happened in Iceland as well as in Greece, where the barbarians were first born as such, was that society itself was shaped in texts – texts that became canonical and therefore continued to frame the perception of propriety and truth. In both cases people were favoured – at first, if later burdened – by a set of *ur-texts*, to which they might refer whenever self-definition was an issue, and against which all new forms were seen as more or less successful variants (Herzfeld 1987; Hastrup 1998). Such ur-texts, defining the Ur-Norsemen and the Ur-Europeans respectively, are cornerstones in the perception of civilisation itself. Even today, we find that Icelandic uniqueness is still claimed with reference to medieval Icelandic history, and a purity of language, life and nature (Magnús Einarsson 1996).

In Greece the classical ur-texts canonised the Ur-Europeans, while in Iceland, the Ur-Norsemen were and often are still portrayed in terms of medieval canonical literature. In both cases, the literature propounds the defining features of civilisation. What connects the classical European and the Icelandic notions of civilisation goes deeper, however, and takes us to a profoundly European view of the world, not only textualising it, but basing it in a profoundly logocentric perspective. This is what makes the Icelandic view of civilisation so distinctly European, while also so remarkably northern. Beyond the *logos* of the literati and the lawmen, vagrants and babblers live another life altogether.

In this study I wanted to show how the idea of civilisation, and its expression in distinct political and other institutions, may be understood in terms of an absolute canon of civilisation, first established in a set of ur-texts, which transcends lesser cultural differences – provided people are still recognisable as civilised. In a logo-centric Europe, textualisation was a prime feature in the politics of recognition. This also applies to Iceland, providing the ur-texts of the early Nordic civilisation.

REFERENCES

Adam of Bremen. 1968. *De hamburgske ærkebispers historie og Nordens beskrivelse*, transl. by C.L. Henrichsen, 2nd ed. Copenhagen: Rosenkilde og Bagger.

Adams, Jonathan and Katherine Holmen, eds. 2004. *Scandinavia and Europe 800–1350. Contact, Conflict, and Coexistence*. Turnhout: Brepols.

Andersen, Øivind. 1989. "The Significance of Writing in Early Greece – a critical appraisal." Karen Schousboe and Mogens Trolle Larsen, eds. *Literacy and Society*. Copenhagen: Center for Research in the Humanities.

Ardener, Edwin. 1989. *The Voice of Prophecy and Other Essays*. Oxford: Blackwell.

Aristotle's Politics. 1943. Transl. by Benjamin Jowett. New York: The Modern Library of the World's Best Books.

Arngrímur Jónsson. 1968. *Brevis commentarius de Islandia* (1593). Preface by Jakob Benediktsson with an English Summary. Íslenzk rit í frumgerð 2. Reykjavík: Endurprent sf.

Arngrímur Jónsson. 1985. *Crymogæa* (1609). *Þættir úr sögu Íslands*, ed. and transl. Jakob Benediktsson. Reykjavík: Sögufélagið.

Bagge, Sverre. 2004. "On the Far Edge of Dry Land: Scandinavian and European Culture in the Middle Ages." Jonathan Adams and Katherine Holmen, eds. *Scandinavia and Europe 800–1350. Contact, Conflict, and Coexistence*. Turnhout: Brepols.

Bloch, Maurice. 1989. "Literacy and Enlightenment." Karen Schousboe and Mogens Trolle Larsen, eds. *Literacy and Society*. Copenhagen: Center for Research in the Humanities.

Brink, Stefan. 2004. "New Perspectives on the Christianization of Scandinavia and the organization of the Early Church." Jonathan Adams and Katherine Holmen, eds. *Scandinavia and Europe 800–1350. Contact, Conflict, and Coexistence.* Turnhout: Brepols.
Burn, A.R. 1972. "Introduction." Herodotus. *The Histories*, transl. by Aubrey de Sélincourt, revised, with an introduction and notes by A. R. Burn. Harmondsworth: Penguin Classics.
Cicero. 1998. *The Republic. The Laws*, transl. by Niall Rudd. Oxford: Oxford World Classics.
Crapanzano, Vincent. 2004. *Imaginative Horizons. An Essay in Literary-Philosophical Anthropology.* Chicago: University of Chicago Press.
Eldevik, Randi. 2004. "What's Hecuba to Them? Medieval Scandinavian Encounters with Classical Antiquity." Jonathan Adams and Katherine Holmen, eds. *Scandinavia and Europe 800–1350. Contact, Conflict, and Coexistence.* Turnhout: Brepols.
Eyrbyggja saga. Brands þáttr ǫrva. Eiríks saga rauða. Grænlendinga saga. Grænlendinga þáttr. 1935. Ed. by Einar Ólafur Sveinsson and Matthías Þórðarson. Íslenzk fornrit IV. Reykjavík: Hið íslenzka fornritafélag.
Flóamanna saga. 1932. Ed. by Finnur Jónsson. Copenhagen: Samfund til Udgivelse af gammel nordisk Litteratur.
Fisher, Robin and Hugh Johnston, eds. 1993. *From Maps to Metaphors. The Pacific World of George Vancouver.* Vancouver: University of British Columbia Press.
Friis-Jensen, Karsten. 1972. *Saxo og Vergil.* Copenhagen: Museum Tusculanum Press.
Grágás. Islændernes Lovbog i Fristatens Tid Ia, Ib. 1852. Ed. by V. Finsen. Copenhagen: Det Nordiske Litteratur-Samfund.
Harbsmeier, Michael. 2002. "Bodies and Voices form Ultima Thule. Inuit Explorations of the Kablunat from Christian IV to Knud Rasmussen." Michael Bravo and Sverker Sörlin, eds. *Narrating the Arctic. A Cultural History of Nordic Scientific Practices.* Science History Publications/USA.
Hastrup, Helene B. 1997. "Det er skythere!" *Sfinx* 20(4)4, 150–155.
Hastrup, Kirsten. 1981. "Cosmology and society in medieval Iceland." *Ethnologia Scandinavica* 1981: 63–78.
Hastrup, Kirsten. 1985. *Culture and History in Medieval Iceland. An Anthropological Analysis of Structure and Change.* Oxford: Clarendon Press.
Hastrup, Kirsten. 1986. "Tracing Tradition. An Anthropological Perspective on Grettis saga Ásmundarsonar." J. Lindow, L. Lönnroth, and G.W. Weber, eds. *Structure and Meaning in Old Norse Literature.* Odense: Odense University Press.
Hastrup, Kirsten. 1990a. *Nature and Policy in Iceland 1400–1800. An Anthropological Analysis of History and Mentality.* Oxford: Clarendon Press.
Hastrup. Kirsten. 1990b. *Island of Anthropology. Studies in Past and Present Iceland.* Odense: Odense University Press.

Hastrup, Kirsten. 1995. *A Passage to Anthropology. Between Experience and Theory*. London: Routledge.
Hastrup, Kirsten. 1998. *A Place Apart. An Anthropological Study of the Icelandic World*. Oxford: Clarendon Press.
Hastrup, Kirsten. 2008. "Shadows of Myth. The Emergence of the Thule Culture." *Facets of Archaeology*. Oslo Archaeological Studies 10.
Hastrup, Kirsten, 2009. "Images of Thule. Maps and metaphors in representations of the far North." Sverrir Jakobsson, ed. *Images of the North. Histories Identities Ideas*. Amsterdam & New York: Rodopi.
Hemmingsen, Lars. 2000. "Middelaldergeografien og *Historia Norwegiæ*." Inger Ekrem, Lars Boje Mortensen and Karen Skovgaard-Petersen, eds. *Olavslegenden og den latinske historieskrivning i 1100-tallets Norge*. Copenhagen: Museum Tusculanum Forlag.
The First Grammatical Treatise. 1972. Ed. by Hreinn Benediktsson. Reykjavík: Institute of Nordic Linguistics.
Herodotus. 1972. *The Histories*, transl. by Aubrey de Sélincourt, revised, with an introduction and notes by A. R. Burn. Harmondsworth: Penguin Classics.
Herzfeld, Michael. 1987. *Anthropology Through the Looking-Glass. Critical Ethnography in the Margins of Europe*. Cambridge: Cambridge University Press.
Herzfeld, Michael. 1995. "Hellenism and Occidentalism: The Permutations of Performance in Greek Bourgeois Identity." James G. Carrier, ed. *Occidentalism. Images of the West*. Oxford: Clarendon Press.
Historia Norwegiæ. Monumenta Historica Norwegiaæ. 1880. Ed. by Gustav Storm. Oslo: Brøgger.
Ingold, Tim. 2000. *Perception of the Environment*. London: Routledge.
Íslendingabók. Landnámabók. 1968. Ed. by Jakob Benediktsson. Íslenzk fornrit. I Reykjavík: Hið íslenzka fornritafélag.
KLNM: Kulturhistorisk Leksikon for Nordisk Middelalder fra Vikingetid til Reformationstid I-XXII. 1956–1978. Copenhagen: Rosenkilde og Bagger.
Lakoff, George. 1987. *Women, Fire, and Dangerous Things. What categories reveal about the human mind*. Chicago: University of Chicago Press.
Landnámabók, Melabók. 1921. Ed. by Finnur Jónsson. København: Kommissionen for det Arnamagnæanske Legat.
Levy, Brian J. 2004. "The Image of the Viking in Anglo-Norman Literature." Jonathan Adams and Katherine Holmen, eds. *Scandinavia and Europe 800–1350. Contact, Conflict, and Coexistence*. Turnhout: Brepols.
Lovsamling for Island I-XXI. 1853–1889. Ed. by O. Stephensen and Jón Sigurðsson. Copenhagen: Høst og Søn.
Lund, Allan A. 1993. *De etnografiske kilder til Nordens tidlige historie*. Aarhus: Aarhus Universitetsforlag.
Lönnroth, Lars. 1969. "The Noble Heathen. A theme in the sagas." *Scandinavian Studies* 41(1), 1–29.

Magnús Einarsson. 1996. "The Wandering Semioticians: Tourism and the Image of Modern Iceland." Gísli Pálsson & E. Paul Durrenberger, eds. *Images of Contemporary Iceland*. Iowa: University of Iowa Press.

Malaurie, Jean. 1956. *The Last Kings of Thule*. London: George Allen and Unwin. (Translated from the French, *Les derniers rois de Thule*. 1955. Paris: Plon)

Meulengracht Sørensen, Preben. 2001. "Literature and Society." *At fortælle Historien/Telling History. Studier i den gamle nordiske litteratur/Studies in Norse Literature*. Trieste: Edizione Parnaso.

Mundal, Else. 2000. "Den latinspråklege historieskrivinga og den norrøne tradisjonen: ulike teknikkar og ulike krav." Inger Ekrem, Lars Boje Mortensen and Karen Skovgaard-Petersen, eds. *Olavslegenden og den latinske historieskrivning i 1100-tallets Norge*. Copenhagen: Museum Tusculanum Forlag.

Nansen, Fridtjof. 1911. *In Northern Mists. Arctic Exploration in Early Time* I–II. London: William Heineman.

Pagden, Anthony. 1986. *The Fall of Natural Man. The American Indian and the Origins of Comparative Ethnology*. Cambridge: Cambridge University Press.

Paine, Robert. 1995. "Columbus and Anthropology and the Unknown." *Journal of the Royal Anthropological Institute* (N.S.) 1: 47–65.

Rosch, Eleanor. 1978. "Principles of Categorisation." Eleanor Rosch and B. Lloyd eds. *Cognition and Categorisation*. New Jersey: Social Science Research Council Committee on Cognitive Research.

Saxo Grammaticus. 1941. *Danmarks Krønike*, fordansket ved Nicolaj Frederik Severin Grundtvig, new edn. by Vilhelm La Cour. Copenhagen: Det Tredje Standpunkts Forlag.

Schier, Kurt. 1975. "Iceland and the rise of literature in "terra nova". Some comparative reflections." *Gripla* I, 168–181.

Seneca. *Medea*. 1927. Transl. Frank Miller. New York.

Sigurður Grímsson, ed. 1946. *Glöggt er gests augað. Úrval ferðasagna um Ísland*. Reykjavík: Menningar- og fræðslusamband alþýðu.

Steensby, Hans Peter. 1917. "Pytheas fra Massalia og Jyllands Vestkyst." *Geografisk Tidsskrift* 24, 12–34.

Stefán Karlsson. 1979. "Islandsk bogeksport til Norge i middelalderen." *Maal og Minne*. 1–2: 1–17.

Stefánsson, Vilhjálmur. 1942. *Ultima Thule. Further Mysteries of the Arctic*. London, Toronto, Bombay, Sydney: George G. Harrap & Co.

Vries, Jan de. 1997. *Altnordisches etymologishes Wörterbuch*. Leiden: Brill.

Weber, Gerd Wolfgang. 1981. "Irreligiosität und Heldenzeitalter. Zum Mythencharacter der altisländischen Literatur." Ursula Dronke et al., eds. *Speculum Norroenum. Norse Studies in Memory of Gabriel Turville-Petre*, Odense: Odense University Press.

SUMMARY

The notion of civilisation implies its own negation – that which is not civilised. For civilisation to register, a negative mirror image must be invoked, located either in another time or in another place. Whether the opposition is constructed temporally or spatially, and whether it is symbolic or real, images of otherness may provide fresh insights into the constitution of the declared civilisation. For the early Nordic civilisation on the edge of the European world, a study of its proposed 'others' reveals how the idea of being civilised owes as much to classical thought as to the contemporary Nordic outlook.

In the case of Iceland, literary and other written sources provide rich material for reflecting on the Icelanders' perceived position in the world; by defining and redefining 'the others', they constantly sought to distinguish themselves and to draw the relevant boundaries of their own civilisation. This paper starts by exposing some of the classical ideas of civilisation and otherness by which the Icelandic singularities may be measured. Having themselves once been perceived as Barbarians of the North, the Icelanders were particularly explicit in redrawing the boundaries of proper culture. Through their literary efforts, they provided canons of a civilisation that is recognisably 'European', yet also quite distinct.

Kirsten Hastrup
Department of Anthropology,
University of Copenhagen
kirsten.hastrup@anthro.ku.dk

PRZEMYSŁAW URBAŃCZYK

DECONSTRUCTING THE "NORDIC CIVILIZATION"

UNTIL the eleventh century, Latin Europe was still "busy" with its internal developments, the most important of which was the northward and eastward political expansion. The post-Romano-Carolingian zone was replaced with a much more pluralistic system of states built upon differentiated cultural traditions. By the year 1000, the political map of the continent had taken the shape that is still recognizable today. There is a tendency to label this process the "Europeanization" of the new territories, which suggests a unilateral expansion of the obviously superior model. I would rather say that it was when the new northern- and central-European Christian states entered the continental stage that Europe became Europe (Urbańczyk 2004). That merging of different traditions and the substantial enlargement of territories where ruling elites felt some supra-regional unity triggered a truly dynamic development across the whole continent. This process is differently understood in various countries, largely depending on individual countries' interpretations of the earlier situation.

In Scandinavia, there is a deeply-rooted scholarly tradition of looking at the northern Viking Age/Early Medieval[1] period, which has established a rather uniform picture of an area that was internally homogenous but at the same time, very different from what was observed elsewhere. The popular idea of a common "Viking Age culture" across the whole North is based on archaeological, linguistic and historical arguments. This vision may be explained as a result of the exceptional richness of vernacular literature that kept historians preoccupied with "internal" northern problems,

[1] There is a traditional "discrepancy" between the Nordic system of subdividing the first millennium AD and the one used elsewhere in Europe. I will use here the general European concept of the Early Middle Ages with its termination period ca. 1000 AD and thus including almost the entire Scandinavian Viking Age.

and also by the material culture which shows continuity from the previous periods. Both resulted in studies focused on the pan-regional commonalities of the Nordic area that were produced in some kind of "splendid isolation".

Thus, the natural geographic and linguistic definition of Scandinavia received an additional historical-cultural dimension. This allowed the inclusion of all of the insular "colonies", which in turn resulted in the enlargement of the Nordic area over the whole of the north Atlantic. There is no doubt that this part of the globe really did show specific traits that sustain these historical generalizations. However, such a perspective may not be scientifically fruitful because it overshadows obvious points of differentiation across the area in question. The dominant trend of looking for the similarities of the "common" Nordic Viking Age culture produced elegant synthetic interpretations but it has made it difficult to understand local and regional variations which eventually resulted in different political and economic developments during the High and Late Middle Ages.

Therefore, I do not like Arnold Toynbee's concept of a specific pre-Christian "Nordic civilization" which was a conscious northern "response" to the breakdown of the imperial Roman world and the ensuing tripartite division into Western Christendom and Byzantium flanked to the south and east by the Islamic world. Such a view is based on a rather simplified contrast between the North and the post-Roman world but at the same time, implies their historical equality in the further development of Europe.

This added an "historiosophic" dimension to the picture of the uniqueness of the homogenous North which had already been established through the combined efforts of Scandinavian geographers, linguists, historians and archaeologists. The idea of an ancient unity and a common destiny is, however, undermined by yet another, equally strong historiographic tradition which divides this huge "Nordic civilization" into original "ethnic" sub-regions. It is generally taken for granted that the earliest history of Scandinavia concerns the primordial Danish, Norwegian, and Swedish peoples who were soon to be followed by the Faroese and the Icelanders. They are all the obvious subjects of national(istic) scholarly interests. Thus, the idea of "national" continuities determined the tracks of the historical narratives that refer to the Nordic early Middle Ages. Even in Iceland, the desire for a deeply-rooted ethno-political continuity is so strong that it is necessary to be reminded that "...those who first settled in Iceland were not Icelanders, but immigrants" (Orri Vésteinsson 2006, 85).

One should ask whether these two somehow contradictory concepts of the original homogeneity promoted mostly by archaeologists, and of the original subdivision of Scandinavia into three "ethnic" parts promoted by historians (and strongly supported by politicians), have a firm foundation in the available data. The study of the problem must be interdisciplinary but I feel that the leading role in such an endeavour will be played by archaeologists who have access to data that are local by their very character, while historians have to deal with sources the majority of which originate (in their extant form) from the geographically limited area of Mediaeval Icelandic scholarly tradition. Optimally, one should apply a combined argumentative approach that refers to both material and written sources of information in order to help cross-check new hypotheses. Unfortunately, this may be impossible in many cases where geographical areas simply lack relevant historical data detailed enough to allow serious discussion of specific problems that may be revealed by archaeological studies.

*

Let us look, then, at some examples of studies that suggest the necessity of including local and regional diversities as an obvious element in further research on mediaeval "Nordic civilization." To challenge the dominating concept or myth of a pan-Scandinavian cultural unity, or even uniformity, one may combine a basic knowledge of the Middle Ages with anthropological experiences of traditional societies, which imply that general ways of life and ideology, and their cultural manifestations, must have somehow differed between the north and the south as well as between the west and the east of such a vast and differentiated area as Scandinavia. This refers not only to the obvious linguistic and ethnic differentiation between the dominating majority of the Germanic people who were, of course, the main object of scholarly interest, and the long overlooked Sami who occupied the far north and the mountainous interior (cf. Hansen and Olsen

2004) [2], and also to the largely neglected presence of the Slavs in southern Scandinavia (cf. Roslund 2001 and Naum 2008). More important for this particular discussion is the internal variability of the "Nordic civilization" itself.

Scandinavian archaeologists traditionally interpreted the visible unevenness of cultural manifestations as merely local variations of one unified cultural tradition. This deeply rooted assumption may be checked by studying collective death rituals that were important for both the external differentiation of particular communities and their internal integration. Fredrik Svanberg's (2003a and 2003b) analyses of south-east Scandinavia during the period 800–1000 AD, indicate that there were eleven quite distinct burial traditions (Svanberg 2003b, Fig. 61). This undermines the popular concept of some homogenous "Viking Age culture" because territorial variability of grave types indicating differentiation in burial customs and death rituals, may be interpreted in terms of religious differentiation. This, in turn, undermines the concept of common pan-Scandinavian religious symbolism and eschatological beliefs because "...it is hard to see how a number of different traditions may all simply be reflections of one and the same coherent mythology or religion" (Svanberg 2003a, 142).

Even in Denmark, most of which is dominated by inhumations, Jutland exhibits a significantly large number of cremations. Unfortunately there are no such detailed regional studies for other parts of Scandinavia but also there are other clear points of differentiation. For Norway we might regard the more general observation that "there were probably major differences in culture and belief" in the area of contemporary Norway (S. W. Nordeide 2006, 222), because the late Iron Age burial customs there seem

---

2 Today, the early contacts between the two populations, Germanic and Sami, are seen as equally important for both parties. The times when mutual relations were interpreted mostly in terms of the forced exploitation of the Sami by Germanic chieftains are long gone, while references to numerous medieval accounts of the use of Sami expertise in magic and the marrying of Sami women to Norse men of high rank are held to be significant. Contacts during pre-Christian times are now discussed in terms of symbiosis and co-operation rather than confrontation and subordination (Hansen and Olsen 2004, ch. 3.3). Rich female graves in the Norwegian zone containing typical Sami ornaments, and females buried in the Sami zone with Scandinavian jewellery, seem to testify to an opportunistic "exchange" of women. This may suggest some institutionalization of the cross-ethnic contacts, which is further suggested by some linguistic connections and place names (Hansen and Olsen 2004, ch. 3.5).

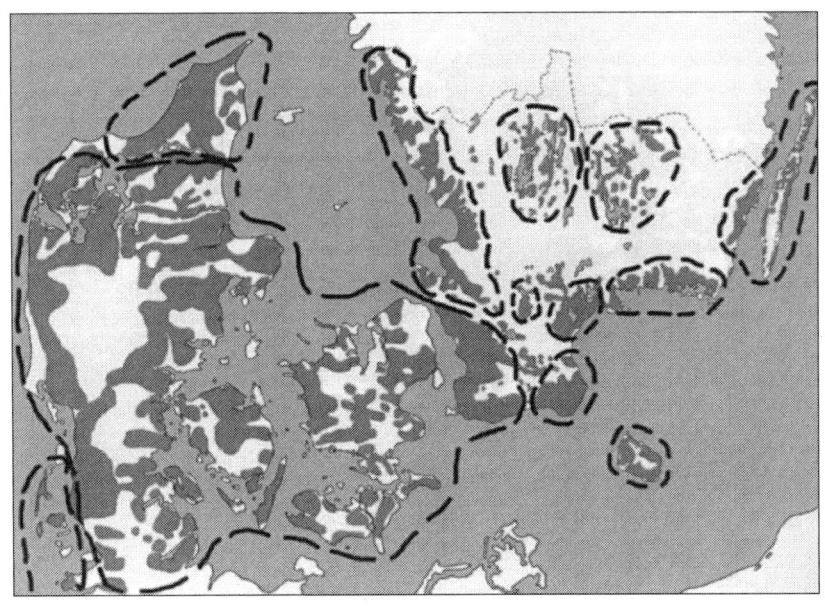

An illustration of the geographical dispostion of different ritual system in south Scandinavian c. AD 800–1000 as argued in this work. (F. Svanberg 2003b, 148).

to be very heterogeneous (S. W. Nordeide 2007, 3f). Other research indicates that while inhumations were the dominant custom in Vestfold, cremations seem to be equally common in western Norway and also became dominant in the north (Stylegar 2007, 87). However, closer analyses of various regions might disclose a more detailed picture. The ritual differentiation observed among various cemeteries of Kaupang — a centre that functioned as a central place visited by various people who traded, lived and occasionally died there — clearly suggests a more complex picture. Unfortunately, this "ethnic" aspect of the site has not provoked deeper reflections (Stylegar 2007, 101). Iceland with its surprising lack of cremations and domination of "one prescribed ritual performance concerning the disposal of the dead" (Þóra Pétursdóttir 2007, 59) showed still another variant of the Nordic world.

Nonetheless, we must accept that obviously, "there were profound chronological, regional, and social differences in pre-Christian religion practice in Scandinavia" (A. Andrén, K. Jennbert and C. Raudvere 2006,

14). This change in critical attitudes results in reflections such as "the source material for Old Norse religion is the expression of a process and a frozen glimpse of a vast universe in motion. It is also a picture of a religion that was part of a much bigger cultural whirlpool and cannot be studied separately" (Bertell 2006, 299);that Scandinavian religion was "an inherent part of the European cultural tradition" (Clunies Ross 2006, 412). In addition, it "may have had large differences within itself" (Bertell 2006, 299).

When discussing the problem of "uniformity vs. differentiation", one should also keep in mind the ambivalence of the Nordic archaeological evidence, which indicates that "the burials of the social elite followed traditions that were primarily supra-regional, while the burial customs of the vast majority of people were primarily connected to ritual traditions more or less limited to relatively small geographical areas and human groups" (Svanberg 2003a, 142). This suggests the dual identity of Scandinavian aristocrats who, in addition to having ties that connected them to their domains, "saw themselves as members of more or less well defined supra-regional communities" with which they maintained intense contacts (Svanberg 2003a, 180; also 2003b, 17). Obviously, it is these rich burials that have always attracted common attention, have dominated literature, and have been the focus of exhibitions, thus obscuring the real differentiation between the prevailing masses of Scandinavian peoples.

The duality of the political elite's cultural affiliations became even more striking and more "cosmopolitan" after the network of Christian monarchies was established in Europe in the late 10th century. One may observe how royal dynasties subsequently began to promote a continental model of rulership with its standard elements such as anointment, coinage, royal titles, iconography, the foundation of churches and monasteries, the introduction of "national" state names, and so on. It was necessary to adopt this conformity with the pan-continental symbolism in order to become acknowledged players on the geopolitical stage. This did not, however, remove attachment of members of the ruling dynasties to their "own/ national" traditions that ensured the cultural coherence of their territorial domains.

One may presume that, apart from the elitist behaviour of the top social levels that signalled their membership in the interregional elite, quite common people too could have belonged to several cultural or symbolic communities through relating themselves differently to available collective perceptions of tradition, mythology or cultural landscape. This could have been the case, first of all, in pre-Christian times when no political power could or would enforce ideological and symbolical uniformity. "Beyond the Vikings, then, lies a world of many cultures, realities and life ways, not just a single and uniform 'Scandinavian Viking Age culture'" (Svanberg 2003a, 202). This should be rather obvious for archaeologists who study precisely localized communities and contemplate the differentiation in these communities' material cultures. For historians, a warning is sounded by those who claim that the authors of the source texts recorded in the 12th and 13th centuries were "...playfully, but quite innocently, playing with forms and contents inherited from a previous, but religiously speaking long dead era" (Simek 2006, 380). Therefore, "...the use of these mythographical, high-medieval texts as source material for a pre-Christian, pre-medieval Scandinavian religion certainly is abuse" (Simek 2006, 380).

Taking into account such results of recent studies on the pre-Christian past, one should not be surprised that Christianization was not uniform in Scandinavia. "There was not a single Christianization process but in fact many different Christianizations" (Svanberg 2003b, 147) that geographically conformed to the identified Viking Age regions of specific ritual systems (*Ibid.*, Fig. 62). It was only the gradual reinforcement of territorial control of the early state centres that enforced relatively homogenous reactions to the eschatological expectations of Christianity. Thus, in the long perspective, Christianity – which raised social consciousness above the individual and local "ethnic" beliefs – helped to overcome cultural differentiations and subsequently eased contradictions, allowing the formation of much broader "national" identities. That is why Christianity may be understood as the corner-stone of the establishment of the stable territorial organizations that took shape in the 10th–11th centuries.

Not so long ago, the Christianization of the areas that bordered the northern and north-eastern edge of the post-Roman core of Europe was viewed as a rather rapid process, initiated by zealous missionaries and effectively executed by devout monarchs. This concept followed the ecclesiastic tradition which equated the end of paganism with the official inclusion of whole peoples (*gentes*) into the Church. The general character of the process was also defined through focusing on similarities between the regional developments that were to follow the continental trend. This generalizing attitude may be questioned by asking whether the similarities are not just superficial manifestations of continental political circumstances.

Similarly, not so evident is the postulated smoothness and linearity of the conversion process, which was, for a long time, considered to be obviously progressive and advantageous for both political organizations and social structures. The recent tendency has been to explore the dialectic aspects of the "acceptance versus resistance" attitudes and to expose the confrontation and the continuation of the "old" and "new" religion-driven socio-political systems (e.g. Kaliff 2007). The research perspective has broadened both by including studies of longer periods "before" and "after" the official conversions, and by looking for details that might shed light on the reality, observed at the regional, local or even individual level (cf. regional studies in Berend ed. 2007).

Religion has always been an important aspect in collective and individual self-definition. Therefore, we may assume that an inter-religious dialogue has played an important role in the processes that shaped the ethnic structure of the continent, and the function of Christianization in inter-ethnic relations deserves closer study. Studies on Christianization must include research on the tensions typical for situations where there is radical ethnic/cultural/linguistic differentiation. The struggle took place not only at the stage of ideological dialogue/conflict (cf. Urbańczyk 2003b) but also in the material expressions of different world views which are manifested in funeral rituals. All this resulted in a long and difficult Christianization and in an actively vigorous or passively stubborn resistance on the part of local people. This is archaeologically witnessed in syncretic practices and pagan burials which are still observed in peripheral regions in the High Middle Ages (for Poland see Urbańczyk and Rosik 2007).

Such differences may be observed in eschatological manifestations that are best visible in burial rites. Here, archaeological records may be the only source of information due to the lack of relevant written sources. However, interpretations of material evidence must be devoid of ready-made clichés that result in circular argumentation. A good example is the easy categorization of early medieval burials as exclusively either of "pagan" or "Christian" character or types. Such exclusive categories are placed separately within two different historical periods: before or after the official conversion. This way, the historiographic tradition of the clear-cut periodisation finds obvious support in archaeological evidence which in fact has been interpreted according to this periodisation. This works in such a way even in Iceland, which obviously had no indigenous traditions that could blur the bi-polar vision of "pagans" versus "Christians". To be honest, one must admit that such logical loopholes were typical also of other historiographies. A good example of the radical separation of two distinct periods is to be found in Polish medieval studies where such an *a priori* scheme, however primitive, also spares the trouble of explaining a transition from one ideology to another.

The way out of this circular argumentation is through complex multidisciplinary studies that must include precise accelerator (AMS) dating of every burial. Only a skilful combination of critically assessed texts and analyses of material evidence, supported by linguistics, theology, numismatics, history of art and historical anthropology, may ensure real progress in our understanding of the fascinating process of Christianization of North Europe. This will reinforce the already visible departure from the simplistic "text-driven" archaeology that concentrates on the "confirmation" of the written sources, and from "item-fascinated" history that uses archaeological data as simple illustrations of ready-made concepts, both of which were parasitic substitutes of the postulated multi-disciplinarity.

There is a need for thoughtful discussion about the Christianization of Iceland which is still viewed through the rather naïve lens of the story constructed by the late "republican" tradition of the peaceful and radical acceptance of religious change. Dominance of this concept saves archaeologists interpretational troubles when discovering early graves and results in a suspiciously clear story devoid of the expected tensions connected to ideological conflict. Instead of contemplating this unique situation of the cleverly negotiated compromise, one should rather ask what could have been the political function of the conversion, viewed as the "capitulation" of the old world (Toynbee 1951, 358).

I suspect that this myth of an unproblematic conversion that hid the real conflicts was consciously created by the Icelandic intellectual elite, perhaps in order to reinforce the idea of the power of negotiability that was deeply embedded in the ideology of the medieval Icelandic political system. Ca. 1130 this was openly expressed by Ari Þorgilsson who in his

Íslendingabók made the Lawspeaker Thorgeir argue that: "We should rather mediate the matters so that each party gets some part of what it desires."[3] This may be taken not as the essence of the historical event but rather as the essence of the political mentality that prevailed in "republican" Iceland.

*

Because of the general premise of the three original ethnicities, the state formation period in Scandinavia is usually viewed as a merely political unification of the hitherto ethno-culturally uniform lands. Therefore, it is interpreted as the final giving of some centrally controlled "law and order", and thus just one more step in the long history of the original existence of the three great nations. From such an evolutionistic perspective, early kings acted as natural "unifiers" who only invigorated the already present process, not as "creators" who triggered and promoted internal unification and external differentiation while striving for the reinforcement and enlargement of their dynastic spheres of political and economic interests.

Scandinavian historiography of the early Middle Ages does not easily acknowledge the theory that in most cases it was the execution of "egoistic" dynastic interests and monopolistic strategies that led to the establishment of the Early Mediaeval states and subsequently resulted in the "production" of political nations. The nineteenth and early twentieth century nationalists "...constructed or even re-invented modern nations, but did so on the historical foundations of older *ethnies* with specific myths, memories, symbols, and values as inspirational sources. In this process the consciousness of a former ethnicity was re-discovered and re-vitalized, and thus formed the roots or origins of the nation..." (Fewster 2006, 401).

A nationalistic reading of early written sources is not, of course, unique to the Nordic part of Europe and such an attitude has been, and still is, typical for many "national" historiographies that more or less consciously respond to dominating political needs to "dig up" the possibly ancient roots of modern nations and states. Neither is the opportunistic manipulation of the past a modern invention. The process of shaping "national" ethnicities can already be discerned in medieval scholarship. This is well represented in Saxo who ca 1200 in his *Gesta Danorum* formulated the idea of a Danish

---

3   Translation in Theodore M. Andersson 2003, p. 91.

identity which served to integrate the social upper class (Fældbek 1996, 133f). To enhance a common identity of previously differentiated communities, which were to be integrated, Saxo invented the legendary king *Dan* as the symbolic protoplast of all Danes. Saxo acted in concordance with the already current method of the conscious and purposeful enriching of the past, which may be illustrated by the similar action taken some twenty five years earlier by the anonymous author of the *Historia Norvegiae* who, in the first chapter of his work, introduced king *Nór*; this character reappeared as king *Nóri* in Oddr munkr's *Óláfs saga Tryggvasonar* (ch. 22) ca. 1190. It is difficult to believe that those medieval historians did not understand the meanings of *Denamarc* and *Nordvegr*. Therefore, one should suspect conscious manipulation introduced in order to produce a past that would "better" fulfill the current political integrational needs. The introduction of eponymic nation-founders, and the establishing of reference points for the "national" identities of all subordinates of competing territorial dynasties, was quite popular throughout medieval Europe, e.g. *Brutus* by Geoffrey of Monmouth, *Bohemus* by Cosmas of Prague, or *Rus* by Nestor.

"Republican" Icelanders did not need to invent any common king-founder because their land was self defined by its insular geography, which automatically determined the common destiny of all those who had chosen the island for settlement. Instead, we may imagine competition between the leading families who challenged each other with alternative visions of the heroic deeds of their ancestors. Just as elsewhere, ownership of the past was important in Iceland as a crucial argument in struggles for power. However, the disappointing shortness of the Icelandic past forced Icelanders to refer to more ancient times. Thus, they recalled the common Nordic past with special stress being put on their Norwegian ancestry. "The sagas of kings contributed to create a Norwegian identity, but at the same time they may have contributed to the creation of an Icelandic identity at least in two ways, both by showing a common Norwegian and Icelandic past and close relations and by telling about conflicts between the Norwegian kings and Icelanders. The *fornaldarsögur* which mostly told about distant past in the Scandinavian mainland may have strengthened the Icelanders' feeling of sharing the history and identity with their Nordic neighbors" (Mundal 2007).

The function of multiple references to the pillars of the high seats, brought from Norway by the emigrants and thrown into water before landing on the Icelandic coast, must have been similar. These references directly symbolized a continuity of tradition and a connection to the Scandinavian mother-land. Such declarations of original Norwegian identity also helped to overcome the multi-ethnicity of the settlers and explained the later "special" relations of Iceland with the overseas kingdom of Norway. The Icelandic "representation of the past, initiated by Ari and elaborated to baroque proportions by the subsequent two centuries of scholarship, had very little to do with any 'genuine' traditions about the *landnám* that may have existed at that time. Instead, it was probably generated by the social and cultural needs of the Icelandic intelligentsia in the High Middle Ages" (Adolf Friðriksson and Orri Vésteinsson 2003, 141).

This relatively common, medieval creative approach to the past proved very effective in achieving "national" identities within various states. Such affiliations were further reinforced by the nationalistic ideology of the late 19th and early 20th century, when European historians searched the early Middle Ages for heroic ancestors, e.g. vikings in Nordic Europe or Gauls in France. Everywhere, archaeologists eagerly supported these evolutionistic concepts of the direct continuation of demographic and cultural traditions by authoritatively appointing "national" monuments of pride and veneration. Gamla Uppsala, Jelling, Oseberg or Thingvellir, however different, all symbolically indicate "ancient roots" and belong to the schoolbook canons of collective identities at both the specific national levels, and at the broad pan-Nordic perspective. Political/ideological reasons for their selection are quite obviously related to national traditions, and symbolically support state ideologies. Thus, in the three kingdoms, three royal burial grounds have been chosen, while in Iceland the assembly site is most venerated. This way, the "national" monarchic and republican ideologies are symbolically anchored in the possibly most distant past in order to prove their ancient origins.

This leads us to the question of the supposed Icelandic anti-monarchism. Taking such a perspective, some scholars identify some kind of a conscious "refusal" of the monarchy on the part of people disgusted with the atrocities connected to the establishment of the Norwegian kingdom (e.g. Byock 2000, 66). Having freedom as their highest value, these people were to choose emigration to a distant island rather than subordination to some monopolistic royal power. And once there, to avoid the domination of one kinship group, they thoughtfully introduced a complex system of keeping a political balance between the numerous local leaders (*goði*) who could aspire to a permanently dominant position. This was viewed as the programmatic "democratic" option that stood at the very foundation of the Icelandic "commonwealth"/"republic"/"free state".

This romantic view of the "republican" farmers, who effectively managed to halt the pan-European process of power centralization and deliberately established a "democracy", is somewhat simplistic. First of all, there is an obvious contradiction between the supposedly anti-monarchic ideology on the one hand, and the message conveyed by many sagas that depict the disastrous results of the obligation for revenge because there was no power strong enough to stop it. That lack of a paramount decision making power, and of a supreme judicial authority, led to the development of a complex system of negotiations which, however, did not furnish final solutions for conflicts that could have lasted for generations.

In my view, medieval Icelandic historians somehow admired the centralized power system even if, at the same time, they were "obligatorily" stressing the hardships introduced by the autocratic monarchy. They were almost obsessed with the effectiveness of radical decisions being taken by rulers, who could apply executive power even if it was achieved by harsh methods. These order-makers immediately dominated the stage whenever they entered the story. The Icelandic intellectuals could have realized that the aim of the monarchic system was not to implement justice but to effectively sustain general social order through immediate intervention, even if this might have left some individuals and their families unhappy. Therefore, despite the open ideological contradiction between the viking ethos of unlimited freedom and the oppressive royal autocracy, the overseas Norwegian court always attracted young men who gained fame there and learned political lessons. Even the Papacy, which in the early Middle Ages had no effective power over distant Christian societies, was looked upon as a semi-legendary paramount authority that was able to pacify even the bloodiest conflicts, as in the famous stories of Njáll and Grettir, whose kinsmen found final reconciliation only in Rome.

Why then was some version of a permanently centralized system armed with executive power not established in Iceland? I suggest dropping the romantic explanations that refer to some original "democratic/anti-monarchic" ideology of the immigrants, and turning to practical reality. Knowing the structure and economic foundations of medieval kingdoms, one should accept the simple fact that monarchy could not have worked in Iceland. There were several reasons for this, which are based on the country's geography, geopolitics, and economy.

The natural borders of the island and its remoteness from the continental network of competing territorial kingdoms excluded the important factor of external political challenge, and the danger of sudden conquest attempt, which could trigger centralizing defensive counter measures. On the other hand, Icelandic territorial expansion was also excluded. Therefore, there were no geopolitical factors which would externally provoke the centralization of political power necessary for both defensive and aggressive military actions. Nor was there any indirect impulse for the local elites to reach for status comparable with the Christian monarchs, who sat too far away from Iceland to pose a permanent challenge.

However, in my view, economic reasons might have been more decisive. A permanent power centre was a very costly solution because a Christian ruler with his family, servants, necessary armed forces (retinue) and clergy (needed for religious and administrative services) must be financed by the rest of society. This meant the regular collecting of a substantial fiscal surplus needed not only for daily consumption but also for the ostentation of the paramount status of the monarch and his entourage. To sustain regular "taxing", some sort of collecting body empowered with executive means must be employed, which adds to the overall running costs because they themselves were also serious consumers.

This was a really heavy burden that posed problems to many medieval kingdoms, even in countries with much more fertile agricultural lands and better climates than Iceland. That was why almost none of the early medieval states (with the significant southern exceptions of Byzantium and the El Andalus caliphate) had capital towns. A king of that time was a *rex ambulans* who was in "permanent" motion. This was not only because the difficult logistics and the personal character of his executive power which necessitated a king's frequent presence in as many places as possible but also because there was simply not enough food to sustain prolonged visits of the numerous and "luxury-hungry" royal court. That was why kings aimed to establish their own local centres (e.g. royal farms or royal strongholds) that furnished them with living conditions but, first of all, with a reliable source of staple food. Otherwise, they had to rely on the more or less voluntary hospitality of local aristocracy, which unavoidably involved some undesirable interdependence.

I believe that the Icelandic economy itself would not have been able to permanently support such expenditure because of the lack of good arable lands and climatic restrictions on cereal production, in addition to the lack of forests full of wild animals. The original settlers arrived with various culturally embedded ideas about the environment and tried to implement them in different geographic circumstances. In many cases, the direct application of strategies common in various parts of the Continent appeared to be catastrophic for both the people and for their natural environments because the delicate ecological balance was seriously disturbed by the newcomers and their animals. The pollen-confirmed removal of birch (Orri Vésteinsson 2000, 167) which was cut or simply burned (Buckland 2000, 147), overpasture by cattle and the results of the presence of pigs and goats (McGovern 2000, 331; also 2003) led to the quick loss of much of the original plant cover (Sigurður Þórarinsson 1974, 49f).

In addition to the negative effects of the overexploitation of the land's resources, which added to the natural shortcomings, the end of the heroic time of the viking expeditions brought an end also to the inflow of luxury imports, e.g. arms and jewellery. Not having substantial quantities of attractive export products, the Icelanders still had to import commodities for daily use (e.g. most metals and steatite pots). Archaeologists studying the early settlement and economy of Iceland may admire how sophisticated the combined exploitation of land and water resources was (cf. numerous analyses by Thomas McGovern), but they also observe how much poorer the level of material culture in medieval Iceland was when compared with the contemporary situation on the Continent. But despite this, the Icelanders managed to finance the building and upkeep of numerous churches, even if these were extremely small and simple.

Economic realities may also explain the weakness of the Icelandic Church, which was much less centralized than elsewhere in Christian

Europe and therefore less effective imposing observation of the strict rules of the universalistic Christian doctrine. The decentralized pagan religion thus found some continuity in the decentralized Church that had no institutionalized backup in the decentralized state. Christianity was attractive for the *goðar* who could reinforce their power by becoming official sponsors and controllers of the ideological centres. The Icelandic Church was "domesticated" through the domination of the *goðakirkjur* which, by their affiliation to central farms, were not only a cheaper solution but also allowed easier manipulation than independent parishes.

However, even such an expenditure must have affected the overall economy and resulted in a generally flatter social structure, with the differentiation between the common people and the elite less obvious than on the Continent. Therefore, Iceland was much less aristocratic than continental Scandinavia which, in turn, was less aristocratic and less centralized than the more southern European societies. And the typical medieval interdependence of political and ecclesiastic spheres made a highly centralized Church "impossible" in a decentralized society such as Iceland. Economic preconditions eventually changed with the adaptation of the Icelandic economy to the demands of the European markets, where *vaðmál*, sulphur and dried fish were in demand during the high Middle Ages. Probably these revenues helped to finance the two bishoprics but were not enough to introduce an ecclesiastical province.

It was the economic inability to support permanent and strictly centralized political and ecclesiastical organizations that made medieval Iceland a special case. Iceland's political organization was not the result of some premeditated ideological programme but rather the necessary outcome of the need to find a specific and effective solution to sustain social order and to avoid devastating military conflicts. Thus, the process of organizational development was halted at some pre-state level where contradictory centralizing and decentralizing tendencies were mutually balanced by the mechanism of collective control institutionalized by the assemblies. Such a stage of achieving a balance between "egalitarianism" and the stately centralization of social power is described in historical anthropology (e.g. Mann 1986). From this perspective, the Alþing resembled "tribal" assemblies where common decisions are carefully negotiated in order to sustain basic social order, and to channel violence. However, such institutions do not have the executive means so typical of central stately powers in order to enforce decisions.

The complicated Icelandic political system and sophisticated law code had to compensate for the lack of a supreme executive power. Collective pressure based on tradition and on common decisions replaced the authoritative implementation of "justice" by some paramount power centre. As the sagas tell us, the results were often not satisfactory for some individuals and their families but in the long term, this programmatically weak system managed to sustain a relative political equilibrium and to curb the possible over-ambitions of leading families which, on the other hand, did not have the economic means to launch long-term warfare or to finance stable domination. This system was definitely not a "democracy" but, rather, some oligarchy of several kinship groups that carefully kept an eye on each other.

One could even rightfully question whether the Icelandic "commonwealth" was a state, at least in the contemporary meaning of the term that requires the permanent centralization of the power sphere's control within a defined territory. It was not even a federation, i.e. a union of self governing regions co-ordinated by a permanent central government. It was a much looser organization that was voluntarily accepted by regional leaders who regulated their mutual relations at the general assembly at Þingvellir once a year. The balance of power and social order were achieved through complex negotiations that were often supported by physical pressure. Lobbying and seeking compromise at the Alþing prevented open military conflicts that would surely have been disastrous for the small insular society, as so clearly became the case during the Age of the Sturlungs.

Thus, the medieval Icelandic "democracy" was not the conscious product of anti-monarchic citizens but rather a necessary but clever response to the lack of a centralized monarchy which could not be introduced because of the reasons explained above. The Icelandic "republic" survived because for a long time, no continental king had any real interest in establishing power there. It would not have been especially difficult for Norwegian rulers of the 11th–12th century to send to Iceland a dozen war ships filled with well-armed warriors who could take the upper hand in the battlefield and declare a conquest. This did not happen because such an "investment" would not pay back dividends. For the Norwegian kings, it was easier to declare a symbolic sovereignty over Iceland as one of the *skattlǫnd* and to use such a claim as an argument for sustaining status on the continental geopolitical stage than to keep garrisons and implement administration which would probably "eat" all possible surpluses.

*

This economy-determined prolonged political decentralization, which resulted in parallel ecclesiastic decentralization, possibly contributed to the survival of ancient tradition and to the development of the vernacular literature. All pre-Christian societies had rich oral traditions but in most cases these were effectively erased by the Church which ideologically supported authoritative monarchy but demanded strict adherence to its universalistic doctrine. The pagan past must have been forbidden and consequently forgotten except for the elements that were effectively Christianized. In striving towards this, the Church was strongly supported by co-operating kings who, in turn, depended on the ideological and bureaucratic support of the clergy. In Iceland, remembrance of the pagan past survived (in a surely contaminated form) because there was no power strong enough to erase it effectively. As a compromise, the pagan ideology there was superficially Christianized when recorded by the monks and priests who mixed the folk tradition with Christian motives. This ideological compromise helped to keep cohesive a society endangered by the hardships of economic crises. The unusual political organization contributed to the development of the unusual literary tradition, without which the pan-Scandinavian identity would surely look very different to how it does today.

The differentiated interdependencies of economic, political and ideological factors have to be considered when discussing the commonalities of the whole "Nordic world" and also the regional specificities of each of its parts. In the context of this discussion one might also refer to the Swedish phenomenon of the carving of rune stones that appeared suddenly and flourished after ca. 990, lasting until the early 12th century. Although these carvings show direct continuity of the vernacular (linguistic and artistic) traditions, the majority of them explicitly endorse Christian values. I think that it is possible to discuss and compare the rune stones with Icelandic literature and to look for common reasons behind both phenomena. The level of political organization in 10th–11th century Sweden was far "behind" its Scandinavian and trans-Baltic neighbors. The territorial power of Erik Sägersal, Olof Skötkonung or Anund Jakob was not comparable to that of other monarchs who managed to implement a high degree of administrative and ideological control over their subordinates, including the aristocracy. The weakness of the early Swedish kings resulted in the weakness of the Swedish Church, which was unable to uproot pagan traditions effectively and had to opt for some compromise. The almost one and a half century long history of the Swedish "Christian" runic stones which were raised in their thousands may be taken as material evidence of the ideological compromise necessary to sustain social order.

However, in contrast to the Icelandic "pagan" literature that survived in the unchanged political circumstances, the Swedish semi-pagan runic stones had to give way to new ideological developments. The raising of these stones ceased after ca. 1130, i.e. when both the monarchy and the Church finally gained the upper hand over the anti-monarchic elites who naturally preferred the pre-Christian/pre-kingship tradition. Thus the two apparently different phenomena of Icelandic "pagan" literature and Swedish "pagan" rune stones can be seen as different solutions to the ideological challenge involved in the process of a long and difficult Christianization that took place in different parts of the "Nordic civilization" where various strategies of direct challenge, but also compromise, adaptation and acceptance were applied.

In such a context one may wonder to what extent the Icelandic vernacular literature and the Swedish "vernacular" stones recorded any real pre-Christian traditions. I am not questioning the obvious continuities from earlier times but rather, asking how big the impact of the expansion of Christianity was on the recording of "pagan" tradition in societies that had a long time to adapt to the new situation. Taking as a point of reference the example of the mutinous Polabian Slavs, who in the late 10th and in the 11th century developed a "new" counter-Christian pagan religion and introduced a theocratic political system (Rosik, Urbańczyk 2007), I suggest seriously considering exactly to what extent the "traditions" recorded on vellum (in Iceland) and on stone (in Sweden) were real traditions or the invention of writers.

*

Still another possible way to challenge the myth of the monolithic common Nordic Viking Age is to promote studies on the multi-ethnicity characteristic of many northern populations. There are numerous examples of such an approach that focus on various parts of the "Nordic civilization" (e.g. Roslund 2001, Urbańczyk 2003a, Hansen and Olsen 2004, Naum 2008). There has even been an attempt to connect the early meaning of the term *víkingr* with some "outsiders" of undefined ethnicity, including the Slavs/ Wends (Jesch 2001, 49–50 and 56).

One of the promising but as yet underdeveloped fields for such research is the peri-Baltic region. Archaeology shows that during the Viking Age and even the High Middle Ages, the Baltic Sea was just a "lake" that was easy to cross and over which intensive demographic and cultural exchange took place. People moved in both directions: Scandinavians settled on the south and east coast and Slavs established their homes in Scandinavia. There were numerous multi-ethnic societies, of which the best known are those of the Wolin and Rügen islands. Cultural traditions penetrated both ways and had a profound impact on local developments. Here, an important scholarly contribution has been offered by Mats Roslund. His studies on south-Scandinavian pottery showed the diverse reception of Slavic tradition in various regions (eastern Denmark, the Mälaren area and Gotland) and proved that "Slavs had a deep impact on Scandinavian culture" (Roslund 2001, 322). Even the ship-building tradition, proudly considered a specifically Scandinavian development, in the Baltic area shows considerable typological parallelism in Nordic and Slavic constructions (cf. Indruszewski 2004, 245f). Evidently, there was an intensive trans-Baltic exchange of experiences between ship builders who shared their local traditions. We know this thanks to dendrochronological analyses that elucidate not only chronology but also provide insights into the histories of individual vessels, i.e. the precise areas of their construction and places where they were subsequently repaired.

Despite these affinities, cultural prejudices expressed by historically based underestimation of some problems or even whole 'directions' of research influenced Scandinavian attitude towards the Slavs. "There seems to be a deeply embedded common premise that the only positive direction of mutual contacts was from the north to the south, of course with Scandinavians as bearers of higher civilization standards and Slavs as simple recipients of the cultural development that took place elsewhere. The obvious disproportion in [Scandinavian] academic didactic referring to the Western Slavs (e.g. in comparison with the always present interest in Russia) results in the lack of research, which further 'proofs' the lack of interesting common problems, which gives excuse for the lack of academic didactic, etc. etc." (Urbańczyk 2005, footnote 3). Ethno-political background of this strange situation has recently been well analyzed by Mats Roslund (2001, chpt. 1).

Archaeology clearly shows the multi-ethnic substrates of the famous peri-Baltic trading centres where cemeteries consist of a "mixture of rites: boat graves, chamber graves, and coffin graves, as well as relatively balanced numbers of cremations and inhumations" (Stylegard 2007, 66). This does not change, however, the traditional narratives that easily "nationalize" early urbanization. Therefore, three Scandinavian original "peoples" must have equally important towns equally early: Hedeby in Denmark, Birka in Sweden and Kaupang in Norway. The emergence or rather, development of early towns is still part of national pride, which may result in exaggerated interpretations (cf. the recently-published volume *Kaupang in Skiringssal*, ed. by Dagfinn Skre, and the discussion in the *Norwegian Archaeological Review* 2008). One may suppose that Iceland will soon join this trend by supplementing this series with its own medieval trading centre in Gásir that has been recently excavated.

Personally, I have tried to promote an inter-disciplinary investigation of the multi-cultural/ethnic origin of the north Atlantic colonies in Iceland and Greenland (Urbańczyk 2003a). Both medieval written sources (e.g. *Grænlendinga saga* and *Landnámabók*) and archaeological evidence (e.g. the series of non-Scandinavian sunken houses built on Iceland during the Viking Age) as well as micro-molecular analyses of the mitochondrial DNA (Helgason et al. 2001), indicate that the picture of the conquering of the north Atlantic was much more complex than the old simplistic "Scandinavian colonization" model.[4] Interpretation clearly depended on national traditions. E.g. for the Norwegian scholars, who eagerly refer to the *Íslendingabók*, "Iceland was settled from Norway"; consequently, this story is a part of Norwegian heritage. At the same time, however, the Irish

---

4 Of course, one should remember that biological descendance does not automatically equal cultural affiliation.

suggest that "the colonists followed the trail of hermit-settlers" and the colonization was, to a large extent, a part of the common Hiberno-Scandinavian history (e.g. MacShamhráin 2002, 79 and ch. 4).

*

The above-quoted recent publications and ongoing discussions "assert that there were many small specific 'regions', 'lands' or similar 'units' in Scandinavia ... but these 'units' are never seen as primary subjects of history. They always exist *within* the general Viking Age culture, *within* the boundaries of the later nation-states and *within* the metahistorical 'unifications' of the later states" (F. Svanberg 2003a: 93). These states, in turn, are often treated first of all as a specific Nordic whole that was relatively isolated from the rest of medieval Europe, which had different kings, different states and different towns. The discussion of possible external connections is usually limited to the "straight east" or "straight west" directions which were established already during the Viking Age. What is completely missing is the new situation that appeared around the Baltic Sea where monarchs of the surrounding states played a complex game of "co-operation versus competition". The dynasties of Ynglings, Skjoldungs, Rurikids, Piasts and Nakonids maintained lively "diplomatic" relations that were strengthened by numerous cross-Baltic inter-marriages. These contacts also included cross-Baltic Christianizing missions and the issue of parallel coinage. When added to the already mentioned diffused contacts indicated by archaeology at the level of the common people, one could argue that in the 10th century, there emerged a sort of a "peri-Baltic civilisation" which is an idea that is surely worth more detailed study.

Anyway, challenging the concept of an isolated, unique and homogenous early medieval "Nordic civilization" is one of the important tasks of the modern medievistic studies.

REFERENCES

Adolf Friðriksson and Orri Vésteinsson. 2003. "Creating a past: a historiography of the settlement of Iceland." *Contact, continuity, and collapse. The Norse colonization of the north Atlantic*, ed. by James H. Barret. Turnhout: Brepols Publishers, 139–162.

Andrén, Anders, Kristina Jennbert and Catharina Raudvere. 2006. "Old Norse religion. Some problems and prospects." *Old Norse religion in long-term perspectives. Origins, changes, and interactions*, ed. by A. Andrén, K. Jennbert and C. Raudvere. Lund: Nordic Academic Press, 11–14.

Berend, Nora (ed.). 2007. "Christianization and state formation in northern Europe." Cambridge: Cambridge University Press.

Bertell, Maths. 2006. "Where does Old Norse religion end? Reflections on the term Old Norse religion." *Old Norse religion in long-term perspectives – origins, changes and interactions*, ed. by Anders Andrén, Kristina Jennbert and Catharina Raudvere. Lund: Nordic Academic Press, 298–302.

Buckland, Paul C. 2000. "The North Atlantic environment". *Vikings. The North Atlantic saga*, ed. by W. W. Fitzhugh, E. I. Ward. Washington: Smithsonian Institution Press, 146–153.

Byock, Jesse. 2000. *Viking Age Iceland*, London: Penguin Books.

Clunies Ross, Margaret. 2006. "The measures of Old Norse religion in long-term perspective." *Old Norse religion in long-term perspectives – origins, changes and interactions*, ed. by Anders Andrén, Kristina Jennbert and Catharina Raudvere. Lund: Nordic Academic Press, 412–416.

Fewster, Derek. 2006. *Visions of past glory. Nationalism and the construction of early Finnish history*. Helsinki: Finnish Literature Society.

Fældbek, Ole. 1996. "Is there such a thing as a Medieval Danish identity?" *The birth of identities. Denmark and Europe in the Middle Ages*, ed. by B. P. McGuire. Copenhagen: Medieval Centre, Copenhagen University, 127–134.

Hansen, Lars Ivar and Bjørnar Olsen. 2004. *Samenes historie fram til 1750*. Oslo: Cappelen Akademisk Forlag.

Agnar Helgason, Eileen Hickey, Sara Goodacre, Vidar Bosnes, Kári Stefánsson, Ryk Ward, and Bryan Sykes. 2001. "mtDNA and the islands of the North Atlantic: Estimating the proportions of Norse and Gaelic ancestry." *American Journal of Human Genetics* 68: 723–737.

Indruszewski, George. 2004. *Man, ship, landscape. Ships and seafaring in the Oder mouth area AD 400–1400. A casestudy of an ideological context*. Copenhagen: National Museum of Denmark.

Jesch, Judith. 2001. *Ships and men in the late Viking Age: the vocabulary of runic inscriptions and skaldic verse*. Woodbridge: Boydell Press.

Kaliff, Anders. 2007. *Water, Heaven and Earth: Ritual Practice and Cosmology in Ancient Scandinavia – An Indo-European Perspective*. Riksantikvarieämbetet.

MacShamhráin, Ailbhe. 2002. *The Vikings. An illustrated history*. Dublin: Wolfhound Press.
Mann, Michael. 1986. *The sources of social power*, vol. 1. Cambridge: Cambridge University Press.
McGovern, Thomas. 2000. "The demise of Norse Greenland", *Vikings. The north Atlantic saga*, ed. by W. W. Fitzhugh, E. I. Ward. Washington: Smithsonian Institution Press, 327–339.
McGovern, Thomas. 2003. "Herding strategies at Sveigakot, N Iceland: an interim report". *Archaeological investigations at Sveigakot*, ed. by Orri Vésteinsson. Reykjavík: Fornleifastofnun Íslands, 48–69.
Mundal, Else. 2007. "Memory of the past and Old Norse identity." [abstract of a paper read at the conference *Medieval memories: Case Studies, Definitions, Contexts*. Prague, September 3–6, 2007].
Naum, Magdalena. 2008. *Homelands lost and gained: Slavic migration and settlement on Bornholm in the early Middle Ages*. Lund: Lunds Universitet.
Nordeide, Sæbjørg Walaker. 2006. "Thor's hammer in Norway. A symbol of reaction against the Christian cross?". *Old Norse religion in long-term perspectives. Origins, changes, and interactions*, ed. by Anders Andrén, Kristina Jennbert and Catharina Raudvere. Lund: Nordic Academic Press, 218–223.
Nordeide, Sæbjørg Walaker. 2007, The Christianization of Norway [MS of a paper presented at the Medieval Europe congress in Paris].
Orri Vésteinsson. 2000. "The archaeology of *landnám*", *Vikings. The north Atlantic saga*, ed. by W. W. Fitzhugh, E. I. Ward. Washington: Smithsonian Institution, 164–174.
Orri Vésteinsson. 2006. "The hall as a shrine." *Reykjavík 871^{+-2}. Landnámssýningin. The settlement exhibition*, ed. by Bryndís Sverrisdóttir. Reykjavík: Reykjavík City Museum, 80–85.
Rosik, Stanisław and Urbańczyk, Przemysław. 2007. "Polabia and Pomerania between paganism and Christianity." *Christianization and the rise of Christian monarchy. Scandinavia, Central Europe and Rus' c. 900–1200*, ed. by Nora Berend. Cambridge: Cambridge University Press, 300–318.
Roslund, Mats. 2001. *Gäster i huset. Kulturell överföring mellan Slaver och Skandinaver 900 till 1300*. Lund: Vitenskapssocieten i Lund.
Sigurður Þórarinsson. 1974. "Sambúð lands og lýðs í ellefu aldir." *Saga Íslands*, vol. 1, ed by S. Líndal, 29–97.
Simek, Rudolf. 2006. "The use and abuse of Old Norse religion. Its beginnings in high medieval Iceland." *Old Norse religion in long-term perspectives – origins, changes and interactions*, ed. by Anders Andrén, Kristina Jennbert and Catharina Raudvere. Lund: Nordic Academic Press, 377–380.
Skre, Dagfinn, ed. 2007. *Kaupang in Skiringssal*. Aarhus: Aarhus University Press.
Stylegard, Frans-Arne. 2007. "The Kaupang cemeteries revisited." *Kaupang in Skiringssal*, ed. by Dagfinn Skre. Aarhus: Aarhus University Press, 65–101.

Svanberg, Fredrik. 2003a. *Decolonizing the Viking Age 1*. Stockholm: Acta Archaeologica Lundensia.
Svanberg, Fredrik. 2003b. *Death rituals in south-east Scandinavia AD 800–1000. Decolonizing the Viking Age 2*. Stockholm: Acta Archaeologica Lundensia.
Toynbee, Arnold. 1951. *A Study of History*, vol. 2. Oxford: Oxford University Press.
Urbańczyk, Przemysław. 2003a. "Breaking the monolith: multi-cultural roots of the North Atlantic settlers." *Vinland Revisited. The Norse World at the Turn of the First Millennium*, ed. by Shannon Lewis-Simpson. St. John's: Historic Sites Association of Newfoundland and Labrador Inc., 45 – 50.
Urbańczyk, Przemysław. 2003b. "The Politics of Conversion in North Central Europe". *The cross goes north. Processes of conversion in northern Europe, AD 300 – 1300*, ed. by Martin Carver. York: York University Press, 15 –27.
Urbańczyk, Przemysław. 2004. "Europe around the year 1000 as seen from the Papal, Imperial and Central-European perspectives." *The European frontier. Clashes and compromises in the Middle Ages*, ed. by Jörn Staecker. Lund: Almqvist & Wiksell International, 35–39.
Urbańczyk, Przemysław. 2005. "A personal view on the *Samenes historie fram til 1750* by Lars Ivar Hansen and Bjørnar Olsen." *Scandinavian Journal of History* 30, no. 11: 83–95.
Urbańczyk, Przemysław and Rosik, Stanisław. 2007. "Poland." *Christianization and the rise of Christian monarchy. Scandinavia, Central Europe and Rus' c. 900–1200*, ed. by Nora Berend. Cambridge: Cambridge University Press, 263–300.
Þóra Pétursdóttir. 2007. "'Deyr fé, deyja frændr'. Re-animating mortuary remains from Viking Age Iceland," Tromsø [manuscript of MA-Thesis].

SUMMARY

Arnold Toynbee's concept of the "Nordic civilization" added a historiosophic dimension to the already popular idea of a common "Viking Age culture" throughout Northern Europe. However, the study of local and regional diversities that may lie hidden behind the attractive products of the elitist "cosmopolitan" culture, must be seen as a necessary element of future research. There is also a need to question the easy separation between the "pagan" and "Christian" periods, by which all the problems of religious transition are avoided. Equally dubious is the tendency to view state formation in Scandinavia merely as the political unification of previously ethno-culturally uniform lands instead of as the ruthless competition of "egoistic" dynasties. And different conversion processes should be recognised in the different parts of the Nordic area involving various strategies of direct challenge, but also compromise, adaptation and acceptance.

Thus, instead of generalizing about an isolated, unique and homogenous early medieval "Nordic civilization", an important task for modern scholars of medieval studies is to explore specific problems that pertain to specific areas. Iceland might be considered to be an ideal testing-ground for this approach with its medieval declarations of original Norwegian identity that helped to overcome the multi-ethnicity of the original settlers; with the romantic view of the "republican" farmers, which concealed the fact that a monarchy could not have worked in Iceland; and with the ideological compromise regarding religion in Iceland, which resulted in survival of the pre-Christian tradition.

Przemysław Urbańczyk
Institute of Archaeology and Ethnology
Polish Academy of Sciences Warzaw
uprzemek@iaepan.edu.pl

MARGARET CLUNIES ROSS

MEDIEVAL ICELANDIC TEXTUAL CULTURE

Surveying the Field

MEDIEVAL Icelandic textual culture was, by common agreement, remarkably rich and varied, yet it was not altogether *sui generis*. In the first place it shared in the wider textuality of Old Norse, which includes Norwegian, Orcadian and other Norse colonial textualities. Some elements of Nordic textuality are uniquely Icelandic, however, principally much skaldic poetry, the mythological poetry of the Elder Edda, and sagas of Icelanders, though in the last-named case the saga writers' debt to medieval European literature more generally is usually acknowledged. Meulengracht Sørensen (2000) assessed the likely causes of the prolific textual output of medieval Icelanders, paying particular attention to the enabling process of what his Aarhus colleague Ole Bruhn (1999) called *textualisation*. Bruhn used this term to refer to the double process of a society's adoption of the technology of writing as a social usage and its consequent understanding of social life as a text. Acknowledging the various hypotheses that have been adduced since the Middle Ages to explain the Icelanders' extraordinarily large and varied investment in textual production, Meulengracht Sørensen characterised its probable motivating forces as: the desire to record and celebrate social and cultural origins; the maintenance of ties with the wider Norse and European world; a concern to record Icelandic settlement history; a concern with the law and its bases, together with the re-formation of politics towards a greater decentralisation than pertained in Norway; the importance of the interest and enterprise of private individuals in literary production; the conversion to Christianity and the various textual prescriptions and possibilities that came into play as a consequence of the Icelanders' incorporation into Western Christendom. Towards the end of his survey he wrote:

> The introduction of Christianity created a new historical consciousness and the country's most important common institutions were inscribed in texts by means of the written word. At the same time it was a decisive factor in the development of Icelandic literature that this early unified social vision was not sustained. In the following centuries it had to give way to a literature that went in the opposite direction and gave textual expression to the decentralized ideology which underlay Icelandic society from the very beginning. Writing was privatized and the result was the sagas of Icelanders and the contemporary sagas, which are characterized by their local and private settings. The forces that combined to shape the oldest literature were not continued (Meulengracht Sørensen 2000, 27).

This statement is accurate only if we privilege one particular kind of Icelandic literary production, the saga, and even then it requires some nuancing. It is true that most sagas of Icelanders, contemporary sagas and even sagas of bishops and kings have a predominantly regional and personal focus, though many of them reach out to more general issues and to the world outside Iceland in various ways. But if we consider the whole of Icelandic textual production during the Middle Ages, the statement is of dubious validity, because a substantial number of medieval Icelandic texts are not local and private in their orientation, but are based on the doctrine and text types of the Christian Church or on the learned literature of the classical world that the Church inherited. Their goals, though they may be inflected towards local tastes and interests, are firmly centralist in the main.

At the heart of the matter, and the topic that is the focus of this essay, is the question of what happens if we give proper weight to all types of Icelandic textual production when we come to consider the placing of Icelandic or even the whole of Nordic civilisation within the wider medieval world. This is not an issue of the evaluation of Icelandic texts on the basis of their literary qualities, as perceived by modern sensibilities. Indeed, it is probably true to say that the modern perception of medieval Icelandic textual culture has been based upon several unstated premises, two of which we need to be aware of if we are to evaluate the nature of medieval Icelandic textual production in the context of medieval European textuality more generally. These are that: a) what is uniquely Icelandic is more valuable and of greater intellectual and artistic worth than what is found in Icelandic texts but largely derived from non-Icelandic sources; and that b) Icelandic prose literature is more valuable than Icelandic poetry, even though such a premise partly contradicts premise a), because it is clear that skaldic poetry is uniquely Norse, and probably, at least after the twelfth century, uniquely Icelandic.

These premises have led many modern scholars and the wider public to a somewhat distorted view of the nature of medieval Icelandic textuality when it comes to evaluating its relationship to the textuality of the medieval world in general, because what is uniquely Icelandic is seen to be better than what is not, better both in terms of cultural importance and better in literary terms. This position can properly be argued by the literary critic but not by the textual historian. Further, one tends to gain an inaccurate sense of the importance of saga literature about native subjects in terms of its actual quantity if one fails to compare it with the very substantial amount of other textual material in vernacular prose, much of it also designated by the term *saga* in Old Icelandic, including hagiography, translated romances, didactic and encyclopedic works, sermons and translations of historical and legendary works originally written in Latin. Old Icelandic prose literature has been privileged over poetry, partly because in the form in which it has been recorded, it has been embedded in prose as a form of prosimetrum, but also because medieval Icelandic poetry is harder to understand for a modern reader, even for a modern Icelandic reader, and, until recently, people have found its convoluted style and largely conventional subject-matter uncongenial. Yet in the traditional culture of medieval Iceland it is clear that poetry, not prose, was the privileged literary form and the form of long standing and, as such, must be given full weight in any discussion of medieval Icelandic textuality.

It is naturally open to anyone to judge a saga like *Laxdœla saga*, say, as a better, more original or more interesting literary work than the Icelandic prose life of Saint Catherine of Alexandria, which is based on non-Icelandic sources. But, if we are to take a clear-eyed view of the whole range of Icelandic textual production from the Middle Ages, we must acknowledge that a great deal of it is the product of translation in the widest sense of that term and thus a product of the mediation of one culture's textuality, that of medieval Latin Christendom for the most part, by another, that of medieval Nordic vernacularity with an Icelandic inflection. Mediation of course implies cultural transformation; transformation in its turn often implies appropriation, and it is these processes that will be investigated here, assuming that such intersections will provide a more balanced view of the nature of the whole of medieval Icelandic textual production.

Vernacularity

On the basis of the Icelandic texts that have survived from the medieval period, one of the most striking characteristics of Icelandic textual production is its vernacularity, its use of the vernacular as the normal means of communication. It seems that, virtually from the beginning of written textuality using manuscripts, the impulse was to translate Latin (and sometimes other languages) into Icelandic rather than to disseminate Latin texts in the original. Surviving works from the late twelfth century, such as fragments of the *Dialogues* of Gregory the Great (Hreinn Benediktsson 1963) and the Old Icelandic *Elucidarius* (Grimstad 1993), bear witness to this impulse, and it continued throughout the medieval period. It is very likely, however, that the number of Latin texts produced in both Iceland and Norway has been seriously underestimated, and the same is probably true of Latin texts emanating from outside Scandinavia (Gottskálk Þ. Jensson 2003). Certainly, we know of a not inconsiderable number of lost Latin works written by Norwegians and Icelanders (some of which were also translated into the vernacular)[1] and there are likely to have been others we do not know about, which have not survived the Reformation, a time when we can assume Latin texts were treated as the products of popery and undervalued or destroyed.

While we can accept that the impulse towards vernacularity was very strong in medieval Iceland, we must not confuse this situation with an imputed ignorance of Latin on the part of either producers or consumers of written texts in Iceland, in terms of their linguistic knowledge or their access to Latin texts. It has been commonly assumed that the reason why

[1] They include Oddr Snorrason's Latin life of Óláfr Tryggvason, Sæmundr fróði's lost Latin history of the Norwegian kings, the *Flos peregrinationis* of Gizurr Hallsson, the Latin life of Bishop Jón Ögmundarson by Gunnlaugr Leifsson (d. 1218/19) and a Latin life of Þorlákr Þórhallsson, of which some fragments remain in AM 386 4to, c. 1200.

so much foreign literature was translated into Icelandic was because most Icelandic audiences would not have known Latin and few Latin works would have been available for people to read. While it is probable that the farm communities who heard saga literature read aloud to them are not likely to have included many – or any – Latinists, this argument does not necessarily hold good for some educated laypeople and, in particular, for religious communities where a great many saints' lives, doctrinal texts, sermons and religious poems are likely to have been composed, as well as many sagas. These religious communities would also have provided audiences for medieval Icelandic texts of all kinds. Further, the evidence of the inventories of religious houses in Iceland during the medieval period indicates that some of them were relatively well supplied with books in Latin and some other European languages, especially German and English (Olmer 1902) and many vernacular texts reveal their authors' acquaintance at either first or second hand with a considerable variety of Latin sources (Lehmann 1937; Sverrir Tómasson 1988). Moreover, there is growing evidence that medieval Icelandic schools may have used both Latin and Icelandic poetic examples in their textbooks (Guðrún Nordal 2001, 22–25), and this practice is clearly reflected in the so-called "grammatical treatises" produced between the twelfth and the fourteenth centuries. These unique products of vernacularity bear witness to the transformation and appropriation of Latin culture and its incorporation into a cultural product that combined Latin and traditional learning in a new synthesis (Clunies Ross 2005, 141–205; Raschellà 2007).

The phenomenon of medieval Icelandic vernacularity is part of a larger and very gradual movement away from Latin as the mainstream language of authoritative communication in Western Europe, a movement that has only really reached its apogee in the last two hundred years, when the vernacular languages have almost completely ousted Latin in religion, literature, politics, law, science and the schoolroom. It is clear from the evidence of medieval European societies in general, that the proportion of writing in the vernacular (as contrasted with writing in Latin) was highest in societies that did not speak Romance vernaculars descended from Latin and that were most remote geographically from Rome. In these circumstances medieval vernacularity becomes something of a statement of socio-politicial and intellectual independence as much as of an inability to understand

Latin, though undoubtedly a poor command of Latin must sometimes have been the spur to vernacularity. In the early medieval period Anglo-Saxon and Irish textuality was much more pronouncedly vernacular than that of Continental Europe, and yet it is hardly the case that English and Irish scholars were less capable Latinists than their Continental counterparts (Lapidge 1993, 1996; Esposito 1990). Characteristically also, these communities both translated learned or ecclesiastical sources into the vernacular and were able to record at least some of their indigenous literary genres in manuscript, though the latter were of course not untouched by either the new written medium or the culture of Christian Latinity. However, the very fact that vernacular literature was permitted to be recorded in manuscript books is an important indicator of its relative acceptance in the world of those who controlled manuscript production and owed some kind of allegiance to the medieval Church.

Thus vernacularity in early medieval Europe is both a trope of translation and a trope of independence and appropriation. Although it may have arisen for pragmatic purposes, to make the doctrine and culture of Latin Christendom available to a non-Latin-speaking and -reading linguistic world, the very act of translating works that were what the Anglo-Saxon king Alfred called "most necessary for all men to know" (*ða ðe niedbeðearfosta sien eallum monnum to wiotonne*)[2] also gave the vernacular a higher official status than it held in societies in which it was not used for such purposes. This is likely to explain why indigenous vernacular literature was able to flourish in such a manuscript environment and why it throve there, appropriating to itself, at least to some extent, the status and privilege that Latin occupied elsewhere. Rita Copeland has written of medieval vernacular academic texts that "these texts have demonstrable relations with exegetical traditions, not simply in terms of content, but in terms of the character of exegesis, which works by displacing and appropriating the materials it proposes to serve" (Copeland 1991, 8). It is arguable that the same sort of phenomenon can be identified in less academic vernacular productions, including those largely developed from indigenous and originally oral textual genres.

[2] From King Alfred's letter (Bodleian Library Oxford, MS Hatton 20, quoted from Whitelock 1967, 6) prefixed to the copy of the Old English translation of Gregory the Great's *Cura Pastoralis* sent to the see of Worcester.

Nowhere did the process of cultural appropriation happen more thoroughly, it seems, than in Iceland. We often tend to forget that medieval Icelandic written textual culture is largely a phenomenon of the later Middle Ages, and seems not to have taken off until the twelfth century. Thus we need to see it in the context of the vigorous textuality, both in Latin and the various European vernaculars, that flourished throughout Western Europe in the twelfth and thirteenth centuries, and which led to many new developments in textual cultures and communities of that period. Within the field of literature, new vernacular genres evolved, many in prose, such as the romance and the chronicle, and these provide an interesting parallel to the development of the prose saga, both chronologically and in terms of compositional technique (cf. Clover 1982; Torfi Tulinius 2009). This does not mean that the Icelandic saga genre is a clone of the romance or the prose chronicle; clearly, it has its own very distinctive character and ideology and its own way of memorialising the past. However, the rise of the Icelandic saga shortly after the rise of new genres of historical writing and the *roman courtois* is unlikely to be fortuitous; the *Zeitgeist* reached to Norway and to Iceland and Icelandic creativity responded with its own version of historicism and memorialising of both past and present.

We can see something similar taking place in the field of poetry. Here, however, vernacular poetry occupied the high social and intellectual ground in indigenous society in both Norway and Iceland, going back as far as we have any evidence. Poetry in eddic measures was traditionally a vehicle for the expression of pre-Christian religious thought and myth; poetry in skaldic measures was the vehicle for expressing encomia in honour of rulers in Norway and other parts of the Norse world, while in Iceland it seems to have taken on other functions in addition, yet still maintained its socially privileged position. Men of high status, or those who composed for them, continued to produce verse in skaldic measures on secular subjects well into the thirteenth century in Iceland (Guðrún Nordal 2001, 117–195), but it was the appropriation of Christian subjects and themes that really shows how far and how thoroughly the vernacular and the latinate were intertwined in the poetic medium both thematically and stylistically. In the fourteenth and fifteenth centuries vernacular Christian poetry became a major vehicle for devotional piety, as witnessed by the composition of many poems in honour of apostles, saints, and, above all, the Virgin Mary (Clunies Ross ed. 2007; Jón Helgason 1936–38). If the Reformation had not come to Iceland in 1550, this strain of vernacular piety may well have continued beyond the sixteenth century.

The Third and Fourth Grammatical Treatises are witness to an Icelandic appropriation of Latin poetic and rhetorical culture which is almost certain to have taken place in the schoolroom and the monastery. They reflect a knowledge of Latin grammar and rhetoric, and, to varying degrees, of the thirteenth-century *poetria nova*, and they show the appropriation of these interpretative frameworks and their application to Icelandic poetics (Clunies Ross 2005, 185–205). Some of the figures they recommend may be found in use in Christian skaldic verse of the thirteenth and fourteenth centuries (Clunies Ross ed. 2007, 1, lv). The fact that many of the figures of Latin poetics did not fit well with indigenous skaldic diction (Tranter 2000, 144–147) does not detract from the ideological assertion of a *translatio studii* in these works and does not necessarily imply a subordination of indigenous poetics to that of the Latin schoolroom. Óláfr Þórðarson, following the lead of his uncle Snorri Sturluson in the Prologue to the latter's *Edda*, boldly claims that poetry in Old Norse and poetry in Latin and Greek operate according to the same principles (Björn M. Ólsen ed. 1884, 60). Whereas Snorri had used the theory of euhemerism to explain how the human Æsir, who represented themselves as gods, migrated to Scandinavia from Troy, bringing classical culture with them and imposing it on the hapless natives of the north, Óláfr sees knowledge and learning coming northwards in the more conventional manner of the literate transmission of cultural knowledge in manuscript books, in his case via the writings of the grammarian Donatus.

Strategies of Appropriation

In theory, medieval Icelandic texuality could be seen to exist on a continuum whose poles are, respectively, dependence on and independence of non-Icelandic texts and cultural influences. At one end would lie almost complete – or apparently almost complete – independence, a condition in which a text reveals no perceptible outside influence, completely indigenous subject-matter and cultural attitudes and a style and structure to match. Perhaps some of the less complex of the *Íslendingasögur*, such as *Droplaugarsona saga*, might be thought to occupy such a position, or, within the field of poetry, some of the royal encomia composed by tenth- and eleventh-century Icelandic skalds, such as Einarr Helgason skálaglamm or Sigvatr Þórðarson, although even here arguments of foreign influence could be adduced. At the other end of the continuum might lie Norwegian and Icelandic works that are close translations of foreign originals, such as various of the over one hundred saints' lives translated mainly from Latin (Widding, Bekker-Nielsen and Shook 1963). Yet such extreme categorisation is rather meaningless, as there are really very few, if any, medieval Icelandic texts that can have been untouched by their relationship to the world beyond Iceland, and even a close translation shows, in its new linguistic dress, how cultural appropriation has taken place.

The fact is that, when Icelanders entered the world of medieval textuality and manuscript culture, they necessarily became part of the wider medieval European cultural world. This is manifested at a number of levels, both textual and paratextual. By the term 'paratextual' is meant the cultural attitudes that shaped people's approach to composing particular kinds of texts in the first place, whether these were for religious reasons or born of the pressures of cultural recuperation of the past. Even though writers of Icelandic saga literature developed their own ways of memorialising the past, the whole project of saga writing can be seen as part of a pan-European movement to place contemporary medieval society in relation both to its legendary and historical indigenous past and to assert links to the still prestigious culture of the ancient Graeco-Roman world.

One pointer to such paratextual influences is the actual choices Icelandic translators made of the texts they decided to translate. Of course, it is likely that some kinds of texts were unavailable to them, but by and large what has been translated probably reflects the interests of Icelandic society and the branches of knowledge Icelanders found valuable or needed to know. Outside the field of ecclesiastical literature, it is striking that works of a historical kind dominate the list of known translations into medieval Icelandic, ranging from *Rómverja saga*, based on Sallust and Lucan, through the Chronicle of Pseudo-Turpin and *Karlamagnús saga*, derived ultimately from Old French *chansons de geste*, to *Breta sögur*, an Old Norse version of

Geoffrey of Monmouth's *Historia regum Britanniae* (c. 1136). A great many other historical works appear to have been known to Icelandic writers (Lehmann 1937, 40–41; Sverrir Tómasson 2006, 93–98). Such an interest in non-Scandinavian history mirrors the dominance of historical writing in the vernacular about Scandinavian subjects, whether set in Iceland or in the wider Scandinavian world. In fact one could say that much vernacular writing has a predominantly historical orientation, with Iceland and Icelandic society as the anchor point: *fornaldarsögur* set in prehistory, *Íslendinga sögur* in the recent past of Icelandic society, *samtíðarsögur* in near-contemporary Icelandic society, *konunga sögur* in Norwegian and wider Scandinavian history, *riddara sögur* in the legendary history of courtly societies of southern Europe and other exotic places. Within ecclesiastical genres, hagiography had a predominantly historical orientation as well. This was a genre vigorously pursued in Iceland as in other parts of medieval Europe, and its influence is felt in the many existing prose translations of the lives of foreign saints (usually from Latin) as well as in the lives of Icelandic saints, both in Latin and the vernacular. To this we must add the many poetic versions of saints' lives and lives of the apostles, ranging from the twelfth-century *Plácitusdrápa* to the fourteenth-century *Kátrínardrápa* and *Pétrsdrápa*, all based on vernacular prose translations (Louis-Jensen 1998, CVII; Louis-Jensen and Wills 2007; Wolf 2007 and Ian McDougall 2007).

Another general area in which there is evidence for substantial Icelandic interest, as reflected in the number and variety of works translated, and one covered in more detail in this volume by Rudolf Simek, is geography, including astronomy and astrology. Although much that has survived from these fields is fragmentary and in many cases obtained indirectly through encyclopedias and florilegia (Clunies Ross and Simek 1993), the range of extant material reveals a predilection for information about the physical world. This interest is manifest beyond translation, and was clearly stimulated by reports from individuals travelling to foreign destinations, including pilgrim experiences and itineraries (Lönnroth 1990). There is a pronounced taste for the exotic in medieval Icelandic literature, revealed through the many narratives set outside Scandinavia, whether west, south or east.

Of equal significance, though the evidence is of a negative kind, are areas in which there is very little indication of an Icelandic interest in translation. The most obvious of these, as Paul Lehmann pointed out in his study of Scandinavia's debt to Latin literature (1937, 15–16, 37), is what he called *Fachphilosophie*, including the writings of classical and medieval philosophers, aside from various of the works of Honorius Augustodunensis and what was transmitted through encyclopedias. In the area of the more theoretically inclined and abstract writings of the Christian Church, too, in contrast to traditional biblical exegesis, there is relatively little to show; few of the Church Fathers seem to have been known directly, although some works like the *Dialogues* of Gregory the Great appear to have been known (Hreinn Benediktsson 1963; Boyer 1993) and Augustine of Hippo's *De doctrina christiana* appears in the inventory of Viðey abbey late in the fourteenth century (Olmer 1902, 7, no. 18). From the later medieval period in Iceland, there does not seem to have been much of a taste for the writings of medieval ascetics and mystics, as was the case in much of the rest of Europe. It is possible, as mentioned earlier, that a great deal has been lost, but, if so, one would have to argue that the losses were particularly heavy in the areas of philosophy and theology, and that is rather improbable, given that some at least of the writings of the Church Fathers were widely distributed in medieval Europe. A more likely hypothesis is that there was no tradition of speculative philosophy and theology associated with pre-Christian Scandinavian religion, and that there continued to be little interest in importing foreign literature from these fields after the conversion to Christianity. To the extent that we are able to judge from the medieval reconstruction of pre-Christian religious thought in Snorri Sturluson's *Edda* and other Icelandic writings, religious and philosophical concepts were primarily expressed through mythic narratives, which tend to particularise and personalise abstractions, at least on the surface.

If we turn from the paratextual evidence for Icelandic participation in the textual world of medieval Europe to the internal evidence of vernacular Icelandic texts themselves, there are a number of levels on which it is fruitful to document their engagement. The first of these is their treatment of sources. In some kinds of texts, Icelandic writers refer specifically to their foreign sources, especially in types of learned or schoolroom literature. They do this largely to authenticate their work. For example, in a piece about the star of Bethlehem published by Kålund and Beckman in *Alfræði* íslenzk (III, 1918, 73), the translator acknowledges his source, John Chrysostom (*Patrologia Graeca* LVI, 637), in detail, although he probably knew it through a Latin digest, writing *Svá segir Jón gullmuðr í glósa yfir Matheo* "Thus says John golden-mouth in [his] commentary on Matthew". Some saga writers acknowledge their vernacular written sources, like the author of *Laxdæla saga*, who refers to two other Icelandic sagas as well as to the work of Ari Þorgilsson (ÍF 5 1934, 7, 199, 202, 226). Direct acknowledgement of oral sources for purposes of authentication occurs widely in Icelandic saga texts, usually in works of a historical nature, and chiefly involves the citation of skaldic poetry to authenticate what the prose writer is claiming. Here oral witnesses are treated by saga writers in the same way as written source texts are used in medieval historiography generally (Whaley 1993; 2007, 82–85; O'Donoghue 2005, 10–77). Oral informants who had the status of eyewitnesses are also frequently mentioned in historical works, in line with the practice of medieval historiography generally; in his *Íslendingabók* Ari Þorgilsson acknowledges three individuals, Teitr Ísleifsson, Þorkell Gellisson and Þóríðr Snorradóttir, whose combined memories put him in touch with the settlement age. Occasionally a poet cites his oral sources, as Einarr Skúlason does in *Geisli* 45/3 (Chase 2007a, 44), when he acknowledges that the Norwegian traveller and mercenary soldier Eindriði ungi was the source of the miracle story of what happened to S. Óláfr's sword Hneitir after it had been bought by the Byzantine emperor. At the time Einarr was composing, this miracle story had probably not yet achieved written form. Interestingly, Snorri Sturluson cites Einarr's *drápa* as the source of *his* account of the same miracle in *Heimskringla* (ÍF 28, 369–371).

Far more frequent than the direct citation of external sources, however, is the use of sources without acknowledgement. This can take one of two forms, the second the more common. In the first case, a vernacular writer indicates that he has used a written source, but does not specify what it is. Such a practice implies the desire to achieve literate *gravitas* more than the desire for authentication. A good example is in stanza 9 of the late fourteenth-century poem *Allra postula minnisvísur*, where the poet composes lines in honour of S. Bartholomew that are strikingly reminiscent of the opening lines of a hymn sung at the feast of this saint and follows this with the interjection *það er ritningar vitni* "that is the testimony of a written text"

(9/6). However, as the poem's editor, Ian McDougall, has indicated (2007, 866), "there seems to be no scriptural parallel".

By far the most characteristic way in which Icelandic vernacular authors use sources, most of which are of foreign origin, is in a free and independent way, so that their sources are often difficult or impossible to trace. This suggests that they felt thoroughly at home with the literature that had come to them from the world outside Iceland and felt little need to acknowledge it directly in their own compositions. We can see such practices, though we can never pin down the sources with absolute certainty, in many works where they are part of the literary whole being created as well as in works of a more scholarly or religious nature. We see it in sagas, such as *Njáls saga*, where likely influences from clerical and chivalric literature have been studied particularly by Lars Lönnroth (1976, 107–164); we see it also in works like Snorri Sturluson's *Edda*, for which no specific written sources have been identified.

Another important Icelandic strategy for the appropriation of non-Scandinavian textuality lies in the various stylistic resources indigenous authors used to assimilate foreign material. This matter cannot be divorced from the paratextual observations made earlier about the kinds of texts that Icelandic translators favoured, nor about their treatment of sources. We have seen that they favoured historical texts above all, and after that texts that gave information about the physical world, much of it exotic. On the whole, Icelandic prose writers favoured a plain, though by no means an artless style, which we tend to identify as typical of the native saga style formed on the basis of oral tradition. Translated texts or texts closely indebted to them were also largely turned into the indigenous preferred style, seemingly as a conscious choice (cf. Lönnroth 1976, 160–164). There are exceptions, though, which show that Icelandic writers were perfectly capable of turning their hands to elaborate, rhetorically complex styles or to abbreviating material substantially; such practices are to be found in some passages of *riddarasögur*, some saints' lives and other prose writing that Ole Widding (1965, 1979) first characterised as *den florissante stil*, "the florid style". Many such florid works date from the fourteenth century. Elaborate, rhetorically complex styles were traditionally also very much characteristic of Old Norse poetry.

Recently, Mats Malm (2007) has argued that most Icelandic writers' conscious choice of a plain, pared back style, even in translations of foreign texts, may be attributable to their awareness of classical rhetoricians' repugnance towards what they termed "effeminate language" in contrast to virile and manly language. As such a preference very much resonated with an Icelandic moral preference for manliness above effeminacy, Icelandic writers were reinforced in their preference for the former, even when the texts they translated were of the "effeminate" variety. Ultimately, such a case cannot be proven, but it is likely that Icelandic writers and translators did act to domicile this aspect of the foreign within the preferred conventions of indigenous style and narrative art.

In the field of poetry, however, the situation was somewhat different, as Malm acknowledges, because poetry "was not associated with decadence, effeminacy, or voluptuousness in Old Norse" (2007, 314–315). On the contrary, its traditional complexity was regarded as manly and of high status. Although, as Malm observes, there was a movement towards a plainer style apparent in some works of the fourteenth century, like *Lilja*, the claims of the *Lilja* poet and others like him cannot be taken at face value. The traditional obscurities of skaldic diction conveyed through the kenning system and fragmented word order here and in some other fourteenth-century poetry gave way to a different kind of rhetorical complexity along the lines Geoffrey of Vinsauf recommended in his *Poetria nova*. The influence of Geoffrey's treatise is clearly apparent in several places in *Lilja* (Chase 2007b, 2, 554–677).

The traditional complexity and high status of skaldic verse arguably protected it from the stylistic simplification accorded to much prose literature, even in cases where poets were translating texts of foreign origin, whether through the medium of an Icelandic prose version or directly from Latin. A great deal of the religious poetry of later medieval Iceland involves either direct translation of Latin ecclesiastical sources or translation through the intermediary of a vernacular prose source, and includes hymns, liturgical sequences, homilies and saints' lives. A large number of elaborate kenning-like phrases for God, Christ and the Virgin Mary, in particular, are calques on well-known Latin epithets for them. The extent of this poetry's debt to foreign sources has been partially recognised by earlier scholars, but its full participation *on its own terms* in the international world of Christian piety, in both Latin and the vernacular European languages, has only recently begun to be fully acknowledged.

As well as other kinds of Icelandic textual production, Christian skaldic poetry demonstrates both dependence on and independence of the larger European cultural world. As a poetic kind, skaldic verse is unique, but the messages it conveyed were part of the culture of Christian Europe translated to Icelandic practices and conditions. The texts in both prose and poetry produced by Icelandic writers to further the cults of Christian saints are very good examples of this kind of translation. Although Iceland did eventually have several of its own native saints, for whom considerable local textual production was undertaken in order to further their cults, and though other Scandinavian saints, particularly S. Óláfr, were of particular importance and again generated indigenous *vitae*, the cults of foreign saints and the apostles were far more numerous. By participating in the cults of foreign saints, and composing vernacular texts in their honour, Icelanders were able to participate themselves in the universal (as it was then seen) and in the local at the same time. There were local cults of foreign saints, both male and female, all over Iceland and a multiplicity of vernacular lives, mostly based on Latin exemplars, to celebrate them. In this, Iceland was little different from the rest of medieval Christendom. What was powerful – what worked for the faithful – were local cults that could be seen to have links to the wider Christian world. As the anonymous fourteenth-century poet of *Heilagra meyja drápa* put it (stanza 18), thinking of S. Cecilia, "The northern world and holy Rome (*Heimrinn norðr og heilög Róma*) receive comfort from a bright maiden" (Wolf 2007, 2, 903), or, as the poet of *Heilagra manna drápa* expressed it (stanza 18/5–8), thinking of S. Blaise, who was known for his ability to cure diseases of the throat, "God's spirit has worked miracles, which are still revealed in our country (*á váru landi*) by means of this dear friend for the healing of a countless number of people" (Wolf 2007, 2, 885). A glance at Margaret Cormack's book on the saints in Iceland (1994) will show that there were active cults of these and many other foreign saints in medieval Iceland, alongside cults of local and Scandinavian saints.

To conclude, in medieval Icelandic texts and practices, largely because of the universalist claims of Christian culture and its dominance throughout medieval Europe, the Icelandic variant of Nordic civilisation was both dependent and independent to varying degrees, preserving, transforming and appropriating. It seems fruitless to try and determine the exact mix of "indigenous" and "foreign" elements in any medieval Icelandic text. The proportions and the nature of the elements vary, but Nordic civilisation was, throughout the Middle Ages, not *in* the medieval world as the title of the symposium *Nordic Civilization in the Medieval World* had it, but *of* it. After Icelanders accepted Christianity, this had to be the case; it was simply not possible to stand outside, and entry into Christendom came with long strings attached. On the whole the Icelandic people managed their entry into this world very well, and the strings appear to have been made of elastic, but they were still there nevertheless.

REFERENCES

Björn M. Ólsen, ed. 1884. *Den Tredje og Fjærde Grammatiske Afhandling i Snorres Edda*. Samfund til udgivelse af gammel nordisk litteratur 12. Copenhagen: Knudtzon.

Boyer, Régis. 1993. "Gregory, St.: Dialogues." *Medieval Scandinavia. An Encyclopedia*, ed. by Phillip Pulsiano and Kirsten Wolf. New York and London: Garland Publishing Inc., 241.

Bruhn, Ole. 1999. *Historien og skriften. Bidrag til en litterær antropologi*. Aarhus: Aarhus University Press.

Chase, Martin, ed. 2007a. "*Geisli*". *Skaldic Poetry of the Scandinavian Middle Ages*. Volume VII, 2 Parts. *Poetry on Christian Subjects*, ed. by Margaret Clunies Ross. Turnhout: Brepols, 1, 5–65.

Chase, Martin, ed. 2007b. "*Lilja*". *Skaldic Poetry of the Scandinavian Middle Ages*. Volume VII, 2 Parts. *Poetry on Christian Subjects*, ed. by Margaret Clunies Ross. Turnhout: Brepols, 2, 554–677.

Clover, Carol J. 1982. *The Medieval Saga*. Ithaca and London: Cornell University Press.

Clunies Ross, Margaret. 2005. *A History of Old Norse Poetry and Poetics*. Cambridge: D. S. Brewer.

Clunies Ross, Margaret, ed. 2007. *Skaldic Poetry of the Scandinavian Middle Ages*. Volume VII. *Poetry on Christian Subjects*. Parts 1 and 2. Turnhout: Brepols.

Clunies Ross, Margaret and Rudolf Simek. 1993. "Encyclopaedic Literature". *Medieval Scandinavia. An Encyclopedia*, ed. by Phillip Pulsiano and Kirsten Wolf. New York and London: Garland Publishing Inc., 164–166.

Copeland, Rita. 1991. *Rhetoric, Hermeneutics, and Translation in the Middle Ages*.

Academic Traditions and Vernacular Texts. Cambridge Studies in Medieval Literature 11. Cambridge: Cambridge University Press.

Cormack, Margaret. 1994. *The Saints in Iceland: Their Veneration from the Conversion to 1400*. Subsidia Hagiographica 78. Brussels: Society of Bollandists.

Esposito, Mario, ed. M. Lapidge. 1990. *Irish books and learning in mediaeval Europe*. Aldershot, Hampshire: Variorum.

Gottskálk Þ. Jensson. 2003. "The Latin Fragments of *Þorláks saga helga* and Their Classical Context". *Scandinavia and Christian Europe in the Middle Ages. Papers of the 12th International Saga Conference Bonn/Germany, 28 July − 2 August 2003*, ed. by Rudolf Simek and Judith Meurer. Bonn: Hausdruckerei der Universität Bonn, 257−267.

Grimstad, Kaaren. 1993. "Elucidarius". *Medieval Scandinavia. An Encyclopedia*, ed. by Phillip Pulsiano and Kirsten Wolf. New York and London: Garland Publishing, Inc., 163−164.

Guðrún Nordal. 2001. *Tools of Literacy. The Role of Skaldic Verse in Icelandic Textual Culture of the Twelfth and Thirteenth Centuries*. Toronto, Buffalo and London: Toronto University Press.

Hreinn Benediktsson, ed. 1963. *The Life of St. Gregory and His Dialogues. Fragments of an Icelandic Manuscript from the 13th Century*. Editiones Arnamagnæanæ, series B 4. Copenhagen: Munksgaard.

ÍF 5 = *Laxdœla saga. Halldórs þættir Snorrasonar, Stúfs þáttr*. 1934. Ed. by Einar Ól. Sveinsson. Íslenzk fornrit 5. Reykjavík: Hið íslenzka fornritafélag.

ÍF 28 = *Heimskringla* III. 1951. Ed. by Bjarni Aðalbjarnarson. Íslenzk fornrit 28. Reykjavík: Hið íslenzka fornritafélag.

Jón Helgason, ed. 1936−38. *Íslenzk miðaldakvæði: Islandske digte fra senmiddelalderen*. 2 vols. Copenhagen: Levin & Munksgaard.

Kålund, Kristian and Nathaniel Beckman, eds. 1908−18. *Alfræði íslenzk. Islandsk encyclopædisk litteratur*. 3 vols. Samfund til udgivelse af gammel nordisk litteratur 37, 41 and 45. Copenhagen: Møller.

Lapidge, Michael. 1993. *Anglo-Latin Literature 600−899*. London and Rio Grande, Ohio: Hambledon Press.

Lapidge, Michael. 1996. *Anglo-Latin Literature 900−1066*. London and Rio Grande, Ohio: Hambledon Press.

Lehmann, Paul. 1937. *Skandinaviens Anteil an der lateinischen Literatur und Wissenschaft des Mittelalters*. Part II. Bayerische Akademie der Wissenschaften. Philosophisch-historische Abteilung, 1937: 7. Munich.

Louis-Jensen, Jonna, ed. 1998. "*Plácitus drápa*". *Plácidus saga*, ed. by John Tucker. Editiones Arnamagnæanæ Series B 31. Copenhagen: Reitzel, 89−124.

Louis-Jensen, Jonna and Tarrin Wills, eds. 2007. "*Plácitus drápa*." *Skaldic Poetry of the Scandinavian Middle Ages*. Volume VII, 2 Parts. *Poetry on Christian Subjects*, ed. by Margaret Clunies Ross. Turnhout: Brepols, 1, 179−220.

Lönnroth, Lars. 1976. *Njáls Saga. A Critical Introduction*. Berkeley, Los Angeles and London: University of California Press.

Lönnroth, Lars. 1990. "A Road Paved with Legends." *Two Norse-Icelandic Studies.* Litteraturvetenskapliga Institutionen, Göteborgs universitet, Meddelanden Nr 7. Göteborg, 17–34.

McDougall, Ian ed. 2007. "*Allra postola minnisvísur.*" *Skaldic Poetry of the Scandinavian Middle Ages.* Volume VII, 2 Parts. *Poetry on Christian Subjects*, ed. by Margaret Clunies Ross. Turnhout: Brepols, 852–871.

Malm, Mats. 2007. "The Notion of Effeminate Language in Old Norse Literature." *Learning and Understanding in the Old Norse World. Essays in Honour of Margaret Clunies Ross*, ed. by Judy Quinn, Kate Heslop and Tarrin Wills. Turnhout: Brepols, 305–320.

Meulengracht Sørensen, Preben. 2000. "Social institutions and belief systems of medieval Iceland (c. 870–1400) and their relations to literary production". *Old Icelandic Literature and Society*, ed. by Margaret Clunies Ross. Cambridge Studies in Medieval Literature 42. Cambridge: Cambridge University Press, 8–29.

O'Donoghue, Heather. 2005. *Skaldic Verse and the Poetics of Saga Narrative.* Oxford: Oxford University Press.

Olmer, Emil. 1902. *Boksamlingar på Island 1179–1490 enligt diplom.* Göteborgs Högskolas Årsskrift II. Göteborg: Wettergren & Kerber.

Raschellà, Fabrizio D. 2007. "Old Icelandic Grammatical Literature: The Last Two Decades of Research (1983–2005)." *Learning and Understanding in the Old Norse World. Essays in Honour of Margaret Clunies Ross*, ed. by Judy Quinn, Kate Heslop and Tarrin Wills. Turnhout: Brepols, 341–372.

Simek, Rudolf. 2009. "The Medieval Icelandic World View and the Theory of the Two Cultures." *Gripla* XX: 183–197.

Sverrir Tómasson. 1988. *Formálar íslenskra sagnaritara á miðöldum.* Stofnun Árna Magnússonar á Íslandi. Rit 33. Reykjavík: Stofnun Árna Magnússonar.

Sverrir Tómasson. 2006. "Old Icelandic Prose." *A History of Icelandic Literature*, ed. by Daisy Neijmann. Histories of Scandinavian Literature 5. Lincoln and London: University of Nebraska Press in cooperation with the American-Scandinavian Foundation, 64–173.

Torfi H. Tulinius. 2009. "The Self as Other. *Iceland and Christian Europe in the Middle Ages.*" *Gripla* XX: 199–216.

Tranter, Stephen. 2000. "Medieval Icelandic *artes poeticae.*" *Old Icelandic Literature and Society*, ed. by Margaret Clunies Ross. Cambridge Studies in Medieval Literature 42. Cambridge: Cambridge University Press, 140–160.

Whaley, Diana. 1993. "Skalds and Situational Verses in *Heimskringla.*" *Snorri Sturluson: Kolloquium anläßlich der 750. Wiederkehr seines Todestages*, ed. by Alois Wolf. Tübingen: Narr, 245–266.

Whaley, Diana. 2007. "Reconstructing Skaldic Encomia: Discourse Features in Þjóðólfr's 'Magnús verses'." *Learning and Understanding in the Old Norse World. Essays in Honour of Margaret Clunies Ross*, ed. by Judy Quinn, Kate Heslop and Tarrin Wills. Turnhout: Brepols, 75–101.

Widding, Ole. 1965. "Jærtegn og Maríu saga. Eventyr." Hans Bekker Nielsen, Thorkil Damsgaard Olsen og Ole Widding. *Norrøn fortællekunst*. Copenhagen: Akademisk forlag, 127–136.
Widding, Ole. 1979. "Den florissante stil i norrøn prosa (isl. skrúðstíllinn) specielt i forhold til den lærde stil." *Selskab for nordisk filologi. Årsberetning for 1977–8*, 7–11.
Widding, Ole, Hans Bekker-Nielsen and L. K. Shook. 1963. "The Lives of the Saints in Old Norse Prose: A Handlist." *Mediaeval Studies* 25: 294–337.
Whitelock, Dorothy, ed. 1967. *Sweet's Anglo-Saxon Reader in Prose and Verse*. 15th rev. edn. Oxford: Oxford University Press.
Wolf, Kirsten, ed. 2007. "*Heilagra manna drápa*" and "*Heilagra meyja drápa*." *Skaldic Poetry of the Scandinavian Middle Ages*. Volume VII, 2 Parts. *Poetry on Christian Subjects*, ed. by Margaret Clunies Ross. Turnhout: Brepols, 2, 872–890 and 2, 891–930.

SUMMARY

This article is a revised version of a paper I presented to the symposium *Nordic Civilization in the Medieval World* held at Skálholt in September 2007. I was asked to address the theme of *Medieval Icelandic Textual Culture* in a workshop whose theme was 'The world-view reflected in texts and practices'. The article surveys the debts of medieval Icelandic textual culture to both indigenous and non-indigenous traditions and suggests ways in which Icelanders showed their awareness that their culture was part of the mainstream medieval European culture of Christendom as well as at the same time maintaining an indigenously inflected vernacular tradition within which literary innovation could and did take place. It reviews the very large range of textual kinds produced in Iceland during the Middle Ages, both in poetry and prose, and builds up a map of Icelandic cultural interests and activities in the context of medieval European civilisation.

Margaret Clunies Ross
University of Sydney
margaret.clunies-ross@sydney.edu.au

RUDOLF SIMEK

THE MEDIEVAL ICELANDIC WORLD VIEW AND THE THEORY OF THE TWO CULTURES

I.

SVERRIR JAKOBSSON postulates that Medieval Icelanders, or at least the writers whose thinking is accessible to us through the written word, did not have a world view in our modern sense of the world, because they did not have a concept of the term "world view".[1] He goes on then to define what he understands as "world view", namely something that "provides meaning to events in the given surroundings, placing them in the context of things known and tangible."[2] In this abstract and hermeneutic meaning, he may be right that as such, the concept did not exist, but I would like to show that we may very well detect a world view in the Middle Ages generally and in Medieval Iceland in particular.

I define the term world view as something more universal than Sverrir, whose book otherwise seems to augment in most respects my own study, *Altnordische Kosmographie*, by using some non-Latin based sources.[3] I, however, would call the given world view of a people at a certain time "the sum of all our concepts of the physical and spiritual world which allows us to come to terms with all the eternal human questions", such as who made this world and in what shape? where do we go after death? and why does it rain so much? to name just a few, but we could also add: where do we come from and who are our ancestors?

Educated Medieval Icelanders were good Christians and as such had read their Latin books in school, as people still do in the Christian world, and therefore they would have had a concept of what many Medieval texts

[1]   Sverrir Jakobsson, *Við og veröldin* (Reykjavík: Háskólaútgáfan 2005), 363.
[2]   Ibid.
[3]   Rudolf Simek, *Altnordische Kosmographie. Studien und Quellen zu Weltbild und Weltbeschreibung in Norwegen und Island vom 12. bis zum 14. Jahrhundert*. Ergänzungsbände zum Reallexikon der Germanischen Altertumskunde 4 (Berlin, New York: de Gruyter, 1990).

call *Imago mundi* ("world picture"), namely not just a physical picture of the world, but a concept of everything that concerns man, including God's role in the world; some examples between the 12th and 14th centuries include Honorius-Augustodunensis's *Imago mundi* (the first version finished before 1110), the *Image du monde* by Gautier de Metz (ca. 1245), and the *Imago mundi* by Pierre d'Ailly (ca. 1390).

I know that Sverrir has loaded his usage of the term *world view* with at the same time more and less. *More* in the way that the world view includes also the individual or group distinctions from other groups, but that of course makes the term *world view* a relative term and therefore also *less*. Less because it thus has no overall validity and may therefore be held only by a very small group of, say, 13th century Icelandic "nationalists", if such a term had existed in the Middle Ages, which it did not.

I use the term *world view* in a much wider sense, insofar as it is the concepts described above held by the majority of those people who actually had an opinion and verbalized that opinion in a way still accessible to us, namely via the parchment. These Icelanders were, however, educated and literate and certainly knew the term *Imago mundi*, probably even beyond its use as a book title, as can be shown by a well-known passage from the manuscript AM 685 d 4to (31 r):

> Svo segir *imago mundi* at heimurinn se uæxinn sem egg & suo sem skurn er utan um eggit sva er elldr umhuerfiss heimenn & sva sem skiall er næst skurni sva er lopt næst elldi & hid huita ur eggi þat er næst skialli sva eru uotn næst lopti & svo sem id rauda er j eggi sva er iordin lukt j þessum hofud skepnum (my italics).[4]

This Icelandic passage answers roughly to a passage by Honorius Augustodunensis (*Imago mundi* I, 1)

> Mundus dicitur quasi undique motus. Est enim in perpetuo motu. Huius figura est in modum pilę rotunda, sed instar ovi elementis distincta. Ovum quippe exterius testa undique ambitur, teste albumen, albumini vitellum, vitello gutta pinguedinis includitur. Sic mundus undique cęlo, ut testa circumdatur, cęlo vero purus ether ut

---

[4] Rudolf Simek, *Altnordische Kosmographie*, 387.

albumen, etheri turbidus aer, ut vitellum, aeri terra ut pinguedinis gutta includitur.[5]

However, in my definition I not only exclude that part of the population about whom we have no factual knowledge but also sources that are, in some cases, impossible to interpret. Here, I have in mind not only cryptic texts but also certain symbols in 12th-century French church sculpture, for example, whose meanings are now lost to us unless there is some written text to unlock the meaning. My use of "world view" is therefore closely connected to the history of the mentality of educated Medieval Icelanders, and it encompasses the worlds of:

Religion & History (*Heilsgeschichte*);
the Scholarly World, especially the Natural Sciences;
Everyday Life, and Literature.

Because I do not subscribe to Sverrir's more hermeneutic and also processual definition of *world view*, I shall not claim to establish the world view of all Medieval Icelanders, but rather those at a given period in time, in my case the 12th century, a period particularly prone to the outside influences because of the massive changes happening in intellectual life across Western Europe, known as the Renaissance of the 12th Century.

That the world view is never ahistorical is obvious, but history is something that permeates all aspects of the world view given above: for the religious aspect it is the *Heilsgeschichte* of the world, for everyday life it is genealogies, family history and local history, for the scholarly aspect both time in the astronomical sense and the continuities of (secular) world history, and in literature the preservation and continuation of stories of old.

But seeing that educated Medieval Christians studied much the same books all over Western Europe, it follows that much of the world view throughout Western Europe will also be consistent, of course allowing for local traditions, superstitions and even mythologies that may preserve elements important to peoples' identities on a lower level than their humanity and Christianity. However, many of these lower concepts may never make it into writing and thus present a certain problem to the modern scholar.

---

[5] "Honorius Augustodunensis Imago mundi," *Archives d'histoire doctrinale et littéraire du moyen age*, 57 (1982): 49.

All that can be gleaned through our manuscripts is only a part of the world view, even though it may still show us complex concepts such as the one of God himself (see p. 187, picture from Schedels Weltchronik, 1492).

II.

In keeping with the topic of this volume, I shall go on to show how much — or rather how little — the Icelandic world view of the 12th century differed from that of Western Europe. It has, been postulated that the world view of the Icelanders (reflected in literature on the one hand, in their political system on the other) was radically different from the rest of Europe and "two cultures" have thus been identified: namely what Lars Lönnroth called "the clerics' and courtiers' European culture" on the one hand, and the "Icelandic farmer's attempts to write down the histories of his home country" on the other.[6]

Sverre Bagge brought this argument to a point towards the end of the last millennium when he talked of the two well known heretics, Hermann Pálsson[7] and Lars Lönnroth, "who interpreted Icelandic culture, including the sagas, as part of the common culture of Western Christendom".[8] Bagge went on to suggest that this "heretic view" had, for some time, become the orthodox view. But he then claimed that history and social anthropology have now again helped us to revert to earlier views, a point with which I can not agree at all.

If we really wanted to establish that there was such a thing as two cultures, firstly, we would have to establish that the one culture, the clerical one, was actually the same in Iceland as the clerical Latin culture on the European continent and thus "foreign" to Iceland. This is a view contested by Jesse Byock in his paper at the International Saga conference in Helsingør held in 1985 where he argued that the situation of the Icelandic church was fundamentally different from the continental one — although

---

[6] "... den isländske bonden, som fjärran från klerkers och hovmäns europeiska kultur roar sig med att skriva ned gamla berättelser från hembygden." Lars Lönnroth, *Tesen om de två kulturerna*. Scripta Islandica 15/1964 (Uppsala and Stockholm: Almqvist & Wiksells Boktryckeri, 1965), 97.

[7] Hermann Pálsson, *Art and Ethics in Hrafnkel's Saga*. (Copenhagen: Munksgaard, 1971).

[8] Sverre Bagge, "Icelandic Uniqueness or a Common European Culture. The Case of the Kings' Sagas," *Scandinavian Studies* 69 (1997): 418–442.

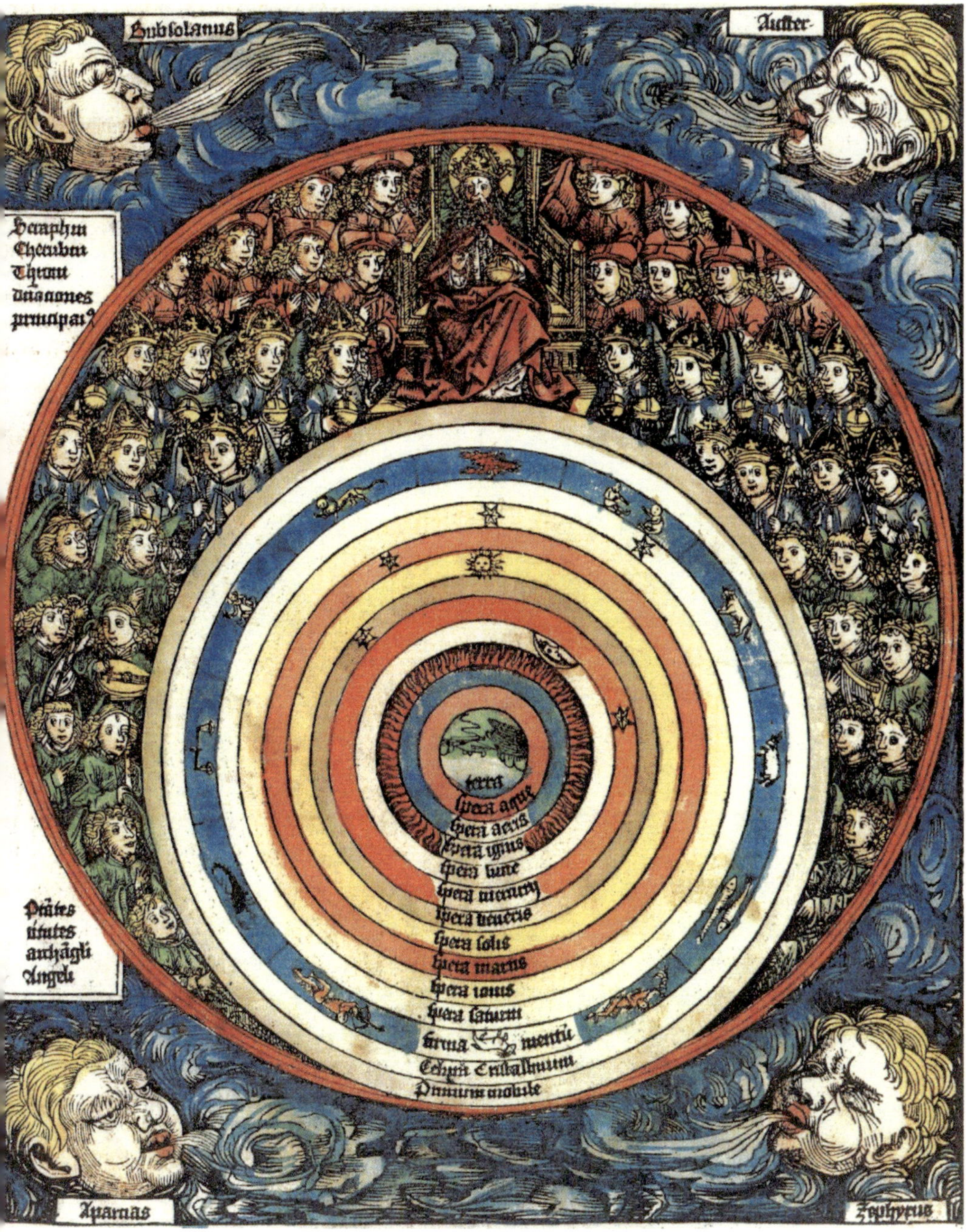
Subsolanus
Auster
terra
spera aque
spera aeris
spera ignis
spera lune
spera veneris
spera solis
spera martis
spera iouis
spera saturni
Primum mobile
Zephyrus

he was specifically talking about political power and not intellectual concepts.[9] Secondly, we would have to establish that the supposed native culture was different to this clerically-dominated culture and substantially so, not just geographically and politico-socially, in the way that the 14th-century Czech culture would have been different from 14th-century Italian culture, for example: nobody ever speaks of "two cultures" in this context, although there would have been obvious differences both politically and culturally.

III.

I will begin with the first point above, in order to try to show how the clerical-learned culture of Iceland was related to the learned world of the continent, when it comes to questions concerning a world view.

A "Division of Science" (*arbor scientiae*) in 13th-century Iceland does not, at first sight, seem to conform with the canonical *Septem Artes*, the Seven Liberal Arts, which we have come to accept as the norm for Medieval subjects mainly on the grounds that the Middle Ages inherited this concept from antiquity via Martianus Capella and other early Medieval authors. However, there is no need to think that the Icelandic "Division of Science" shows a deviant picture of the Seven Liberal Arts, because there is also a multitude of different distinctions in Medieval Latin mss concerned with *arbor scientiae*.

Within the Seven Liberal Arts, the single arts are very well represented in Icelandic manuscripts: the four Grammatical Treatises even cover aspects of the *trivium* (rhetoric, grammar, and dialectics). The Icelanders seem to have had a particular predilection for the quadrivium, however; although musical manuscripts are not overly well preserved (perhaps because many of them contained Latin hymns and were therefore destroyed during the reformation),[10] we find tracts on mathematics and geometry (AM 194 4to, AM 685 d 4to, GkS 1812 4to, AM 764 4to) and especially astronomy. It seems that Iceland was particularly up-to-date in the field of astronomy: we find the latest 12th-century theories, like that concerning the heliocentricity of Mercury and Venus, as well as far more traditional

---

[9] Jesse Byock, "The Power and Wealth of the Icelandic Church: Some Talking Points," *Proceedings of the 6th Saga Conference* (Helsingør, 1985), 89–101.

[10] Cf. John Bergsagel, "Music and Musical Instruments," *Medieval Scandinavia: An Encyclopedia*, (New York and London: Garland, 1993), 420–423.

THE MEDIEVAL ICELANDIC WORLD VIEW 189

theories derived ultimately from the Venerable Bede. Although not necessarily evident from theoretical tracts, in Medieval practice, cosmography and geography were closely related to astronomy. Illustrations and texts for both appeared side by side and sometimes even within the same picture (as in AM 764 4to).

Medieval Icelandic maps, of which a surprising number are to be found in manuscripts, show us not only an intense interest in geography, but also an interesting addition to the contemporary European world views, namely with regard to the transatlantic discoveries and a very particular concept of Greenland as part of Northern Europe. This is reflected in the maps of Henricus Martellus[11] which were based on the calculations by the Dane Claudius Clavus (fl. ca. 1420),[12] and also in the early modern Skálholt maps, but not in Medieval central European maps of the same time (such as the widely known early Ptolemaic map in Hartmann Schedel's *Chronicon universale* of 1492). But not only was the North West better known to Scandinavians than to any other European scholars, obviously through the Scandinavian voyages of discovery undertaken in the 10th and 11th centuries, even Eastern Europe is presented in considerably more detail in Icelandic manuscripts than it is in concurrent European maps.[13] Examples include the location of the Biarmones, or of the town of Kiev, on the largest of the Medieval Icelandic *Mappae mundi*, the one in GkS 1812 4to (5v–6r), but also the naming of a whole series of towns in Icelandic geographical treatises (such as AM 736 I 4to, 1r–1v, and especially Hauksbók, AM 544 4to, 2r–4r). While Miklagarðr (Constantinople) is of course known, and is shown on most European Medieval maps, towns like Garðar (Kiev), Hólmgarðr (Novgorod), Palteskja (Polotzk) and Smalenska (Smolensk) are only marked on maps in Icelandic manuscripts.

A very specialized but fascinating aspect of Medieval Icelandic map-

---

[11] Werner Kreuer, ed., *Monumenta Cartographica: Tabulae mundi* (Gotha: Perthes, 1998), 55–58.

[12] Rudolf Simek, "Elusive Elysia, or: Which Way to Glæsisvellir? On the Geography of the North in Icelandic Legendary Fiction," *Sagnaskemmtun. Studies in Honour of Hermann Pálsson*, ed. by R. Simek, J. Kristjánsson, H. Bekker-Nielsen (Wien: Braumüller, 1986), 247–275.

[13] Rudolf Simek, "Skandinavische Mappae Mundi in der europäischen Tradition," *Ein Weltbild vor Columbus. Die Ebstorfer Weltkarte. Interdisziplinäres Colloquium 1988*, ed. by Hartmut Kugler in Zs.-arbeit mit Eckhard Michael (Weinheim: Acta Humaniora 1991), 167–184.

making is the plan of Jerusalem.[14] It is quite astonishing that out of 15 maps of Jerusalem that survive worldwide from the Middle Ages, three come from Iceland, and these are practically identical to the Flemish source of all those 15 plans, namely Lambert of St. Omer's mighty encyclopedia *Liber floridus* – which I believe was the model for Hauksbók.[15]

When it comes to the more obscure sides of the Medieval world view, Iceland was certainly not behind in soaking up knowledge which was fashionable and up to date in western Europe, even if it was of limited value to Icelanders (or humanity as such). Teratology, the lore of the wonderful as represented by the so-called Marvels of the East, reached Iceland as early as the 12th century, and the Icelanders showed their characteristic lack of exact discrimination between the simply odd, like the elephant (as depicted twice in the Old Icelandic *Physiologus* in AM 673 a 4to, 7r–7v),[16] or the absolutely fictitious, like various types of fabulous creatures, both zoomorphic and anthropomorphic.[17] As is well known, one of these men even made it into *Eiríks saga rauða*, obviously to prove the fact that Vinland did indeed extend from Africa, a point made in the short cosmography in AM 736 I 4to (written around 1300).[18]

This extensive cosmographical knowledge of the Icelanders extended even to mythical creatures from Greek and Latin mythography, which is hardly surprising, seeing that this clerical culture permeated all areas of life. These depictions are not limited to their representation as the symbols of the zodiac (as in AM 249 b fol, or in GKS 1812 4to, 3r ff), but are also found in other contexts outside mere astronomical interpretations of mythological figures (cf. GKS 1812 4to, 3v).

---

[14] Rudolf Simek, "Hierusalem civitas famosissima. Die erhaltenen Fassungen des hochmittelalterlichen *Situs Jerusalem* (mit Abbildungen zur gesamten handschriftlichen Überlieferung)," *Codices manuscripti* 16 (1992) [1995]: 121–153.

[15] Rudolf Simek, "Warum sind *Völuspá* und *Merlínuspá* in der *Hauksbók* überliefert?" *Deutsch-Nordische Begegnungen. 9. Arbeitstagung der Skandinavisten des deutschen Sprachgebiets 1989 in Svendborg* (Odense, 1991), 104–115.

[16] *The Icelandic Physiologus*, ed. by Halldór Hermannsson. Islandica. 27. (Ithaca, New York: Cornell Univ. Library, 1938; reprint: Kraus Reprints, 1966).

[17] Rudolf Simek, "Wunder des Nordens. Einfoetingar, Hornfinnar, Hundingjar und Verwandte," *triuwe. Studien zur Sprachgeschichte und Literaturwissenschaft. Gedächtnisbuch für Elfriede Stutz*, ed. by Karl-Friedrich Kraft, Eva-Maria Lill and Ute Schwab. Heidelberger Bibliotheksschriften 47 (Heidelberg: Winter 1992), 69–90.

[18] Rudolf Simek, *Altnordische Kosmographie*, 429–432.

Nor did the learned Icelanders of the 12th and 13th centuries stop at just taking over or borrowing from continental sources, but just like their European colleagues the foundations of their learned culture (perhaps monastic and academic but nevertheless very lively) were so secure that they could play with and develop novel ideas from learned roots. A good example is the unique Icelandic table of fabulous creatures in BL Add. 11250 which does not rest directly on a continental source, but presupposes a knowledge of high Medieval teratology which then was used in a playful way elsewhere, like in the margins of *Flateyjarbók* or in copies of *Jónsbók*.

IV.

All of these examples have been taken from the world of scholarship, which formed only one aspect of the world view as defined above. As the purely religious aspects of the Medieval world view, apart from the local variations of popular religion, were not likely to vary too much in the book-based religion of Christianity, this leaves two more aspects to investigate, namely everyday life and literature. The former is, for all accounts and purposes, out of our reach as it is visible to us only through literature for one thing, and may well, to some extent, be even out of the reach of literature, as the banal occurrences of everyday life were not the topic of literary elaboration even in the pseudo-realistic Icelandic sagas. Thus we are left with the world of literature to establish any significant deviations of Iceland, in terms of the world view, from the rest of the Western world. As all three major genres of Icelandic literature, namely sagas, skaldic poetry and Eddic poetry, have no direct formal counterpart in European literature, it may be worthwhile investigating whether these genres may not be deceptive and whether similar types of literature were not represented on both sides of the North Atlantic as far as themes and topics are concerned. The following table should thus serve as a tentative experiment to look at literary genres as far as their protagonists are concerned, something that has traditionally been done with the subdivision of Icelandic saga literature.

	Iceland	Western Europe
Early Saints, Martyrs and Church Fathers	Heilagra manna sögur Religious skaldic poetry	Latin and Vernacular Hagiography in prose and poetry
New Saints and Churchmen	Biskupa sögur Religious skaldic poetry	Local politico-hagiographical literature in prose and poetry
Rulers of Antiquity	Sagas of Antiquity	Epics of antiquity
Heroic Rulers and Heroes	Heroic Eddic poetry Fornaldar sögur	*Lais* *Chansons de Geste*
Kings and Emperors	Skaldic poetry Konunga sögur	*Gesta*, *Historiae*, Chronicles
Arthurian Knights	Riddara sögur	Vernacular court epics and prose romances, Lais
Comic and Romantic Heroes	Legendary romance	Late court epics, prose *Volksbücher*, *Schwank*-literature
Lokal Chieftains and Farmers, past	Skaldic poetry Íslendinga sögur	*Spielmannsepik*, Moral tales, *bispel*
Lokal Chieftains and Farmers, present	Samtíðar sögur	– (Wernher der Gärtner: *Meier Helmbrecht*)
Gods and Powers (non-Christian)	Mythological Poetry O.N. Mythography	(Mythological poetry) Latin Mythography

As indicated by the brackets in the right hand column of the last two groups, stories about contemporary farmers seem to have been underrepresented on the continent as was mythological poetry, although it did exist. However, as the farmer-chieftains of the Sturlung age represent the highest social stratum of 13th-century Iceland, we should perhaps not compare them with the occasional tales found about farmers but rather about nobility – and there is plenty of that in German, French, and English Medieval literature.

This leaves us with the problematic genre of mythological poetry, which is limited to a relatively small group of 12th-century French clerics, who used poetry based on classical mythology in their philosophical writings and nearly all of whom belonged to the so-called School of Chartres. For us, their most important protagonists are Bernhardus Silvestris and Walter of Chatillon.

However, even despite these attempts at composing mythological poetry and even mythography (notably the work of Remigius of Auxerre), the corpus of mythological poetry on the continent is even smaller than in Iceland (where Codex Regius contains 10 strictly mythological poems and few others are found outside). Also, the unique combination of mythology with historiography that we find in, for example, the myths of Odin's immigration in Snorri, Ari and a few other Icelandic texts, never seems to have been produced on the continent.[19] We may therefore safely state that mythological writings (especially in combination with mythological historiography) in Iceland was a far wider and more varied genre than on the continent.

To sum up, in the areas of the scholarly and the literary worldview, Iceland produced a cognitive surplus in two major fields: firstly, in the field of geography, where not only detailed knowledge of Iceland and Greenland as well as the transatlantic discoveries, but also a relatively intimate knowledge of north-eastern and eastern europe is reflected both in scholarship and in literature; secondly, in the field of mythological writings, with the inclusion of genealogies of mythological and heroic ancestry.

V.

The second question posed in section II above concerned the possible difference between a (supposed) native culture and the clerically dominated culture of an intellectual elite. An excellent way of investigating this question is by looking at the actual context of texts as found in the Medieval manuscripts. This "material philology" (or more conservatively: codicology) has been sadly neglected in Old Norse studies until quite recently and

---

[19] Cf. Heinz Klingenberg, "Trór Thórr (Thor) wie Trōs Aeneas. Snorra Edda Prolog, Vergil Rezeption und Altisländische Gelehrte Urgeschichte," *alvíssmál* 1 (1992): 17–54; Heinz Klingenberg, "Odin und die Seinen. Altisländischer Gelehrter Urgeschichte anderer Teil," *alvíssmál* 2 (1993): 31–80; Heinz Klingenberg, "Odins Wanderzug nach Schweden. Altisländische Gelehrte Urgeschichte und mittelalterliche Geographie," *alvíssmál* 3 (1994): 19–42; Rudolf Simek, "Der lange Weg von Troja nach Grönland. Zu den Quellen der gelehrten Urgeschichte in Island," *Germanisches Altertum und christliches Mittelalter. Festschrift für Heinz Klingenberg*, ed. by Bela Brogyanyi and Thomas Krömmelbein (Hamburg: Kovacs, 2001), 315–327.

this neglect has led to many editions presenting "works" of Old Norse prose or poetry quite unconnected from their actual position with the transmission process in Medieval manuscripts. However, this is about to change and more attention is now being paid to the actual place given to texts in their Medieval contexts.

The manuscripts studied by me in the context of the two genres mentioned above, namely geographical and mythological knowledge, give no indication that there was a distinction between a "popular" and a "learned" culture in Iceland: cosmographical information was frequently used to preface historical or pseudo-historical works, such as in Snorri's writings, but also in manuscripts like Eirspennill (AM 47 fol)[20] and AM 764 4to[21] as well as Hauksbók.[22] Hauksbók is also a good example of the merging of native and "foreign" learned material within one manuscript: it uses many native saga texts, as well as texts translated from the Latin, to create a very personal encyclopedia along the lines of a Flemish model known to the collector.[23]

As far as mythography is concerned, we only have to look at the manuscripts of *Snorra Edda* to see what accompanied Snorri's work. Despite the fact that Snorri covered indigenous material only and took great pains to preserve the mythographic, heroic, and poetic lore according to the skaldic sources, of which he quotes 509 stanzas in *Skáldskaparmál* alone (not to mention the skaldic 583 stanzas quoted in *Heimskringla*), the *Edda* is always found in the company of learned works representing the "elite" clerical culture: works like the Grammatical Treatises that deal with grammar and rhetoric, as well as distinctly native texts like poems of the Poetic Edda (see table).

---

[20] The case of Eirspennill is particularly interesting, as Finnur Jónsson in his 1916 edition chose to ignore the cosmographical introduction on fol. 1r, cf. R. Simek, *Altnordische Kosmographie*, 428.

[21] Ibid., 436

[22] Ibid., 449.

[23] Cf. Rudolf Simek, "Warum sind *Völuspá* und *Merlínuspá* in der *Hauksbók* überliefert?", 104–115; Sverrir Jakobsson, "Hauksbók and the construction of an Icelandic World View," *Saga-Book* 31 (2007): 22–38, chooses to ignore this model, which leads to his assumption of Hauksbók as merely the manifestation of a private "world view" (Ibid. 29).

Manuscripts of Snorra Edda with accompanying texts

Codex Upsaliensis 11, DG 11 8vo (U), 1300-1320: *Snorra Edda* + 2nd Gramm. Treatise + *Skáldatal* + *Ættartal Skjöldunga* + *Lögsögumannatal* + *Rígsþula* (fragm.)
AM 748 I 4to (A), fragm., after 1300: *Skáldskaparmál* + *Þulur* of *Snorra Edda* + 7 Eddic Poems of *Codex Regius* + *Baldrs draumar* + 3. Gramm. Treatise
Codex regius of Snorra Edda, GKS 2367 4to (R), ca. 1325: *Snorra Edda* + *Grottasöngr* + *Jómsvíkingadrápa* + *Málsháttakvæði*
Codex Wormianus, AM 242 fol (W), ca. 1350: *Snorra Edda* + 4 Gramm. Treatises + *Rígsþula*
AM 757 a 4to (B), fragm., ca. 1380–1400: *Skáldskaparmál* + *Þulur* of *Snorra Edda* + 3rd Gramm. Treatise
AM 748 II 4to (C), ca. 1400: only *Skáldskaparmál* + *Þulur* of *Snorra Edda*
Codex Trajectinus, MS Utrecht 1374, (T), ca. 1595: *Snorra Edda* + *Grottasöngr*

There are, of course, exceptions to the rule, such as the *Codex Regius* of the Poetic Edda (GKS 2365 4to), which only contains poems and accompanying prose and contains nothing of learned lore with Latin origins.

Such exceptions (we may add *Flateyjarbók*, but this late and sumptuous manuscript is an unsuitable example for demonstration of the establishment of an indigenous lay culture) are hardly sufficient to justify talking about a completely separate culture that only rested on native lore to the exclusion, or at least part-rejection, of Latin clerical learning (from Andreas Heusler to, in milder form, Einar Ólafur Sveinsson). On the contrary: although the Icelanders managed to surpass the continent in knowledge in the two fields of geography and mythography, and managed to make the best of it both politically (by settling Greenland and attempting to settle Vinland, and at least keeping the knowledge about these places alive) and culturally (by keeping both skaldic poetry and the mythological knowledge necessary for understanding it alive in mythography and Eddic poetry), they also managed to integrate very successfully both native and foreign learning into a single culture. This culture was, at least in the 12th and 13th century, on a par with continental European culture.

If there had been two cultures — rather than one literary and social elite, interrelated and interacting in life as in literary production — we would have to imagine two different social groups of (say, monastic-clerical and secular) Icelanders that had a very different outlook. Despite the well-known political clashes between the higher clergy and some secular chieftains in the 13th century, the manuscript tradition gives us no clue that this may have been the case when it came to the actual world view of Medieval Icelanders. The examples of geographical knowledge in maps and in cosmographies shows how unlikely it is that it was two different sets of people who preserved the Latin and such native additional information of the "cognitive surplus" to be found in Iceland. The social setup of Iceland in Christian times, as represented by the institution of the Goðakirkja (or Eigenkirchenwesen) makes it even more improbable that priests and farmers who were in daily physical and mental contact could, over a prolonged period of time, preserve or develop two differing world views. [24]

But in saga writing, too, it is unlikely that the Icelandic *literati* who composed hagiography, political history in the kings sagas, or the courtly texts of the *riddarasögur*, would have handed over their quill to somebody else to compose *Eiríks saga rauða* or *Eyrbyggja saga*. Therefore, I see no need to talk of two cultures, of a particular (and unexplained) Icelandic uniqueness or an Icelandic *Sonderkultur*.[25] What the Icelanders achieved, and could rightly be proud of, was a not insubstantial cognitive surplus.

---

[24] Cf. Gunnar Karlsson, *Goðamenning* (Reykjavík 2004).
[25] Klaus von See, "Snorris Konzeption einer nordischen Sonderkultur," *Snorri Sturluson. Kolloquium anläßlich der 750. Wiederkehr seines Todestages*, ed. by Alois Wolf. Ergänzungsbände zum Reallexikon der Germanischen Altertumskunde 4. Berlin, New York: de Gruyter, 1993, 141–177.

REFERENCES

Bagge, Sverre. "Icelandic Uniqueness or a Common European Culture. The Case of the Kings' Sagas." *Scandinavian Studies* 69 (1997): 418–442.
Bergsagel, John. "Music and Musical Instruments." *Medieval Scandinavia: An Encyclopedia*. New York and London: Garland, 1993, 420–423.
Byock, Jesse. "The Power and Wealth of the Icelandic Church: some Talking Points." *Proceedings of the 6th Saga Conference* (Helsingør, 1985), 89–101.
Hermann Pálsson. *Art and Ethics in Hrafnkel's Saga*. Copenhagen: Munksgaard, 1971.
Gunnar Karlsson. *Goðamenning*. Reykjavík: Mál og menning, 2004.
"Honorius Augustodunensis 'Imago mundi'," ed. Valerie Flint. *Archives d'histoire doctrinale et littéraire du moyen age*, 57 (1982).
The Icelandic Physiologus, ed. by Halldór Hermannsson. Islandica 27. Ithaca, New York: Cornell University Library, 1938. Reprint: Kraus Reprints, 1966.
Klingenberg, Heinz. "Odin und die Seinen. Altisländischer Gelehrter Urgeschichte anderer Teil." *alvíssmál* 2 (1993): 31–80.
Klingenberg, Heinz. "Odins Wanderzug nach Schweden. Altisländische Gelehrte Urgeschichte und mittelalterliche Geographie," *alvíssmál* 3 (1994): 19–42.
Klingenberg, Heinz. "Trór Thórr (Thor) wie Trōs Aeneas. Snorra Edda Prolog, Vergil Rezeption und altisländische Gelehrte Urgeschichte." *alvíssmál* 1 (1992): 17–54.
Kreuer, Werner, ed. *Monumenta Cartographica: Tabulae mundi*. Gotha: Perthes, 1998.
Lönnroth, Lars. *Tesen om de två kulturerna. Kritiska studier i den isländska sagaskrivningens sociala förutsättningar*. Scripta Islandica 15/1964. Uppsala, 1965.
See, Klaus von. "Snorris Konzeption einer nordischen Sonderkultur," *Snorri Sturluson. Kolloquium anläßlich der 750. Wiederkehr seines Todestages*, ed. A. Wolf. Berlin, New York: de Gruyter, 1993, 141–177.
Simek, Rudolf. *Altnordische Kosmographie. Studien und Quellen zu Weltbild und Weltbeschreibung in Norwegen und Island vom 12. bis zum 14. Jahrhundert*. Berlin, New York: de Gruyter, 1990.
Simek, Rudolf. "Der lange Weg von Troja nach Grönland. Zu den Quellen der gelehrten Urgeschichte in Island." *Germanisches Altertum und christliches Mittelalter. Festschrift für Heinz Klingenberg*, ed. by Bela Brogyanyi and Thomas Krömmelbein. Hamburg: Kovacs, 2001, 315–327.
Simek, Rudolf. "Elusive Elysia, or: Which Way to Glæsisvellir? On the Geography of the North in Icelandic Legendary Fiction." *Sagnaskemmtun. Studies in Honour of Hermann Pálsson*, ed. by R. Simek, J. Kristjánsson, H. Bekker-Nielsen. Wien: Braumüller, 1986, 247–275.
Simek, Rudolf. "Hierusalem civitas famosissima. Die erhaltenen Fassungen des

hochmittelalterlichen *Situs Jerusalem* (mit Abbildungen zur gesamten handschriftlichen Überlieferung)." *Codices manuscripti* 16 (1992) [1995]: 121–153.

Simek, Rudolf. "Skandinavische Mappae Mundi in der europäischen Tradition." *Ein Weltbild vor Columbus. Die Ebstorfer Weltkarte. Interdisziplinäres Colloquium 1988*, ed. by Hartmut Kugler and Eckhard Michael. Weinheim: Acta Humaniora, 1991, 167– 184.

Simek, Rudolf. "Warum sind *Völuspá* und *Merlínusp*á in der *Hauksbók* überliefert?" *Deutsch-Nordische Begegnungen. 9. Arbeitstagung der Skandinavisten des deutschen Sprachgebiets 1989 in Svendborg.* Odense 1991, 104–115.

Simek, Rudolf. "Wunder des Nordens. Einfoetingar, Hornfinnar, Hundingjar und Verwandte." *triuwe. Studien zur Sprachgeschichte und Literaturwissenschaft. Gedächtnisbuch für Elfriede Stutz*, ed. by Karl-Friedrich Kraft, Eva-Maria Lill and Ute Schwab. Heidelberger Bibliotheksschriften. 47. Heidelberg: Winter, 1992, 69–90.

Sverrir Jakobsson. *Við og veröldin*. Reykjavík: Háskólaútgáfan, 2005.

Sverrir Jakobsson. "Hauksbók and the construction of an Icelandic World View." *Saga-Book* 31 (2007): 22–38.

SUMMARY

The paper takes the Medieval Icelandic world view as its subject and attempts to demonstrate how closely related that world view was to that of the rest of Europe, from the 12th century onwards. However, given the nature of our sources in surviving manuscripts, we only have access to the conceptions and ideas of an intellectual elite. But as this is also true for Medieval Europe as a whole, there is no reason to assume that the world view to be found in Icelandic manuscripts is less representative than elsewhere. Although in Medieval Iceland, the Renaissance of the Twelfth Century was accepted with amazing speed, there were also two areas of learning where the Icelanders exceeded the knowledge attained in continental Europe. The first of these was pre-Christian mythology which was preserved through Skaldic poetry, the second was the geography of the North and the transatlantic coasts, where the Icelanders managed to preserve knowledge gained through their ancestors' Viking Age voyages of discovery. In these fields of knowledge, we can talk of a substantial cognitive surplus within Medieval Icelandic learning.

Rudolf Simek
University of Bonn
simek@uni-bonn.de

TORFI H. TULINIUS

THE SELF AS OTHER

Iceland and Christian Europe in the Middle Ages

THE SOCIETY and culture of medieval Iceland have two characteristics that make them a very interesting and stimulating object of study for the historian or literary scholar. On the one hand, the society was original, especially in the way it was organized. On the other, its culture was very rich, at least when we consider the amount of texts that remain and were composed in this comparatively small society that evolved in a land far away from any other European country, literally at the periphery of Christian Europe.[1] However, for a long time scholars did not usually think about the culture of medieval Iceland in terms of its relationship to the rest of Christian Europe. On the contrary, for the country was considered to be a sort of repository. Up there in the far North, the original culture of the Germanic peoples – or at least of the Scandinavian or northern Germanic peoples – was cultivated and preserved in the isolation of the North Atlantic. Interestingly enough, this point of view on Iceland's medieval culture is not the Icelandic one originally. Even though some Icelanders have adopted it, it is more correct to say that it is the point of view of the continental European, that is, of someone at the centre who is looking at the periphery.

It is not necessary to view medieval Iceland in this way. And in fact, over the last half a century at least, a considerable number of scholars have established new ways of considering the country's relationship to the rest of Christian Europe in the medieval period. Progressively over the years, a

---

[1] An attempt at comparative quantification has been made by Gunnar Karlsson in his *Goðamenning. Staða og hlutverk hinna fornu goðorðsmanna* (Reykjavík: Heimskringla, 2004), 423–434. When compared to what is left of medieval texts from all other Scandinavian countries, the difference is staggering. For a description of the large Icelandic corpus, see for example Kurt Schier, *Sagaliteratur* (Stuttgart: Metzler, 1970).

new and better understanding has been emerging of the connections between the exceptional wealth of Iceland's medieval literature and its participation in the culture of the Medieval West. These connections can be expressed in terms of otherness and integration as well as in terms of identity formation. The Icelanders were aware that their pagan heritage was different. However, they integrated this otherness into an image of themselves as a Christian people that they constructed through their literary production.

Before elaborating on this, let us look at how the older conception may have originated.[2] Many factors of the history of Europe explain how we have perceived the mystery of Iceland's cultural 'miracle' over the last two hundred years or so. One of them may be that we do not measure sufficiently the length of time and the degree of historical change that has occurred since this Icelandic miracle took place. Eight centuries ago, Europe was an area where states were weak but the Church was both unified and comparatively strong as an organisation. Though it might be said that there is a parallel in the direction in which Europe is evolving today, with the weakening of states and the strengthening of a common institution, the European Union, the period in between was quite different. Indeed, in the period separating the Middle Ages and our era, states grew stronger, as did the idea of nationhood. In addition, the Reformation created a cultural divide across Europe. We have every reason to believe that both these factors have distorted our perceptions of Northern Europe and its medieval culture, as we will see in greater detail shortly.

Another explanation is that when scholars started to think about Medieval Iceland in the 18th and 19th centuries, they perceived it in the following terms: Iceland was the repository of a culture common to all the Nordic – or even Germanic – peoples. It was maintained and preserved in Iceland, unadulterated by influence from southern Europe. We have here a

[2] For a recent overview of the history of the reception of medieval Icelandic culture and literature over the last centuries, see Andrew Wawn's and Jón Karl Helgason's contributions to the *Companion to Old-Norse Icelandic Literature and Culture* (Oxford: Blackwell, 2005), 64–81 and 320–337. See also Margaret Clunies Ross's cogent remarks in her "Medieval Iceland and the European Middle Ages," *International Scandinavian and Medieval Studies in Memory of Gerd Wolfgang Weber*, ed. by M. Dallapiazza, O. Hansen, P. Meulengracht-Sørensen and Y. S. Bonnetain (Trieste: Edizioni Parnaso, 2000), 111–120; *The Manuscripts of Iceland*, ed. by Gísli Sigurðsson and Vésteinn Ólason (Reykjavík: Árni Magnússon Institute, 2004), 101–169.

THE SELF AS OTHER 201

certain way of thinking which is very outdated but is, however, still quite persistent among the general public, if not among scholars. It is characterised by the use of the concepts of purity and influence. They can be expressed by the following propositions: "the culture of medieval Iceland is the purest conserved manifestation of Germanic culture" and "it is not yet under the influence of Christian European culture with its basis in Latinity."

The reason for this persistence is linked to a very strong desire in several countries of Northern Europe at certain times in their respective histories for an identity which was distinct from the rest of European culture. That is why medieval Icelandic studies flourished in Germany, England and Scandinavia – and finally in Iceland itself, each of these scholarly traditions giving the study of medieval Icelandic culture its special twist, linked to the ideological purposes it was meant to serve.[3]

Let us take one example, that of the so-called "Icelandic school" in saga studies. This school evolved among Icelandic scholars in the first half of the 20th century, a period in which the country was progressively gaining its independence from Denmark. Scholars such as Björn M. Ólsen, Sigurður Nordal and Einar Ól. Sveinsson were eminent representatives of this approach to the sagas. They emphasized the originality of Icelandic culture, i.e. the fact that – though Germanic and Scandinavian in its origins – it was also the original creation of the people living in Iceland at the time.[4]

The rise of the Icelandic school was of great cultural significance for the people of Iceland while they were taking their last steps on the road to independence. It also opened the way for a re-examination of the relationship between its medieval culture and what was going on in the rest of Europe at the same time. By viewing the society of 13th-century Iceland as the centre of production of this culture, it opened up the possibility of

[3] For Germany and Britain, see among others Klaus von See, *Barbar, Germane, Arier : Die Suche nach der Identität der Deutschen* (Heidelberg: Winter, 1994) and Andrew Wawn, *The Vikings and the Victorians: Inventing the Old North in Nineteenth-century Britain* (Cambridge: D. S. Brewer, 2000). For the Scandinavian countries, see *The Waking of Angantyr: the Scandinavian past in European culture*, ed. E. Roesdahl and P. Meulengracht-Sørensen (Aarhus: Aarhus Universitetsforlag, 1996).

[4] Jesse L. Byock, „Þjóðernishyggja nútímans og Íslendingasögurnar," *Tímarit Máls og menningar* (1993:1): 36–50. The best recent representative of the Icelandic school's view of Icelandic literary history can be seen in Jónas Kristjánsson, *Eddas and Sagas. Iceland's Medieval Literature*, tr. P. Foote (Reykjavík: Hið íslenska bókmenntafélag, 1988).

looking at how its actors had access to material from other cultures. Indeed, many things have been uncovered by the last two or three generations of scholars that indicate that the image of Iceland as the repository of an ancient Germanic culture, unadulterated by influence from the South, does not hold up to scrutiny. It is quite sufficient merely to read through the great amount of texts which have been left to us from the period in order to discover evidence of the very close links between Iceland and the rest of Christian Europe in every field.

The Christianization of Iceland

If we begin by considering the field of religion, it is an inescapable fact that Iceland became part of the Catholic Church when the leaders of the country decided to convert to Christianity at the Alþing, or Parliament, of the year 1000. It stayed Catholic until the Reformation in 1550. Throughout the period in which all the literature was created, therefore, Iceland was a Christian country.

The Conversion had an enormous impact on Iceland. This impact was not only immediate but shaped the development of the society for years to come. An important factor in this development was the need to educate clerics. Though the first priests came from abroad, this could not be a permanent situation. It was necessary to train young Icelanders for the priesthood. Many of those chosen appear to have belonged to the upper echelons of society and within two generations, there seems to have developed quite a large group of educated Icelanders from the dominant classes who were ready to take control of and administer the new Church of Iceland. There is no reason to believe that these local clerics were any less educated than their counterparts elsewhere in Europe, though usually members of the higher clergy in Iceland had to travel abroad to study. What is important is that their training involved studying Latin and therefore gaining access to the world of clerical learning. There is overwhelming evidence that this knowledge was quite widespread in Iceland, at least from the late 11th century onwards.[5] It is safe to assume that access to a body of knowledge com-

---

5   For an overview of this see for example Sverrir Tómasson, *Formálar íslenskra sagnaritara á miðöldum* (Reykjavík: Stofnun Árna Magnússonar, 1988), 15–43.

mon to all of Christian Europe did not remain the sole possession of Icelandic clerics but was disseminated to other social groups, especially to the lay chieftain class.[6]

One of the reasons for this is that many of the clerics belonged to this latter class. Indeed, the Icelandic Church of the 11th and 12th centuries has been called a "goðakirkja" by scholars wishing to highlight the fact that the most powerful members of the clergy belonged to families of lay chieftains (sing. *goði*, plur. *goðar*).[7] Many clerics continued to exercise their secular powers despite their ordination until the late 12th century when this was forbidden by the archbishop of Trondheim, whose province encompassed Norway, Iceland, the Faroe Islands, the Orkneys, the Hebrides and the Isle of Man. During the first two centuries of Christianity in Iceland, one could say that the Church and the lay chieftains formed a joint dominant class which did not begin to separate until the late 12th century or even the middle of the 13th century. The consequence was an unwillingness on the part of the Icelandic Church to implement some of the policies of Rome, especially if they went against the interests of the lay chieftains. Even though the lay chieftains showed, in their culture, an interest for pre-Christian times and the pagan religion, this does not mean that they did not also use what they needed from clerical culture.

Another reason is that the lay chieftains were themselves in need of access to at least some aspects of the learning of the Church. One example is the practice of law. Though Icelandic law from the Free State period (i.e. before 1262) has roots in an important and probably ancient Germanic legal tradition, it also shows evidence of learning from continental Europe. Moreover, during both the 12th and 13th centuries, it is known to have incorporated important changes stemming directly from changes in canon law.[8] These changes were implemented by lay chieftains since they had control over the legislative assembly or *Alþingi*.

A fine example of a lay chieftain who manifestly acquired knowledge

---

[6] See Margaret Clunies Ross's contribution to this volume.
[7] See Gunnar Karlsson, *Goðamenning*, 411–428.
[8] See Sveinbjörn Rafnsson, „Grágás og Digesta Iustiniani," *Sjötíu ritgerðir helgaðar Jakobi Benediktssyni*, 2 vols. (Reykjavík: Stofnun Árna Magnússonar, 1977), 720–732, Torfi H. Tulinius, „Guðs lög í ævi og verkum Snorra Sturlusonar," *Ný Saga. Tímarit Sögufélags* 8 (1996): 31–40, and Sigurður Líndal, „Um þekkingu Íslendinga á rómverskum og kanónískum rétti frá 12. öld til miðrar 16. aldar," *Úlfljótur* 50:1 (1997): 247–273.

from southern Europe is the magnate from the Westfjords, Hrafn Sveinbjarnarson. The saga which tells his biography emphasises his travels to France and Spain. It also dwells at length on his abilities as a physician, describing in detail some of his methods of curing ailing individuals. *Hrafns saga* even describes how its protagonist removes a kidney stone which had been obstructing the urethra of one of his neighbours. Scholars have shown that the medical acts that Hrafn is said to have accomplished are quite in keeping with what was being taught in the new schools of medicine in 12th-century Europe.[9] As for the law, this type of knowledge would have been very useful to the lay chieftain, enabling him to gain support from his underlings who would be indebted to him for medical services rendered, in the same way that they depended on his ability to uphold their rights in lawsuits.

If clerical learning was useful, the ethics and morals of the Church were also exercising their sway over the hearts and minds of medieval Icelanders and by the time the sagas were written, they had been Christian for four to six generations. Even though some traces of paganism probably survived marginally, it is not likely that the Christian ethic was just a superficial veneer. In fact, the sources show evidence of deeply Christian behaviour among the people of Iceland in the 12th and 13th centuries, both clerics and laymen. There is no reason to believe that by the year 1200 the behaviour or minds of Icelanders were any less (or more) shaped by Christianity than in other parts of Europe.[10]

What may interfere with our perception of this deeply Christian mentality is that the best known Icelandic texts from the period are the sagas of Icelanders. Written in the 13th century (at least most of the important ones), they tell of the ancestors who settled the country at the end of the ninth century and their descendants until the country was converted to Christianity in the year 1000. Each and every one is a sort of history of the establishment of the society, not only as a Christian one, but also about how political power was acquired through settlement and noble ancestry. One could say that one of the roles of these sagas was to establish through

---

[9] See Guðrún P. Helgadóttir, ed, *Hrafns saga Sveinbjarnarsonar* (Oxford: Clarendon Press, 1987), xciii–cviii and 4–6.

[10] For an exhaustive study of what the sources tell us about religious life in Iceland during this period, see Régis Boyer, *La vie religieuse en Islande 1116–1264. D'après la Sturlunga saga et les sagas des évêques* (Paris: Fondation Singer-Polignac, 1979).

the writing of history an identity for 13th-century Icelanders.[11] Though they have been shown to be shaped by Christian ethics, the world they portray is not only a pagan one; it is also one which celebrates a heroic ethos that seems to us in contradiction with a Christian world-view. However, I believe that this is an anachronistic misinterpretation and that one must conceive of these sagas as written by and for the lay chieftains and the people surrounding them. These people were Christian but also had to defend themselves or attack others in the recurrent power struggles of the period. Therefore, they had to strike a balance between their Christian morals and a more aggressive aristocratic ethic. Indeed, quite a few of these sagas can be read as working through the contradictions and conundrums of these two types of ethical standards that compete for the souls and minds of the lay chieftain class. The opposition between paganism and Christianity has nothing to do with this. Recently, Margaret Clunies Ross has proposed the term of 'Christian secularity', to characterize the culture of the social group which gave us the sagas.[12]

In an important book, Orri Vésteinsson gives us a careful study of "The Christianization of Iceland".[13] What is perhaps the most interesting result of his work is that he shows how the history of the Icelandic Church and the evolution of society in the first two centuries of Christianity in the country were inextricably related. The Church shaped the society and evolved with it, as the society evolved either to accommodate or to react to the Church's new demands upon society. Moreover, this evolution can be shown to follow more or less the same lines as those by which Church and society evolved elsewhere in Europe during the same period.[14]

---

[11] For a more elaborate presentation of these ideas see my "The Matter of the North. Fiction and uncertain identities in 13th century Iceland," *Old Icelandic Literature and Society*, ed. M. Clunies Ross. Cambridge studies in medieval literature 42 (Cambridge: Cambridge University Press, 2000), 242–265.

[12] Margaret Clunies Ross, "Medieval Iceland and the European Middle Ages," p. 113.

[13] Orri Vésteinsson, *The Christianization of Iceland. Priests, Power and Social Change 1000–1300* (Oxford: Oxford University Press, 2000).

[14] Richard W. Southern, *Western society and the Church in the Middle Ages* (London: Penguin, 1970).

Skaldic poetry, sagas and continental literature

By the 13th century, Christianity had therefore shaped the lives of medieval Icelanders in a very deep way on all levels. In this, they were participants in the common "civilisation of the medieval West".[15] The consequences for their cultural production were wide-ranging. Mention has already been made of the subtle dialectic between religious morals and warrior ethics in the sagas of Icelanders. In what follows, I will present the results of recent studies which show how the contact with Europe was decisive in fostering and shaping the development of Icelandic literature in the twelfth and thirteenth centuries.

In her 2001 book, *Tools of Literacy*, Guðrún Nordal undertakes to show that what can be conceived of as the most ancient and least Christian of Icelandic cultural practices in the 13th century is actually heavily influenced by Latin learning.[16] I am referring here to skaldic poetry, probably the most hermetic type of ancient Germanic poetry, characterized by complex metrics and an elaborate system of poetic speech based on the "kenning".[17] The "kenningar" very often refer to the ancient pagan myths and are a good example of intertextuality, since the skaldic poets used their audience's knowledge of myth to convey their message. Skaldic poetry was practised in pagan times but seems to have been adapted to Christian purposes by court poets of the missionary kings of Norway. These poems are believed to have been memorized and transmitted more or less unchanged from one generation to another until they were written down in the late 12th or 13th century.[18]

---

[15] I have, of course, Jacques Le Goff's great book in mind here, *La Civilisation de l'Occident médiéval* (Paris: Arthaud, 1964). English translation: *Medieval civilization, 400–1500*, transl. by Julia Barrow (Oxford: Blackwell, 1990).

[16] Guðrún Nordal, *Tools of Literacy. The Role of Skaldic Verse in Icelandic Textual Culture of the Twelfth and Thirteenth Centuries* (Toronto: University of Toronto Press, 2001).

[17] A useful presentation of skaldic poetry is Roberta Frank's *Old Norse Court Poetry: the Dróttkvætt Stanza* (Ithaca: Cornell University Press, Islandica 42, 1978).

[18] This is actually a debated subject within the field of medieval Icelandic studies. See Bjarni Einarsson's *Skáldasögur. Um uppruna og eðli ástarskáldsagnanna fornu* (Reykjavík: Menningarsjóður, 1961). See also Theodore M. Andersson's response "Skalds and Troubadours," *Mediaeval Scandinavia* (1969): 7–41. The debate has gone on since then, see for example Alison Finlay, "Skald Sagas in their literary context 3: the love triangle theme," *Skaldsagas. text, vocation and desire in the Icelandic Sagas of poets*, ed. Russell Poole (Berlin: Gruyter, 2000), 232–271.

But original skaldic poetry continued to be composed by poets of the 12th and 13th centuries and the significant contribution to be found in Nordal's book is a meticulous study of how the practice, transmission and study of this poetry was shaped and transformed by an intimate knowledge of grammar, versification and rhetoric, as these disciplines were taught in cathedral schools and universities all over Christian Europe. In this, she brings to light an interesting dynamic that one also sees evidence for in other aspects of Icelandic medieval culture: structures, ideas, and practices current elsewhere in Western Christendom being borrowed and put to use by the dominant groups within Icelandic society (laymen and clerics) for specific cultural practices and for the creation of a distinct local culture on which this society based its identity.

Another Icelandic scholar, Ármann Jakobsson, has written two books in recent years in which he considers another cultural product of medieval Iceland, the sagas of kings or royal biographies, in the context of the common culture of Europe in the High Middle Ages.[19] Indeed, the earliest prose narratives that we call sagas are biographies of kings of Norway and Denmark which date from the second half of the 12th century. The interaction between oral story-telling and learned models of history writing is particularly interesting to study within this genre. A series of texts have been preserved which can be used to show how a form which in its beginning adhered to clerical conventions for writing history evolved into lively and complex biographical narratives of the lives and times of past kings. The kings' sagas or *konungasögur* bloomed fully as a genre in the first half of the 13th century, notably in Snorri Sturluson's famous *Heimskringla*, a history of the kings of Norway from mythological times to the second third of the 12th century. Ármann Jakobsson also contends that a slightly earlier kings' saga, called *Morkinskinna*, is equally sophisticated. He has written a doctoral dissertation devoted to the saga in which he shows that in many ways, its aesthetics betray knowledge and appreciation of developments in the art of narrative in southern Europe.[20] By so doing, he deep-

---

[19] Ármann Jakobsson, *Í leit að konungi. Konungsmynd íslenskra konungasagna* (Reykjavík: Háskólaútgáfan, 1997) and *Staður í nýjum heimi. Konungasagan Morkinskinna* (Reykjavík: Háskólaútgáfan, 2002). A briefer presentation of his position can be found in "Royal biography," his contribution to the already cited Blackwell *Companion to Old Norse-Icelandic Literature and Culture*, 388–402.

[20] See Ármann Jakobsson, *Staður í nýjum heimi*, 61–107.

ens and makes more complex the evolutionary history of the genre. As has already been said, *Morkinskinna* is believed to have been composed earlier than *Heimskringla* and to have influenced it considerably. If this is true it means not only that clerical techniques and traditional story-telling, but also literary fashions from the other European countries, formed the crucible in which the kings' sagas were shaped.

This is not surprising in a period when the Norwegian kingship was being strengthened and endeavoured to model itself on the more established monarchies in France and England. Indeed, at the same time as the composition of *konungasögur* was flourishing in Iceland and to a lesser degree in Norway, there seems to have been great interest in the literature of these same countries at the Norwegian court. From the 1220s (and maybe earlier), a considerable number of literary works seem to have been translated from French to Norse.[21] The translations travelled to Iceland and quite a few autochthonous sagas can be shown to have borrowed motifs, situations, even themes from the *riddarasögur*.

It is tempting to consider the totality of the literary and cultural production of medieval Iceland as participating more or less directly in the courtly culture that was evolving in Norway and which seems to have fascinated Icelanders, especially the chieftains, many of whom were, by the 13th century, members of the Norwegian court. Not only did these chieftains spend time at the court of the king of Norway, but they seem also to have endeavoured to import courtly practices to Iceland, an indication that they viewed themselves as aristocrats in the same way as the nobility of Europe.[22]

The amazing development of literature in Iceland during the same period is in many ways linked to the rise of a courtly culture in the area. It has been argued that kings' sagas such as *Heimskringla* and *Morkinskinna* were written for the court, not only to honour the ancestors of the rulers but also as narratives of how to behave at court and on the risks and bene-

---

[21] The most recent presentation of this translated literature is by Jürg Glauser, "Romance (Translated *riddarasögur*)," *Companion to Old Norse-Icelandic Literature and Culture*, 371–387.

[22] That this is not a new observation can be seen from Einar Ól. Sveinsson's remarks on courtly influence on Icelandic chieftains in the thirteenth century, see *The Age of the Sturlungs*, p. 35–42.

fits of serving kings.[23] Other saga forms also participate in this. In my 1995 book *La « Matière du Nord »* I write about legendary sagas, which are prose narratives often based on older eddic lays that sing the adventures of heroes of the very distant Nordic past. The thesis I defend there is that in the retelling (and often re-invention) of these tales, the authors were working through contradictions and constraints that were all related to the evolution of Icelandic society towards models which were dominant in southern Europe.[24] In order to create an identity for themselves as members of the Icelandic chieftain class – the social group that was in a position to produce literature – they exploited material they perceived as belonging to their past much in the way French and English *trouvères* had used the three "matières", that of Rome (*romans antiques*), France (*chansons de geste*) and Bretagne (*romans courtois*).

Historical events, social change and cultural production all show that Icelandic society and culture were evolving along the same lines as other societies and cultures during the same period. Once this is established, we are in a position to ask why the literature of medieval Iceland is, despite this, so intensely original.

Integrating the Other

In a recent monograph on one of the most important of the sagas of Icelanders, *Egils saga Skalla-Grímssonar*, I attempt to interpret the saga by putting it into the context of the first half of the 13th century when it is believed to have been composed.[25] The saga tells us of several generations of the same family. Originally from Norway, they flee to Iceland at the end of the 9th century because King Harald Finehair's unification of the country leads to a conflict in which he takes the life of Þórólfr Kveld-Úlfsson, the most valiant member of his generation of the family. Þórólfr's younger brother, Skalla-Grímr, settles the area of Borgarfjörður in western Iceland

---

[23] Ármann Jakobsson, *Staður í nýjum heimi*, 285–287.
[24] Torfi H. Tulinius, *La « Matière du Nord ». Sagas légendaires et fiction dans la littérature islandaise en prose du XIIIe siècle* (Paris: Presses de l'Université de Paris-Sorbonne, 1995). English translation: *The Matter of the North. The Rise of Literary Fiction in 13th century Iceland*, transl. Randi C. Eldevik (Odense: Odense University Press, 2002).
[25] Torfi H. Tulinius, *Skáldið í skriftinni* (Reykjavík: Hið íslenska bókmenntafélag, 2004).

and one of his sons, Egill, is the main protagonist of the saga. Born a pagan, Egill is not only a fierce warrior, avid for wealth and jealous of his power, he is also one of the greatest practitioners ever of skaldic poetry. He will kill a man in a most savage way and shortly afterwards, declaim a poetic strophe that is remarkably complex and finely wrought.

Of course, the Egill of the saga is a fictional character, even though a real person may have existed with this name. It might therefore be interesting, in light of the subject of this paper, to examine how the author goes about telling his story and to try to understand the meaning he gives it. When studied carefully, it becomes clear that the saga is very elaborately composed. It is divided into two parts where one is exactly twice as long as the other. In addition, episodes and themes tend to repeat themselves with variations in a very regular way. Finally, the plot is both intricate and complex, doubling a surface conflict with the Norwegian royal family with a more subterranean one, involving Egill, his father and brother.

To this structural refinement, the author also brings a highly sophisticated use of intertextuality. As we have already seen, the skaldic kenning is partly based on intertextual play, since it is necessary to know the pagan myths in order to understand some of them. In his narrative, the author of *Egils saga* also refers covertly to pagan myths in different ways, for example through nicknames of his characters or by transposing mythic situations into the reality he is creating with his story. In this way he suggests a meaning to his narrative: by naming a character Hǫðr, for example, i.e. the blind god who killed his brother Baldr, the author thereby sounds the theme of fratricide, which is one of the undercurrents in the saga.[26]

One of the ways in which skaldic poetry was adapted after the Conversion was by using references to Christian learning in the poems composed for religious purposes. An example of this can also be found in one of the poems ascribed to Egill in the saga, though it does not present itself as a religious poem. In the fifth strophe of *Sonatorrek* ("On the difficulty of avenging one's sons"), Egill develops an extended metaphor for praise poetry: *þat berk úr orðhofi mærðar timbr máli laufgat* ("I carry out of the word-temple the timber of praise which has been made to sprout leaves by the action of language"). This *nýgerving*, i.e., an extended congruent metaphor based on a series of periphrases or kennings, also echoes the follow-

---

[26] Torfi H. Tulinius, *Skáldið í skriftinni*, 53–116.

ing tale from the Bible. The twelve tribes of Israel are in the desert squabbling about who should become high priest. Moses asks Yahweh what to do, and Yahweh tells Moses to make a wooden rod for each of the tribes:

> And Moses laid up the rods before the Lord in the tabernacle of witness, and, behold, the rod of Aaron for the house of Levi was budded, and brought forth buds, and bloomed blossoms, and yielded almonds. And Moses brought out all the rods from before the Lord unto all the children of Israel: and they looked, and took every man his rod (Numbers 17: 8–9).

Egill's extended metaphor has in common with the biblical tale that cut wood is brought out of a temple and has blossomed. In the Bible it is by the action of the Holy Spirit, in the poem it is through the inspiration of the poet. The allusion to the Bible suggests a spiritual dimension to the art of the poet. It is in a way divinely inspired.[27]

This adds one more religious aspect to the portrait of Egill, which is also, as most representations of the past in Icelandic medieval literature, informed by an Augustinian vision of history as a story of fall and redemption. God establishes covenants with humanity at different times: with Abraham, Moses and then in the Incarnation of God as man in Jesus Christ. When this Christian historical schema is transposed to Nordic history, it is seen to parallel Biblical history. The pagan past of the North is part of mankind's march towards redemption, the Conversion being parallel to the Incarnation. This was very important for the evolution of Icelandic culture since it allowed the construction of a positive image of pagan ancestors. Despite the fact that they had not had access to the Revelation, they were nevertheless noble heathens and even eligible for being saved at the end of time.[28] One consequence of this was the possibil-

---

[27] For a more detailed exposition of the implications of this biblical material in *Sonatorrek* for our understanding of the poem, see my „The Conversion of *Sonatorrek*," *Analecta Septentrionalia. Beiträge zur nordgermanischen Kultur- und Litteraturgeschichte*, Ed. W. Heizmann, K. Böldl and H. Beck (Berlin and New York: Walter de Gruyter, Reallexikon der germanischen Altertumskunde, Ergänzungsbände 65, 2009), 698–711.

[28] For a more detailed presentation of the impact of Augustinian history on the construction of a pagan past in Old Norse-Icelandic literature, see Gerd W. Weber, "Intellegere historiam. Typological perspectives of Nordic prehistory (in Snorri, Saxo, Widukind and

ity of integrating aspects of the pagan culture, for example skaldic poetry, into the contemporary Christian secular culture.

Conversion is one of the important though hidden themes of *Egils saga*. It is possible to understand the history of the saga's main character as one of conversion in the widest sense of that term in medieval times.[29] Egill receives the "prima signatio" when serving the Christian king of England, i.e. he submits to a rite that is equivalent to the shorter baptism that a layperson can give to newborns in the absence of a priest. This does not mean that he converts; he is, however, brought into the orbit of Christianity and becomes eligible for salvation.[30]

But Egill is also a sinner, as the saga suggests. By suggesting parallels between his story and those of Cain and Abel, Judas, and most significantly that of King David, especially David's affair with Bathsheba and its consequences, the saga offers itself to be read as the story of the conversion of Egill's soul, from savage Viking to a poet of pre-Christian times capable of expressing his inner life in terms close to Christianity. Though the saga probably makes many complex references to events and persons in 13th-century Iceland, as I have tried to show in my book, one can also read it as a story of the conversion of the old pagan poetry, as a pendant in many ways to *Heimskringla*, authorizing the kings' sagas' use of this poetry as a source of knowledge about the distant past. The account of what is done with Egill's bones after his death in the last chapter of the saga is symbolic of this. He dies before Iceland has been converted. Therefore, his remains are buried in a mound. Shortly after the advent of Christianity, Egill's niece has Egill's bones taken out of the mound and buried under the altar of a Church that her husband has built on their estate. When a learned priest finds these bones several generations later, he removes them from under the altar and has them buried on the outskirts of the cemetery, which is appropriate for those who are only prime-signed. The pagan poet's relationship to Christianity is thus being defined, as well as the proper

---

others)," *Tradition og historieskrivning. Kilderne til Nordens ældste historie*, ed. by Kirsten Hastrup and Preben Meulengracht Sørensen. Acta Jutlandica LXIII:2. Humanistisk Serie 61 (Aarhus: Aarhus Universitetsforlag, 1987), 95–141.

[29] For a wide-ranging discussion of this theme, see Jean-Claude Schmitt, *La Conversion d'Hermann le Juif. Autobiographie, histoire et fiction* (Paris: Seuil, Librairie du XXIe siècle, 2002).

[30] Torfi H. Tulinius, *Skáldið í skriftinni*, 97–105.

Christian attitude to his poetry: the pagan Other is accepted, albeit with necessary precautions.[31]

Integrating the Other is a major characteristic of European culture. One could even say that it is based upon this integration, since Christianity, which is the dominant ideology of the Medieval West, is founded on a fusion of Jewish religion and Greco-Roman culture. One could continue to say that the vibrant culture of laymen throughout the countries of Western Europe is a consequence of the integration of the Celtic and/or Germanic cultural heritages into the mainstream. The best example of this is the importance of the Celtic "matière de Bretagne" in the development of medieval literature. The way Icelanders integrated their pagan heritage while at the same time participating in producing a culture common to all Christian countries in the West is quite in line with this tendency; this is why the concepts of purity and influence are not useful to understanding Iceland's relationship to Southern Europe in the Middle Ages. I would prefer a more dynamic concept, that of culture as something which is continually reinventing itself, both in its relationship to the cultures of others but also in relationship to itself as other. Medieval Icelanders constructed their own identity and culture by viewing their pagan past as other but also by integrating this particular otherness of their past into the Christian secular culture of their own time.

REFERENCES

Andersson, Theodore M. "Skalds and Troubadours." *Mediaeval Scandinavia* (1969): 7–41.

Ármann Jakobsson. *Í leit að konungi. Konungsmynd íslenskra konungasagna.* Reykjavík: Háskólaútgáfan, 1997.

Ármann Jakobsson. "Royal biography." *A Companion to Old Norse-Icelandic Literature and Culture*, ed. by Rory McTurk. Oxford: Blackwell, 2005, 388–402.

Ármann Jakobsson. *Staður í nýjum heimi. Konungasagan Morkinskinna.* Reykjavík: Háskólaútgáfan, 2002.

---

[31] For a discussion of Egill's theological status, see Torfi H. Tulinius, "Le statut théologique d'Egill Skalla-Grímsson," Hugr. *Mélanges d'histoire, de littérature et de mythologie offerts à Régis Boyer pour son 65e anniversaire* (Paris: Presses de l'Université de Paris-Sorbonne, 1997), 279–88.

Bjarni Einarsson. *Skáldasögur. Um uppruna og eðli ástaskáldsagnanna fornu.* Reykjavík: Menningarsjóður, 1961.

Boyer, Régis. *La vie religieuse en Islande 1116–1264. D'après la Sturlunga saga et les sagas des évêques.* Paris: Fondation Singer-Polignac, 1979.

Byock, Jesse L. „Þjóðernishyggja nútímans og Íslendingasögurnar." *Tímarit Máls og menningar* (1993:1): 36–50.

Clunies Ross, Margaret. "Medieval Iceland and the European Middle Ages." *International Scandinavian and Medieval Studies in Memory of Gerd Wolfgang Weber*, ed. M. Dallapiazza, O. Hansen, P. Meulengracht-Sørensen and Y. S. Bonnetain. Trieste: Edizioni Parnaso, 2000, 111–120.

Clunies Ross, Margaret. "Medieval Icelandic Textual Culture." *Gripla* XX (2009): 163–181.

Einar Ól. Sveinsson. *The Age of the Sturlungs. Icelandic Civilization in the Thirteenth Century.* Islandica 36. Ithaca: Cornell University Press, 1953.

Finlay, Alison. "Skald Sagas in their literary context 3: the love triangle theme." *Skaldsagas. text, vocation and desire in the Icelandic Sagas of poets*, ed. Russell Poole. Berlin: Gruyter, 2000, 232–271.

Frank, Roberta. *Old Norse court poetry: the Dróttkvætt Stanza.* Islandica 42. Ithaca: Cornell University Press, 1978.

Glauser, Jürg. "Romance (Translated *riddarasögur*)." *A Companion to Old Norse-Icelandic Literature and Culture* ed. by Rory McTurk. Oxford: Blackwell, 2005, 371–387.

Guðrún Nordal. *Tools of Literacy. The Role of Skaldic Verse in Icelandic Textual Culture of the Twelfth and Thirteenth Centuries.* Toronto: University of Toronto Press, 2001.

Gunnar Karlsson. *Goðamenning. Staða og hlutverk hinna fornu goðorðsmanna.* Reykjavík: Heimskringla, 2004.

Hrafns saga Sveinbjarnarsonar, ed. Guðrún P. Helgadóttir. Oxford: Clarendon Press, 1987.

Jón Karl Helgason. "Continuity? The Icelandic Sagas in Post-Medieval Times." *A Companion to Old Norse-Icelandic Literature and Culture*, ed. by Rory McTurk. Oxford: Blackwell, 2005, 320–337.

Jónas Kristjánsson. *Eddas and Sagas. Iceland's Medieval Literature*, transl. P. Foote. Reykjavík: Hið íslenska bókmenntafélag, 1992.

Le Goff, Jacques. *La Civilisation de l'Occident médiéval.* Paris: Arthaud, 1964. English translation: *Medieval civilization, 400–1500*, transl. by Julia Barrow. Oxford: Blackwell, 1990.

The Manuscripts of Iceland, ed. by Gísli Sigurðsson and Vésteinn Ólason. Reykjavík: Árni Magnússon Institute, 2004.

Roesdahl, E. and P. Meulengracht Sørensen, eds. *The Waking of Angantyr: the Scandinavian past in European culture.* Aarhus: Aarhus Universitetsforlag, 1996.

Schier, Kurt. *Sagaliteratur.* Stuttgart: Metzler, 1970.

Schmitt, Jean-Claude. *La Conversion d'Hermann le Juif. Autobiographie, histoire et fiction*. Paris: Seuil, Librairie du XXIe siècle, 2002.
Southern, Richard W. *Western society and the Church in the Middle Ages*. London: Penguin, 1970.
Sverrir Tómasson. *Formálar íslenskra sagnaritara á miðöldum*. Reykjavík: Stofnun Árna Magnússonar, 1988.
Torfi H. Tulinius. *La « Matière du Nord ». Sagas légendaires et fiction dans la littérature islandaise en prose du XIIIe siècle*. Paris: Presses de l'Université de Paris-Sorbonne, 1995. English translation: *The Matter of the North. The Rise of Literary Fiction in 13th century Iceland*, transl. Randi C. Eldevik. Odense: Odense University Press, 2002.
Torfi H. Tulinius. "Le statut théologique d'Egill Skalla-Grímsson." *Hugr. Mélanges d'histoire, de littérature et de mythologie offerts à Régis Boyer pour son 65e anniversaire*. Paris: Presses de l'Université de Paris-Sorbonne, 1997, 279–288.
Torfi H. Tulinius. *Skáldið í skriftinni*. Reykjavík: Hið íslenska bókmenntafélag, 2004.
Torfi H. Tulinius. "The Matter of the North. Fiction and uncertain identities in 13th century Iceland." *Old Icelandic Literature and Society*, ed. M. Clunies Ross. Cambridge studies in medieval literature 42. Cambridge: Cambridge University Press, 2000, 242–265.
Torfi H. Tulinius. „The Conversion of *Sonatorrek*." *Analecta Septentrionalia. Beiträge zur nordgermanischen Kultur- und Litteraturgeschichte*, ed. by W. Heizmann, K. Böldl and H. Beck. Berlin and New York: Walter de Gruyter, Reallexikon der germanischen Altertumskunde, Ergänzungsbände 65, 2009, 698–711.
Wawn, Andrew. "The Post-Medieval Reception of Old Norse and Old Icelandic Literature." *A Companion to Old Norse-Icelandic Literature and Culture*, ed. by Rory McTurk. Oxford: Blackwell, 2005, 64–81.
Weber, Gerd W. "Intellegere historiam. Typological perspectives of Nordic prehistory (in Snorri, Saxo, Widukind and others)." *Tradition og historieskrivning. Kilderne til Nordens ældste historie*, ed. by Kirsten Hastrup and Preben Meulengracht Sørensen. Acta Jutlandica LXIII:2. Humanistisk Serie 61. Aarhus: Aarhus Universitetsforlag, 1987, 95–141.

SUMMARY

This article discusses links between medieval Iceland and contemporary medieval European culture. The notion that Icelandic medieval culture was, for the most part, free from European cultural influence still has some currency—at least amongst the general public. However, the central argument of the article is rather that Icelandic literary culture could not have emerged had not the Icelanders already begun to engage with European culture, and had not medieval Icelandic society—both clerical and lay—already adapted to it. In this context, reference is made to Margaret Clunies Ross's concept of 'Christian secularity' in order to explain the specific characteristics of Christian Icelandic society during the twelfth and thirteenth centuries, and recent work by other scholars is reviewed to provide further support for this perspective. Finally, reference is made to *Egils saga* and to the present author's recent book on the saga: the aim is to demonstrate how the concepts of 'self' and 'other' may be used to define the attitude of the authors of medieval Icelandic sagas (especially the *Íslendingasögur*) to their own heathen past. It was by integrating the heathen 'otherness' of the past with their own contemporary 'self' that the Icelanders created for themselves a national identity as inhabitants of the Christian cultural world.

Torfi H. Tulinius
University of Iceland
tht@hi.is

VILHJÁLMUR ÁRNASON

AN ETHOS IN TRANSFORMATION: CONFLICTING VALUES IN THE SAGAS

THIS PAPER is divided into two parts. In the first part, I discuss how interpretations of saga morality harbour different conceptions of honour. I am critical of attempts to analyze the "moral outlook" of the sagas in terms of ideas and character traits, taken out of social context. Though I stress the close relationship between saga morality and social structure, I warn against the tendency to reduce morality to a mere function of social processes. It follows from my basic approach that in order to compare ethical models and value orientations, thorough knowledge and analysis of the societies in question is required. I lack the resources to evaluate to what extent saga morality is unique but I rely largely on Jesse Byock's analyses of medieval Icelandic society which provide reasons for showing why the saga virtues take on a distinctive form.

In the second part of the paper, I argue that the overarching values related to unconditional claims for honour on the one hand, and social need for peace on the other hand, exemplify a tension between two different types of morality. I discuss examples of classical virtues in *Njál's saga* which require both genuine moral analysis but also awareness of how they are channelled in distinctive ways because of the special social and political structure of the Icelandic Free State. This structure relies heavily on personal characteristics and the saga demonstrates how virtues are by themselves inadequate to solve the main task of morality. I argue that the uniqueness of saga morality resides primarily in describing virtues and political processes that contribute to peaceful settlements.

I

There is no framework of ethics in the sagas, no reflective attempt to analyze moral behaviour or norms. By telling about human interaction in a social world, however, the sagas of the Icelanders inevitably describe a morality, portray an ethos impregnated with values and virtues, norms and obligations. The narrative of the sagas is rather silent about orderly domestic life but is fuelled by disruption or conflicts of interest that have consequences in the public sphere. Hence they tell us more about public morality relating to conflict resolution than about private morality. These two aspects of morality are inevitably related, however, because every morality requires a political environment which facilitates orderly existence and protects values that are sought after in people's everyday dealings. This has been recognized by all the major thinkers in the history of ethics, most explicitly by Aristotle who regarded politics as the master science of the good for man: "For even if the good is the same for the individual and the state, the good of the state clearly is the greater and more perfect thing to attain and to safeguard."[1] According to my reading, the sagas are concerned with politics in this grand sense, morality in "the headless polity", as Jesse Byock has referred to the Icelandic Free State.[2] Morality in the narrower sense of mundane interaction is often left to the silence mentioned in phrases like "var nú kyrrt um hríð", "now everything was quiet for a while".

Everyday interaction takes place against a more or less tacitly assumed background of norms. When conflicts occur, they tend to make some of these norms more explicit and to provide reasons for reconsidering their validity.[3] From the standpoint of narrative this emphasis on conflict is understandable, there is no need to tell about the ordinary. But by telling about the extraordinary – the episodes when orderly co-existence was disrupted – the sagas place basic values and social norms into sharp focus. At the same time, they portray interaction where individuals' virtues and vices, as well as their ability to uphold their obligations, are put to the test.

---

[1] Aristotle, *Nicomachean Ethics* (Indianapolis: The Bobbs-Merrill Company, 1962), 4–5 [1094b].

[2] Jesse Byock, *Viking Age Iceland* (London: Penguin Books, 2001), 2.

[3] "Moral judgment serves to clarify legitimate behavioural expectation in response to interpersonal conflict resulting from the disruption of our orderly coexistence by conflict of interests." Jürgen Habermas, *Justification and Application* (Cambridge: Polity Press, 1993), 9.

AN ETHOS IN TRANSFORMATION

In this way the ethos of the Free State appears clearly, yet admittedly from a limited perspective.[4]

Let me explain this by means of an example. It has been convincingly argued that in the context of the sagas, *sæmd*, or honour, was "at stake in virtually every social interaction".[5] This interaction takes place against a rich normative background which provides meaning and validity to everyday conduct and underpins the self-understanding and identity of the actors. Presumably, these elements would not become subjects of a narrative unless they were somehow threatened so that they had to be explicitly defended. It is the means of defending them, the ways in which conflicts are handled that are in focus in the sagas. A major reason why the procedural aspects of honour come to the fore is that it affects the entire society how conflicts are handled. So conflict brings not only the normative background to awareness but also makes at least some of the actors aware of its relevance for the entire polity. Personal honour – how it is regarded and the way in which it is upheld and defended – thus becomes a concern of the state or of the community at large.

There are various interpretations of the morality of the sagas and elsewhere I have roughly divided them into three main categories.[6] I will briefly summarize them here, draw out their distinctive characteristics and relate them to recent interpretations of saga morality. I do this in light of the question concerning whether or not the sagas portray value orientations and ethical models that may be considered part of a distinctive Nordic civilisation. Since interpretations agree that *sæmd*/honour is a key concept of saga morality, but conflict as to how *sæmd* is to be understood in the context of the sagas, I use their portrayal of this notion to tease out their differences.

I distinguish between romantic and humanistic interpretations of saga morality which imply a radically different understanding of honour. In the

---

[4] In her book, *Ethics and action in thirteenth-century Iceland* (Odense: Odense University Press, 1998), Guðrún Nordal provides a rich general analysis of ethical norms and behaviour which goes far beyond the political.

[5] William Ian Miller, *Bloodtaking and Peacemaking. Feud, Law, and Society in Saga Iceland* (Chicago: The University of Chicago Press, 1990), 29.

[6] Vilhjálmur Árnason, "Morality and Social Structure in the Icelandic Sagas," *The Journal of English and Germanic Philology* 90 (1990:2): 157–174; also "Saga og siðferði. Hugleiðingar um túlkun á siðferði Íslendingasagna," *Tímarit Máls og menningar* 46 (1985:1): 21–37.

romantic view, *sæmd* is understood as a personal sense of honour and pride, and saga morality is analyzed primarily in terms of individual qualities and attitudes. This also explains the dynamics of the sagas: disputes were started when somebody's sense of honour was hurt and he or his family had to make up for it. For the hero, life without honour was worthless, and the only thing of lasting value was an honourable reputation.[7] Gísli Súrsson provides a good example of a hero from the romantic point of view.[8] Gísli was a great man, who in his killings was fulfilling his duty to his fosterbrother and defending his family honour, even though it meant killing his sister's husband, who was also his brother's best friend and the family's chieftain. Typically seen as a tragic figure, the romantic hero is said to exemplify values and virtues of Nordic heathen origin which were radically opposed to Christian ideals.

Under the heading of "romantic" readings of the sagas, I have drawn out the typical views of many saga scholars, especially those from the nineteenth and early twentieth century. But no less important is the "layman's view of the sagas and the principles they embody: a reading which", the Icelandic philosopher Kristján Kristjánsson recently argued, "still prevails in the public consciousness".[9] Kristján has reconstructed this popular reading of saga morality and argues that it "represents a virtue based ethics where he or she who achieves moral excellence becomes a great minded person (*mikilmenni*)."[10] "Great minded persons," Kristján writes, "are paragons of moral virtue, guided by a strong sense of self-respect, and they are not lacking in self-esteem either, being well aware of their own merits."[11] Kristján observes that "every saga reader has their favorite exemplar" of a hero who portrays this great mindedness.[12]

Kristján does not think that the moral outlook of the sagas is unique.

---

[7] Cf. Ólafur Briem, *Íslendinga sögur og nútíminn* (Reykjavík: Almenna bókafélagið, 1972), 32–33.

[8] Gísla saga Súrssonar, *Vestfirðingasögur*, ed. by Björn K. Þórólfsson and Guðni Jónsson. Íslensk fornrit 6. (Reykjavík: Hið íslenzka fornritafélag, 1943), 3–118. In English: *The Saga of Gisli the Outlaw*, transl. by George Johnston with Notes and Introduction by Peter Foote (Toronto: University of Toronto Press, 1963).

[9] Kristján Kristjánsson, "Liberating Moral Traditions: Saga Morality and Aristotle's *Megalopsychia*," Ethical Theory and Moral Practice (1998:1): 407.

[10] Ibid., 412.

[11] Ibid., 410.

[12] Op.cit.

He compares saga morality to the ancient moral outlook of the Greeks and contrasts both with what he calls the modern moral outlook. The modern moral outlook is characterized by Christian and Kantian assumptions about purity of heart and moral equality of persons. Kristján is critical of sociological readings of the sagas and makes no attempt to relate these moral outlooks to different social structures or to historical development. For him, moral values and virtues can be liberated from their original traditions and made viable in the contemporary world. Instead of seeing it as parochial, he argues that there is good reason to study saga morality "as an atemporal, universal moral outlook, relevant to modern concerns."[13] According to Kristján, the sagas of the Icelanders, as the Greek ethics of antiquity, present us with an option "at which we need to take a hard look; or at any rate as a potential sources of values to be incorporated into other moral outlooks."[14]

Another Icelandic philosopher, the late Þorsteinn Gylfason, argues in his introduction to *Njáls saga* that some of the moral characteristics that people take to be peculiar to the sagas, such as honour, are very much alive today. He writes: "The importance of honour in *Njála* (and other sagas) is often said to reflect a special morality of honour which is sometimes said to be characteristic of shame cultures, for instance that of the Greece of Homer and the tragedians."[15] Þorsteinn rejects this reading and, on the basis of a few examples which show that in Iceland "the language of honour and dishonour is perfectly colloquial to this day" and still a major motivation for conduct, he concludes that the "fundamental moral conceptions of *Njála* are shared by us."[16]

Kristján and Þorsteinn both reject the sharp distinction sometimes made between moral cultures of shame and the more modern one of guilt, the former being primarily motivated by received opinion and the latter by more independent conscience or moral conviction of the individual.[17] Both refer to examples where a saga character's conception of his own honour

[13] Ibid., 407.
[14] Ibid., 422.
[15] Þorsteinn Gylfason, "Introduction" *Njal's Saga*, transl. by C.F. Bayerschmidt and L.M. Hollander (Ware: Wordsworth Classics of World Literature, 1998), xxvii–xxviii.
[16] Ibid., xxviii, xxx.
[17] On this distinction, see Bernard Williams, *Shame and Necessity* (Berkeley: University of California Press, 1993).

invites him to go against received opinion (the famous example of Síðu Hallur in *Njáls saga*). But there is an important difference between the positions of Kristján and Þorsteinn. Kristján's reading is characteristically romantic in the sense that he admires the individual qualities of the saga characters and nostalgically inquires about ways to make their virtues – especially that of *stórmennska*, which he takes to be the Icelandic equivalent to the Greek *megalopsychia* – more viable in a contemporary context. Þorsteinn, on the other hand, who maintans that the Icelandic medieval society "was in all essentials the same as that of the rest of medieval Europe, with frequent feuds between clans," defends two contentions that draw him closer to what I call the humanist position.[18] First, he talks about many acts that in romantic vocabulary would be regarded as tragic result of the duty of vengeance, such as Flosi's action in the burning of Njáll, as "an heinous crime by the laws of his society as well as by his Christian faith."[19] Secondly, as mentioned before, he takes the fundamental moral conceptions of the sagas to be largely shared by contemporary Icelanders, who are often motivated by a conception of their honour, independent of received opinion.

The major spokesman for the humanist position, Hermann Pálsson, invites us to concentrate on the moral ideas of the text rather than the qualities of individuals.[20] If we do so we will see, he argues, that the sagas are to be understood as Christian lessons about the deserving defeat of those who show excessive pride and arrogance. The sagas were not written in order to glorify the so called pagan heroes but rather to preach peace and moderation in the spirit of medieval Christianity. They have the conscious moral objective of teaching people what to aim for and what to avoid in their own lives. The duty of vengeance, which according to the romantic view is a major vehicle of the heroic virtues, becomes a cruel criminal act from the humanistic perspective. From this viewpoint, Gísli Súrsson is a coldblooded criminal who murders his brother-in-law and therefore justly deserves his defeat.[21]

It follows from the humanistic reading that the value orientation and

---

[18] Ibid., xii.
[19] Ibid., xxi.
[20] Hermann Pálsson, *Úr hugmyndaheimi Hrafnkelssögu og Grettlu* (Reykjavík: Menningarsjóður, 1981), 15.
[21] Hermann Pálsson, "Icelandic Sagas and Medieval Ethics," *Medieval Scandinavia* 7 (1974): 64–65.

ethical models portrayed in the sagas of the Icelanders are shared by Christian medieval culture at large, both in their condemnation of pagan conduct and in their presentation of Christian ideas. Both the romantic and the humanistic interpretations can be substantiated by textual references. But they are limited by their guiding hermeneutic ideas that saga morality can be analysed primarily in terms of the moral conceptions or ethical elements – values, virtues, rules and obligations – as such, without inquiring about the particular shape they take in the context of medieval Iceland. In this way, these positions prematurely and erroneously invite comparisons with other cultures. For example, the virtues of the Greek *megalopsychos* are nurtured by a moral context which is radically different from the "modern" ethos and will, therefore, hardly be revived within it.

While similar basic features of morality can be found in every social interaction, they take on a distinctive shape in their interplay with the particular culture of which they are a part. Although there is a common core at the surface or at the abstract level, a study of a concrete, socially conditioned morality cannot isolate the moral elements from the social context.[22] If this is not taken into account, then otherwise interesting interpretations of saga morality are endangered by subjectivistic and idealistic reductionism, reducing saga morality to abstract moral values, religious ideas or personal character traits. Such interpretations deal with the subject matter without tracing its roots to the socio-moral substance: the duties and norms of conduct that were peculiar to the Free State, and their relation to the social institutions and political processes which enveloped the distinctive *ethos* of saga society.

It is here that the third interpretation of saga morality marks its field of investigation. It is difficult to generalize about sociological readings of the sagas but they account for individual actions portrayed in the sagas in light of the social structures and political institutions, or rather the lack of them, in the Icelandic Free State.[23] Such readings of the sagas have enabled us to place actions and attitudes in a social setting against which they can be better understood. One of the most interesting and important questions in

[22] For an interesting discussion of this point and its relation to relativism, see Stuart Hampshire, *Morality and Conflict* (Harvard: Harvard University Press, 1987), 36–43.
[23] See, for example, Gísli Pálsson, ed. *From Sagas to Society. Comparative Approaches to Early Iceland* (London: Hisarlik Press, 1992), and Richard Gaskins, "Félagsvísindamannasaga", *Skírnir* (1997): 237–259.

this context is how the Free State managed to function without executive institutions. An intricate account of this is found in Jesse Byock's theory about feud in the Icelandic sagas.[24] Byock argues that the sagas demonstrate how an original system of decision-making and conflict-solving functioned. This "system of advocacy" structured feuds in the Free State, directed disputes into socially accepted channels and brought them to a resolution.

Byock's structural analysis provides a background for understanding and explaining saga morality which differs from both romantic and humanistic interpretations. What is most striking in his account is the displacement of individual heroism in the sagas: "In saga literature brokerage is characterized as a form of worldly societal interchange rather than as the heroic actions of an individual."[25] Moreover, some of the most cherished heroes of the sagas, like Gísli Súrsson, are characterized as socially inept individuals who do not know how to employ the socially accepted and available tools. They are like misplaced Vikings, unable to honour the norms of an agrarian society where peace and order are vital. Gísli, for example, makes a deadly mistake, Byock argues, by following "the traditional Norse code of family honour which was no longer appropriate to the settled conditions of Icelandic society."[26]

The fruitfulness of Byock's analysis lies in the grounding of these phenomena in the social order. Instead of abstracting individuals from their social conditions, he carefully analyzes the social systems and processes which channel and condition human interaction. Byock discusses the framework of human behaviour in medieval Iceland in terms of power relations, creation and distribution of wealth and the specific life conditions of a small nation on a large island in the North Atlantic. He shows how the society of the Icelanders was built both on Scandinavian heritage but also developed in a distinctive direction, mainly due to a unique "protodemocratic" political process. The following words from Jóhann Páll Árnason's book, *Civilizations in Dispute,* can be used to describe the differences between Byock's structural analysis of the sagas on the one hand, and the romantic and humanistic readings on the other hand: "The most funda-

[24] Byock, *Feud in the Icelandic Saga* (Berkeley: University of California Press, 1982).
[25] Ibid., 42.
[26] Ibid., 193.

mental change of perspective is a shift towards relational conceptions of power: the focus is now on structures, constellations or apparatuses rather than on subjective capacities or dispositions."[27]

Within this sociological hermeneutical frame, *sœmd* tends to be regarded primarily as a social asset or commodity that people acquired in their interaction with other people or which was assigned to them by other social actors. Byock calls it an "honorable recompense" paid to a third party for intervening in the affairs of others.[28] In a similar vein, William Ian Miller analyzes the "economy of honor" and refers to it as "a precious commodity in very short supply," even though it was, as cited earlier, "at stake in virtually every social interaction."[29] Preben Meulengracht Sørensen has a similar idea about *sœmd* as a limited social good.[30] This objectification or commodification of *sœmd* implies that one person's honour cannot increase except at the cost of somebody else's honour.

As Helgi Þorláksson has argued and substantiated with convincing counterexamples, this position is not tenable.[31] Helgi makes a distinction between personal and social honour and maintains that much depends on making this distinction clear. He argues that only the latter can be regarded as goods in short supply, continually competed for by those who were in positions of power or had ambition to gain them.[32] Helgi describes personal honour in terms of improving oneself, showing greatness of mind and readiness to defend oneself against attacks. "This personal honour would not be increased by attacking others," Helgi writes, invoking some of the themes of the romantic reading.[33] I believe that Helgi is right in rejecting the reduction of *sœmd* to a social commodity and thus depriving it, in effect, of important moral features.

[27] Jóhann Páll Árnason, *Civilizations in Dispute. Historical Questions and Theoretical Traditions* (Leiden: Brill, 2003), 202.
[28] Jesse Byock, *Medieval Iceland* (Berkeley: University of California Press, 1988).
[29] William Ian Miller, *Bloodtaking and Peacemaking. Feud, Law, and Society in Saga Iceland* (Chicago, London: University of Chicago Press), 30 and 29.
[30] Preben Meulengracht Sørensen, *Fortælling og ære. Studier i islændingesagaerne* (Aarhus: Aarhus Universitetsforlag, 1993).
[31] Helgi Þorláksson, "Virtir menn og vel metnir," *Sæmdarmenn. Um heiður á þjóðveldisöld*, ed. by Helgi Þorláksson et. al. (Reykjavík: Hugvísindastofnun Háskóla Íslands, 2001), 15–22, especially 17–19.
[32] Ibid., 20–21.
[33] Ibid., 21.

Interpretations of the complex concept of honour in the sagas require a careful contextual reading.[34] Honour has both personal and social dimensions and must not be reduced to either. Moreover, the distinction between the personal and the social cannot always be clearly drawn in this context, especially in the cases of powerful men who could bring conflicts to a resolution. Byock writes: "The *goðar* early became political entrepreneurs adept at forming ad hoc interest groups of often unrelated backers. They specialized in advocating client's interests through arbitration both in and out of courts, and found it honourable and profitable to engage in resolving moderately mature, that is 'court ready', conflicts."[35] Byock argues convincingly that in order to succeed in playing the role of an advocate, the individual had to be "a *hófsmaðr*, a person of justice and temperance".[36] It is hard to imagine a person reaching that kind of moral maturity without engaging in the efforts of self-improvement and self-restraint characteristic of personal honour. At the same time, these elements are preconditions for gaining the social capital of increased estimation among the public. In this way, the personal and social aspects of honour seem to be interwoven.

This relates to the question dealt with by both of the aforementioned Icelandic philosophers Kristján Kristjánsson and Þorsteinn Gylfason, whether "honour and shame essentially depend on the received opinion of a community,"[37] or whether they reside in the self-conception of the individual, independent of received opinion. If the former, sometimes seen as characteristic of shame cultures, honour is in effect reduced to a social product, leaving little room for genuine moral excellence. This must not be too sharply stated: the question is not about the personal *or* the social, in the sense that personal virtues can be independent of social reputation. Since socialization is individualization the two are obviously interrelated.

A more interesting question in this context concerns the nature of moral thinking and whether it is primarily a strategic or instrumental skill of those who are clever readers of the social landscape of praise and blame, or whether moral prudence is of a more distinctive nature. Sociological

---

[34] Excellent examples of such a reading are found in Vésteinn Ólason, *Samræður við söguöld* (Reykjavík: Heimskringla, 1998).
[35] Byock, *Viking Age Iceland*, 218.
[36] Ibid., 190.
[37] Þorsteinn Gylfason, "Introduction" to *Njal's Saga*, xxx.

readings usually disregard this distinction. Byock writes that "Iceland exhibits many aspects of a shame society, in which the conviction of members of the peer group and public opinion at large carried significant influence."[38] To flesh out his point he refers to the episode in *Njáls saga* when Hrútur gives a precious ring to a boy who ridicules him. Byock writes: "Though Hrut is the object of the joke and is shamed by the children's antics, he is able to prevent utter disaster to his reputation by demonstrating both restraint and generosity. With a sense of graciousness and a largeness of spirit, which he is wise enough to know will be held in high regard and spoken of long after the event, he gives the boy a fine gift."[39]

There is a striking shift in this passage, which goes to the heart of the question I am pondering. In one sentence, Byock describes Hrútr's action as exemplifying "a sense of graciousness and a largeness of spirit" which Kristján takes to indicate the moral excellence of the one who desires to *be* virtuous and not merely to be *seen* as virtuous.[40] (It might be noted here that in a purely social conception of *sœmd* or *virðing*, seeming to be virtuous could be sufficient; cf. the etymological relations between "seem" and "sœmd", "virðing" and "virðast".) In the next sentence, Byock threatens to undermine Hrútr's largeness of spirit by explaining it in terms of his wisdom of knowing that his noble acts "will be held in high regard and spoken of long after the event." This makes the nobility of Hrútr's act dependent on its social reception rather than being the fruit of his fine character and exercise in self-improvement. This and other examples indicate that Byock's shrewd analysis of medieval Iceland shares, to some extent, the shortcomings of sociological readings when it comes to evaluating the moral dimension of the sagas.

It is instructive to make use of Jóhann Páll Árnason's civilizational analysis to evaluate the shortcomings of all three interpretations of saga morality that we have considered. He writes: "it seems appropriate to distinguish between economic, political and ideological spheres of the social world. The task of civilizational analysis would then be to show that the constitution, differentiation and interaction of these recurrent clusters of

---

[38] Byock, *Viking Age Iceland*, 226.
[39] Ibid, 227.
[40] Kristján Kristjánsson, "Liberating Moral Traditions", 415.

social practices take a specific turn at the civilizational level."[41] One way to describe the limitations of the romantic and humanistic interpretations is that they give the ideological sphere too much independence from the political and economic spheres of the social world, by analyzing the moral constellations in abstraction from social structures of wealth and power. From this viewpoint of civilizational analysis, the major limitation of sociological interpretations is, to the contrary, their tendency to see the ideological sphere as a too passive reflection of the political and economic spheres of the social world. Structural and functionalist perspectives of sociological analyses tend to reduce morality to a function of social processes. As a consequence, human actions in the sagas are not interpreted in the light of moral characteristics but as manifestations of material and societal interests perpetuated by the social system.

In the conceptual framework of Jóhann Páll Árnason's civilizational analysis, this limitation amounts to a neglect of the ideological sphere, a disregard of the "constellations of meaning" that play a major role in any worldview or articulation of society. In his theory, Jóhann Páll draws upon the implications of Castoriadis' analysis of the imagination for social theory. "At the most fundamental level, social imaginary significations set up an ontological framework: 'every society defines and develops an image of the natural world of the universe in which it lives'."[42] In the words of Alfred North Whitehead: "Without metaphysical presupposition there can be no civilization."[43] If this is correct, one must ask which metaphysical presuppositions are behind the civilization in the Icelandic Free State. Surely, "the ideology of honour", as Vésteinn Ólason has described it,[44] has metaphysical elements which require careful textual analysis and need to be placed in the social context portrayed in the text. The notion of fate is a good candidate for this.

As is to be expected, views on the role of fate in the saga narrative differ radically in the different hermeneutical grids of scholars. For Kristján Kristjánsson, fate serves as this metaphysical underpinning in the sagas. Kristján has been critical of interpretations of saga morality such as my

[41] Jóhann Páll Árnason, *Civilizations in Dispute*, 207.
[42] Ibid., 227. Jóhann quotes Castoriadis.
[43] This is the motto of Árnason's book, *Civilizations in Dispute*.
[44] Vésteinn Ólason, *Dialogues with the Viking Age*, 226.

own, which emphasize the relation of saga morality to the social structure and play down the role of religious and other conscious moral ideals. Kristján writes: "any significant ethics must rest on metaphysical presuppositions and I am of the opinion that the sagas are shot through with at least one: ideas about *freedom* and *necessity*." He argues that the "morality of the saga heroes can only be understood as reactions to outer necessity and inner freedom."[45] Kristján rejects the view that the saga characters act unreflectively and takes the words of Gunnarr á Hlíðarendi about his relative reluctancy to kill people as an example of moral reflection. Kristján writes: "Indeed saga characters are constantly reflecting upon, hesitating, rejoicing over or regretting their deeds. And in at least one area their moral ideas had profound metaphysical underpinnings, namely, in the upholding of a view about destiny and free will ... a kind of Stoic fate-leads-the willing-and-drags-the-reluctant attitude to their destiny."[46] Kristján argues that the objective style of the saga narrative is delusive in this regard, by neither delving into the depths of the human soul and emotional life nor telling about the complex philosophical ideas the characters had about the nature of the universe.

In his introduction to *Njáls Saga*, Þorsteinn Gylfason considers the role of fate and concludes that there is no fatalism in the saga: "Generally speaking, not a single action of any consequence is presented in *Njála* as being necessitated by fate or planned by any external power."[47] This wording shows how radically the notion of fate is decontextualized because the Icelandic fate is interwoven with self-understanding and immanent worldview but does not have an explicit reference to external power. Much in the way as Þorsteinn argued that the fundamental moral notions of *Njála* are shared by us, he states that the author of *Njála* "conceives of *gæfa* and *ógæfa* in the same ways as we do. Hence it is only through an overinterpretation of these words that scholars have been able to read fatalistic beliefs into them".[48] Fate plays little or no role in Byock's interpretations of actions in the sagas. In light of the emphasis he places on "the choice that

---

[45] Kristján Kristjánsson, "Að geta um frjálst höfuð strokið," *Þroskakostir* (Reykjavík: Rannsóknastofnun í siðfræði, 1992), 169 and 172. My translation.
[46] Kristján Kristjánsson, "Liberating Moral Traditions," 406.
[47] Þorsteinn Gylfason, "Introduction" to *Njal's Saga*, xxiv.
[48] Ibid., xxiv.

individuals faced between violence and compromise"[49] in the Free State, one could argue that from his standpoint the reference to fate is used as a justification for resorting to violence or at least for evading consensual solutions.

There are reasons to believe that in their own way, each of these three accounts of the role of fate in the sagas are misleading, one-sided: mainly because they do not give due consideration to the way in which the metaphysics of fate is related to the ideology of honour that is rooted in cultural conditions which are foreign to the new Icelandic society. The metaphysics of fate provides a perfect background to the old morality of unconditional honour, the rigid imperative of revenge, which does not give people much leeway for deliberation and doubt but provides them with an interpretative key to their personal existence and social world. When the conditions that nourished this old morality are undermined in the transformation of the ethos in the Icelandic Free State, the bonds of the metaphysics of fate inevitably slacken and a space opens up for a rationalizing use of the idea. This goes hand in hand with the opening up of options between responding to the imperative of revenge on the one hand, and adopting a more consensual view towards honourable conflict resolution on the other. Playing on a famous title by John Rawls, I will suggest that what is of primary importance for the distinctive morality and civilization described in the sagas is political, not metaphysical.

II

In my discussion so far I have tried to show how different interpretations of the sagas lead to different understandings of *sæmd*. But there is another general value that is prominent in the sagas, though it is more in the background of the narrative. This is the value of *peace* and the related cluster concepts of *grið*, *sættir* and other things conducive to peace. Some of the sagas show how the traditional ideal of unconditional *sæmd*, which is associated with the standing of individuals and families, clashes with efforts to secure peace which is of general interest to society as a whole. Vésteinn Ólason has called this "the tension between the desire for revenge and the

---

[49] Byock, *Viking Age Iceland*, 2.

impulse for reconciliation".[50] Considered from this perspective, the morality of the sagas is primarily procedural in the sense that the main issues are how conflicts are dealt with and peace restored.

Obviously, *sœmd* and peace are not comparable concepts. *Sœmd* is intimately bound up with the self-understanding, self-respect and reputation of the actors on the social scene. Its internal logic relates to the (special) interests of the persons involved but not to the general welfare of the community. It is a thick substantial morality with rigorous imperatives rooted in vulnerable identity.[51] This leads to certain competitive ways of handling disputes – e.g. duty of revenge and duelling – which can threaten the social order. Peace, however, is in the interest of all and co-operative attempts to secure it may require the sacrificing of individual interests. This marks a tension in the sagas between elements of an ethos characterized by particular interests, and moral features which secure the more general interests of the community. This also implies a different understanding of honour; the traditional unconditional *sœmd* is in conflict with a more reflective notion of honour which relates to the co-operative virtues and processes conducive to peace.

One way to account for this moral tension or ethos in transformation is to see how the virtues are depicted in the saga narrative and how they reflect conflicting values. This will help us see how classical virtues take on a distinct shape in the early Icelandic cultural context. It also illustrates how moral elements call for a separate interpretation and cannot be reduced to mere functions of social processes. Classical moral analysis of the virtues can throw light on different characters in the sagas which is not revealed from sociological perspectives.

There is a cluster of characters in *Njáls saga* which exemplify different types of virtues and vices. For the sake of analysis, I will focus on four different positions represented by four typical characters, or rather two types of positions and their antitheses. The first is the traditional hero who thinks primarily of his *sœmd* and is ready to uphold it by performing the duty of vengeance or by duelling. A clear example of this type in *Njála* is

---

[50] Vésteinn Ólason, *Dialogues with the Viking Age*, 201. The wording of the Icelandic original text, "Átök milli hefndarkröfu og sáttavilja ..." (*Samræður við söguöld*, 168), is somewhat stronger; "hefndarkrafa" denotes an imperative or demand for revenge rather than desire.

[51] On thick and thin morality, see, for example, Michael Walzer, *Thick and Thin: Moral Argument at Home and Abroad* (Notre Dame, IN: Notre Dame University Press, 1994).

Gunnarr of Hlíðarendi. The description of him emphasizes his physical characteristics and fighting skills as well as his uprightness and spontaneity. Even though he says at one point: "Sáttgjarn hefi ek jafnan verit" – "I have always been ready and willing to make a peaceful settlement" (Ch. 56),[52] he proves the opposite when he decides not to hold the agreement to leave the country in the wake of his killings. It is a proof of his heroic character that he does this in spite of knowing that it will lead to his death, as Njáll had premonitorily warned him. But Gunnarr's flaw is revealed in the way that he dishonours the workings of the social system on which peace in the 'Great Village Community', as Byock calls the Icelandic Free State, depended.[53] In so doing, he chooses to resort to violence although the saga suggests that this action is a mixture of fate and heroism. The unconditionality of the heroic virtues places a fatal weight on the shoulder of the hero and does not provide leeway for options that open up more reconciliatory thinking.

Gunnarr's example demonstrates clearly the relationship between morality as (i) a system of moral/social norms: in this case the demand to uphold one's honour and reputation; (ii) the real behaviour of individuals observing or defying these norms: Gunnarr observes the norm of honour while defying the norm of keeping a settlement; (iii) individual self-formation and self-understanding in light of these norms: Gunnarr accepts his fateful choice with courage and serenity.[54] It is significant that throughout his story he does not, unlike Skarphéðinn for example, instigate the disputes that lead to his killings.

The opposite of this heroic type is a man like Hrappur who has much the same characteristics as a hero – physical strength, fighting skills, spontaneity and the strength of character that is needed for courage. However, this strength is not a virtue in his case because it is deliberately used for reprehensible objectives and lacks the relationship with wisdom and moderation (these clearly need to go together). He even exhibits a kind of naïve

---

[52] *Brennu-Njáls saga*, ed. by Einar Ólafur Sveinsson (Reykjavík: Hið íslenzka fornritafélag 1954), 145. *Njal's Saga*, transl. by C.F. Bayerschmidt and L.M. Hollander. (Ware: Wordsworth Classics of World Literature 1998), 114.

[53] Cf. Byock, *Viking Age Iceland*, 228–229.

[54] This distinction is made by Michel Foucault in *The Use of Pleasure. The History of Sexuality* 2 (New York: Vintage Books, 1990), 25–29.

honesty that also marks the hero, as well as loyalty to Hallgerður, his guardian. This type of man is, in fact, not driven by honour, which has channelled the hero's life forces into a coherent unconditional pattern, but more instinctively by jealousy and aggression. The most common label used in the saga about this character is *ójafnaðarmaður*, although it is rather associated with a man of a higher social standing than Hrappur (who does not get a separate introduction in the saga). The incentive for action of the *ójafnaðarmaður* is also different since he is preoccupied with power which he seeks to increase through means that are not accepted in society. In their own way, each of these types can pose a threat to the need for peaceful co-existence in an agrarian society.

The other main type serves the major role of channelling disputes into processes that could lead to peace and settlement. In this role we find more reflective and diplomatic characters who exemplify, at best, the virtues of *hóf*, benevolence and friendship. Heinrich Beck has described such persons as social heroes with a "clear insight into the existing social rules" and with "the reputation, wealth, and authority to guarantee a balance, like Óláfr pái", or as bargainers aware of "all the shrewd ways of handling social affairs, like Snorri Goði".[55] But in order to be worthy of the title "social hero" this man needs to be well-intentioned. Moreover, he must not be guided by the unconditional demand of *sœmd*, even though he is aware of the importance of honour in all social affairs.

Using Aristotle's distinction, social heroes are characterized more by reflective intellectual virtues than non-reflective moral virtues, which are the distinctive mark of the romantic hero. The former is a matter of good judgment while the latter is a state of character shaped in upbringing and socialization, such as courage and moderation. However, full virtue requires a proper interplay of both types of virtues. Gunnarr of Hlíðarendi displays moral virtue but it is not enlightened by practical wisdom (which he usually seeks in Njáll's advice). *Njáls saga* creates the "illusion" that the characters get their virtue and vice stamp from their very first appearance in the saga but the effects of their actions are much more ambiguous as they weave into a complex web of interaction; "því at allt orkar tvímælis,

---

[55] Heinrich Beck, "Laxdæla saga: A Structural Approach", *Saga Book of the Viking Society*, XIX (1974–77), 383–402.

þá er gǫrt er", says Njáll, "once a deed has been done there will always be two opinions as to whether it was justified or not" (Ch. 91).[56]

Wisdom is a prominent virtue in Old Icelandic literature and is distinguished from mental capacities exercised for ignoble objectives. Njáll is introduced in these terms: "vitr var hann ok forspár, heilráðr ok góðgjarn," or as it says in the long-winded English translation: "He was learned and had the gift of second sight. He was benevolent and generous in word and deed, and everything which he adviced turned out for the best" (Ch. 20).[57] In his case, wisdom is related to good advice and is thus primarily practical wisdom. Mǫrðr Valgarðsson, on the other hand, is said to have been "slœgr maðr í skapferðum ok illgjarn í ráðum"; "He was a sly and wily fellow and the worst troublemaker" (Ch. 25).[58] As Byock puts it, he "skillfully uses the political tools of his own society to his own advantage,"[59] while caring less about how they may affect his fellow men in the process. Mǫrðr is neither guided by an unconditional demand of honour nor is he benevolent in his dealings. He lacks the virtue of *góðgirnd*, benevolence. But he can play the game to his own advantage. In fact, he exhibits a certain type of intellectual virtue but is lacking in moral virtue. In *Njála*, a man is not regarded as wise or prudent unless his advice is given with benevolence or *góðgirni*. If they are given with malevolence, *illgirni*, it is mere cleverness or knavery. Sociological analyses of the sagas which reduce honour to a response to received opinion and conflate social success with moral virtue have difficulties in separating such clever scoundrels from social heroes.

The deliberation of benevolent men in the sagas has two major aims. The first is that a man can bring conflicts to a resolution in such a way that his honour is increased or at least not damaged. An example of this is the plan that Njáll lays out for Gunnarr in his dealings with the brothers Hrútr and Hǫskuldr. The plan is quite cunning and implies deception and play-acting in order to lead Hrútr into a trap. This deliberation is mainly instrumental or strategic, finding the necessary means to reach a desired end.

---

[56] *Brennu-Njáls saga*, Einar Ólafur Sveinsson, ed., 226. *Njal's Saga*, translation by C.F. Bayerschmidt and L. M. Hollander, 181.

[57] *Brennu-Njáls saga*, Einar Ólafur Sveinsson, ed., 57. *Njal's Saga*, translation by C.F. Bayerschmidt and L. M. Hollander, 40.

[58] *Brennu-Njáls saga*, Einar Ólafur Sveinsson, ed., 70. *Njal's Saga*, translation by C.F. Bayerschmidt and L. M. Hollander, 49.

[59] Byock, *Feud in the Icelandic Saga*, 200.

The saga concludes: "ok hafði Gunnarr ina mestu sœmð af málinu", "and Gunnarr won great acclaim from the suit" (Ch. 24).[60] In this case, the benevolence of Njáll's advice is judged from the individual point of view of Gunnarr's *sœmd* and the personal relations of friendship between Gunnarr and Njáll. Most deliberated advice which Njáll gives in the saga is of this kind.

The most striking example in the saga of malevolent deliberation is when Mǫrðr, on the advice of his father, manages to deceive the sons of Njáll into killing Hǫskuldr. "Svá kom, at hann kom sér í svá mikla vináttu við þá, at hvárigum þótti ráð ráðit, nema um réðisk við aðra." "In the end they got to be such close friends that no counsel was taken but all shared in it" (Ch. 108).[61] Njáll comments on this: "Ekki em ek í ráðagerð með þeim ... sjaldan var ek þá frá kvaddr, er in góðu voru ráðin." "I am not in their plans ... in the past I was rarely kept out when something good was being considered" (Ch. 110).[62] It is clear that Mǫrðr is determined to get Hǫskuldr killed and for most people, his death is "hǫrmulig tíðendi", "most distressing tidings". But even though this is considered to be an evil deed, it makes sense in the saga ethos; it can even be "justified" by following the reasoning or internal logic of the *sœmdar*/feudal morality. In that web of reasoning, Njáll's benevolent advice and actions contribute to the tragedy by "surcharging the father-son bond with excessive burdens," as William Ian Miller has argued.[63] As has often been pointed out, Njáll's well-intended advice has unintended consequences which culminate in tragic events. This is one manifestation of the limits of virtue-based morality in the sagas.

The other main aim of benevolent deliberation is that conflicts can be brought to a peaceful resolution through an agreement which will hold. Some of Njáll's advice is clearly aimed at this objective. But the most striking and distinctive deliberation of this kind is that of Síðu-Hallr near the end of the saga. What makes his position remarkable is that it goes directly

---

[60] *Brennu-Njáls saga*, Einar Ólafur Sveinsson, ed., 68. *Njal's Saga*, translation by C.F. Bayerschmidt and L. M. Hollander, 48.
[61] *Brennu-Njáls saga*, Einar Ólafur Sveinsson, ed., 276. *Njal's Saga*, translation by C.F. Bayerschmidt and L. M. Hollander, 215.
[62] *Brennu-Njáls saga*, Einar Ólafur Sveinsson, ed., 280. *Njal's Saga*, translation by C.F. Bayerschmidt and L. M. Hollander, 219.
[63] William Ian Miller, "Justifying Skarphéðinn," *Scandinavian Studies* 55 (1983): 316–344.

and consciously against the prevailing ideas of greatness and honour. His famous words: "Mun ek nú sýna þat, at ek em lítilmenni." "Now I shall again show that I am a humble man [small minded or ignoble man]" (Ch. 145),[64] express his decision not to ask for reparations for his son, Ljótr, while at the same time offering his adversaries "pledges of peace". This rather unexpected and apparently revolutionary move does not, however, meet with astonishment: "varð rómr mikill ok góðr gǫrr at máli hans, ok lofuðu allir mjǫk hans góðgirnd." "His words were received with loud approval, and all praised his good will."[65] And later he receives fourfold reparations for Ljótr. This act by Síðu-Hallr breaks the vicious circle of violence by upsetting the feudal scales of payment and repayment. Neither Njáll nor Hallr are warriors, both are men of good will and practical wisdom, but Hallr exceeds Njáll in understanding the roots of the problems that they are both apparently fighting. This is underlined by Njáll's explanation for not accepting the offer of leaving his burning house: "Eigi vil ek út ganga, því at em ek maðr gamall ok lítt til búinn at hefna sona minna, en ek vil eigi lifa við skǫmm." "No, I will not come out, for I am an old man and little fit to avenge my sons, and I do not want to live in shame" (Ch. 129).[66]

The words of Síðu-Hallr are revolutionary because they break with the "old morality" of *sœmd* and shame. This amounts to breaking the "first person perspective" and adopting a more general perspective which takes the common interest into account. When I say that the virtues-based morality of honour is limited to the first person perspective, I do not only mean that it is fuelled by personal emotions but also and primarily that it aimed to protect and defend the vulnerability of the particular person and thereby his family. In the context of the sagas, Hallr's position sounds unrealistic since there is no institutional structure to uphold it. Síðu-Hallr's position is often associated with Christianity but as such, it is only an abstract idea that lacks all concrete content except the pledge. The pledge is dependent upon the will and virtues of individuals but cannot be

---

[64] *Brennu-Njáls saga*, Einar Ólafur Sveinsson, ed., 408. *Njal's Saga*, translation by C. F. Bayerschmidt and L. M. Hollander, 316.
[65] *Brennu-Njáls saga*, Einar Ólafur Sveinsson, ed., 412. *Njal's Saga*, translation by C. F. Bayerschmidt and L. M. Hollander, 318.
[66] *Brennu-Njáls saga*, Einar Ólafur Sveinsson, ed., 330. *Njal's Saga*, translation by C. F. Bayerschmidt and L. M. Hollander, 258.

substantiated by a community and therefore appears in the form of hope or a vision. In this way, Síðu-Hallr's position points beyond the ethos of the Free State while the apparently conflicting position of others does not. The case of Síðu-Hallr shows that the narrative does not dissolve the perspective of ideal morality in ethical substance (in Hegel's sense). His position provides a critical vision that works against the ruling moral order and, in fact, reveals its own limitations.

Among several things, *Njáls saga* demonstrates the enormous effect that individual vices can have on society: repeatedly, defects of character and individual inability or unwillingness to control temper are mentioned as reasons for unfortunate chains of events. Virtues and vices are all the more important where institutions are weak.

One of the effects of a good social structure is to neutralize the effects of personal virtues and vices. This requires political processes that are conducive to peace and flourishing of the community, a system of political institutions that channels conflicts and secures the rights of citizens. A well-functioning political system is a precondition both for social peace and the flourishing of individuals. The virtues are necessary in moral life but the precondition for this is a political structure which reduces the effect of personal virtues and vices upon the handling of social affairs. This is a political reading of the virtue-based morality of the sagas. It rests on the argument that the morality of virtue is, as such, insufficient to solve the main task of morality, i.e. to resolve conflicts that threaten our very co-existence.

On the basis of this reading, it makes sense to say that *Njála* describes a society that is groping its way toward the rule of law.[67] From a primarily ideological perspective, it makes sense to say that the saga describes an ethos in the process of transformation from heathen values to Christian values. But a political interpretation emphasizes the role of the social need for peace and sees the ethical transformation as one from a rigid imperative of revenge to a more deliberative means of handling conflict resolution. The latter breeds a culture of negotiation and reconciliation which fosters a strong emphasis on good will, moderation and *sáttgirni*. A case can be made for the position that this "willingness to find compromise solutions"

---

[67] Cf. Þorsteinn Gylfason, "Introduction" to *Njal's Saga*, xxvii.

is the spirit of the unique political structure of the Icelandic Free State.[68] The political structure provided space for fundamental choices between resorting either to violent, or to consensual means in the handling of conflicts. This resulted in a transvaluation of values, where honour became gradually more linked to peaceful settlements.

The main lessons about virtues I draw from this moral-political reading of *Njála* are the following. (i) The virtues that are necessary to uphold the morality of unconditional honour, which are partly sustained by the social structure of the Free State, must be rechannelled and harnessed for peace and social order. (ii) The virtues of those wise and benevolent men whose efforts aim at seeking peace and reconciliations, e.g. by giving good advice and acting as intermediaries in conflicts, are by themselves doomed to failure in the social structure of the Free State. (iii) At the heart of saga morality there is a conflict between the unconditional morality of personal honour and the social need for peace which promotes more conciliatory values. It is my contention that the uniqueness of saga morality resides more in these characteristics than in the virtues of individual great-mindedness that are found in some form or other in all heroic societies.

REFERENCES

Aristotle, *Nicomachean Ethics*, transl. by M. Ostwald. Indianapolis: The Boobs-Merrill Company, 1962.
Brennu-Njáls saga, ed. by Einar Ól. Sveinsson. Íslensk fornrit XII. Reykjavík: Hið íslenzka fornritafélag, 1954. In English: *Njal's Saga*, translation by C. F. Bayerschmidt and L. M. Hollander. Ware: Wordsworth Classics, 1998.
Byock, Jesse. *Feud in the Icelandic Saga*. Berkeley: University of California Press, 1982.
Byock, Jesse. *Medieval Iceland.* Berkeley: University of California Press, 1988.
Byock, Jesse. *Viking Age Iceland.* London: Penguin Books, 2001.
Foucault, Michel. *The Use of Pleasure. The History of Sexuality*, vol. 2. English translation Robert Hurley. New York: Vintage Books, 1990.
Gaskins, Richard. "Félagsvísindamannasaga," *Skírnir* 171 (1997): 237–259.
Gísla saga Súrssonar, *Vestfirðingasögur*, ed. by Björn K. Þórólfsson and Guðni Jónsson. Íslensk fornrit VI . Reykjavík: Hið íslenzka fornritafélag, 1943, 3–118. In English: *The Saga of Gisli the Outlaw*, transl. by George Johnston with Notes and Introduction by Peter Foote. Toronto: University of Toronto Press, 1963.

[68] Byock, *Viking Age Iceland*, 209.

Gísli Pálsson, ed. *From Sagas to Society. Comparative Approaches to Early Iceland.* London: Hisarlik Press, 1992.
Guðrún Nordal. *Ethics and action in thirteenth-century Iceland.* Odense: Odense University Press, 1998.
Habermas, Jürgen. *Justification and Application,* transl. by C.P. Cronin. Cambridge: Polity Press, 1993.
Hampshire, Stuart. *Morality and Conflict.* Cambridge, Mass.: Harvard University Press, 1987.
Helgi Þorláksson. "Virtir menn og vel metnir," *Sæmdarmenn. Um heiður á þjóðveldisöld.* Reykjavík: Hugvísindastofnun Háskóla Íslands, 2001, 15–22.
Hermann Pálsson. *Úr hugmyndaheimi Hrafnkelssögu og Grettlu.* Reykjavík: Menningarsjóður, 1981.
Hermann Pálsson. "Icelandic Sagas and Medieval Ethics." *Medieval Scandinavia* 7 (1974): 64–75.
Jóhann Páll Árnason. *Civilizations in Dispute. Historical Questions and Theoretical Traditions.* Leiden: Brill, 2003.
Kristján Kristjánsson. "Að geta um frjálst höfuð strokið." *Þroskakostir.* Reykjavík: Rannsóknastofnun í siðfræði, 1992, 157–173.
Kristján Kristjánsson. "Liberating Moral Traditions: Saga Morality and Aristotle's *Megalopsychia.*" *Ethical Theory and Moral Practice* (1998:1): 397–422.
Meulengracht Sørensen, Preben. *Fortælling og ære. Studier i islændingesagaerne.* Aarhus: Aarhus Universitetsforlag, 1993.
Miller, William Ian. "Justifying Skarphéðinn." *Scandinavian Studies* 55 (1983): 316–344.
Miller, William Ian. *Bloodtaking and Peacemaking. Feud, Law, and Society in Saga Iceland.* Chicago: The University of Chicago Press, 1990.
Ólafur Briem. *Íslendinga sögur og nútíminn.* Reykjavík: Almenna bókafélagið, 1972.
Vésteinn Ólason. *Samræður við söguöld. Frásagnarlist Íslendingasagna og fortíðarmynd.* Reykjavík: Heimskringla, 1998. English transl. by Andrew Wawn: *Dialogues with the Viking Age. Narration and representation in the sagas of the Icelanders.* Reykjavík: Heimskringla, Mál og menning, 1998.
Vilhjálmur Árnason. "Morality and Social Structure in the Icelandic Sagas," *The Journal of English and Germanic Philology* 90 (1990:2): 157–174.
Vilhjálmur Árnason. "Saga og siðferði. Hugleiðingar um túlkun á siðferði Íslendingasagna." *Tímarit Máls og menningar* 46 (1985:1): 21–37.
Williams, Bernard. *Shame and Necessity.* Berkeley: University of California Press, 1993.
Þorsteinn Gylfason. "Introduction." *Njal's Saga,* translation by C.F. Bayerschmidt and L.M. Hollander. Ware: Wordsworth Classics of World Literature, 1998, xi–xxxi.

SUMMARY

In this article I seek to show how in the representation of morality in the *Íslendingasögur* a tension is discernible between two different concepts of honour, both of which need to be understood in the light of the particular social and historical circumstances of the Icelandic commonwealth. On the one hand, there are those notions of honour that go with the duty of revenge in a kinship society; on the other hand, there is the honour that accrues to individuals who succeed in resolving disputes and securing settlements. I analyse a variety of characters in *Njáls saga* from these perspectives, arguing that full understanding of such portrayals depends on detailed analysis of individuals' vices and virtues. Such analysis must take account of the distinctive social circumstances described in the *Íslendingasögur*; comparisons with different societies provide, in my view, only a limited insight into the values of saga heroes. I argue that the sagas reveal the severe limitations of human virtue when confronted by problems rooted in the basic structure of society; this helps to explain why the advice of benevolent and peaceable men can prove so ineffective. *Njáls saga* depicts a society that disintegrates for the want of institutions able to transform the desire for reconciliation into the rule of law, and to direct conflicts into a legal process. Such institutions create conditions for a political morality intended to guarantee people access to due judicial process, thereby reducing the importance of an individual's vices and virtues.

Vilhjálmur Árnason
Faculty of History and Philosophy
School of Humanities
University of Iceland
vilhjarn@hi.is

SVAVAR HRAFN SVAVARSSON:

HONOUR AND SHAME: COMPARING MEDIEVAL ICELAND AND ANCIENT GREECE

THE NOTIONS of honour and shame have been used in different ways to describe the moral and social world evidenced in the saga literature of medieval Iceland, that of its creators and that of its subject matter; these notions are commonly held to be fundamental to this social world. I propose to consider two specific ways in which scholars have utilised and scrutinised these notions in the context of saga literature. Both involve a comparative effort, whereby the notions of honour and shame at work in saga literature are compared to those of Archaic and Classical Greek literature. One effort is guided by the hope of *clarifying a moral outlook* that holds good in important respects for both literatures and reflects a certain social structure. The other aims less at clarification than at *liberation*; past notions of honour and shame, seemingly remote and alien, primitive even, are morally precious and should be salvaged for the modern world.

I. Four theses in studies of ancient Greece

The comparative approaches I have in mind are fairly recent ones, influenced no doubt by at least four intertwined but distinct theses that gradually emerged and became influential in the latter part of the last century in studies of ancient Greek literature and morality. All of them focused on features relating (directly or indirectly) to honour and shame, and offered opportunities (sometimes quite explicitly) for comparisons with similar social worlds, such as that of medieval Iceland. The ground was fertile, since the use of these concepts was commonplace in the study of saga literature.

The first and earliest of these theses is based on the distinction between shame-cultures and guilt-cultures; it underlines the distinction's validity and interpretative significance as applied to specific periods in the history of ancient Greece. It gained currency after it appeared in E. R. Dodds' widely admired *The Greeks and the Irrational* (1951), in which he adopted the well known formulation of the distinction made by the anthropologist Ruth Benedict in 1947: "True shame cultures rely on external sanctions for good behavior, not, as true guilt cultures do, on an internalized conviction of sin. Shame is a reaction to other people's criticism."[1] Using this concept Dodds claimed that "Homeric man's highest good is not the enjoyment of a quiet conscience, but the enjoyment of *tīmē*, public esteem: "Why should I fight," asks Achilles, "if the good fighter receives no more τιμή than the bad [*Il*. 9.315 ff.]? And the strongest moral force which the Homeric man knows is not the fear of god, but respect for public opinion, *aidōs*: αἰδέομαι Τρῶας, says Hector at the crisis of his fate [*Il*. 22.105], and goes with open eyes to his death."[2] Other classical scholars followed suit, but sometimes applied this conceptual apparatus not only to the moral world of the Homeric poems, as Dodds had done, but also to that of later Archaic and then Classical Greece.[3] By the early nineteen-nineties, the conceptual soundness and usefulness of the distinction for the study of the Archaic and Classical Greek world seemed uncontroversial.[4]

[1] Ruth Benedict, *The Chrysanthemum and the Sword: Patterns of Japanese Culture* (Boston: Turtle, 2003 [1946]), 223. Benedict's influential passage continues: "A man is shamed either by being openly ridiculed and rejected or by fantasying to himself that he has been made ridiculous. In either case it is a potent sanction. But it requires an audience. Guilt does not. In a nation where honor means living up to one's own picture of oneself, a man may suffer from guilt though no man knows of his misdeed and a man's feelings of guilt may actually be relieved by confessing his sin."

[2] E.R. Dodds, *The Greeks and the Irrational* (Berkeley and Los Angeles: University of California Press, 1951), 17–18.

[3] Conspicuous examples are Arthur W. H. Adkins, *Merit and Responsibility: A Study in Greek Values* (Oxford: Clarendon Press, 1960), and Hugh Lloyd-Jones, *The Justice of Zeus* (Berkeley and Los Angeles: University of California Press, 1971), ch. 1. Dodds (*ibid.*, ch. 2) did indeed trace the gradual emergence of a guilt-culture discernable, for example, in Sophocles.

[4] Probably the last major study to make unproblematic use of the distinction is that of N. R. E. Fisher, *Hybris: A Study in the Values of Honour and Shame in Ancient Greece* (Warminster: Aris and Phillips, 1992). Fisher claims that "Homeric, and later, Greek has many words for feelings of 'shame', and none specifically for feelings of moral guilt; and it is right to classify Ancient Greece as more of a 'shame-culture' than a 'guilt-culture'" (180, n110).

The second thesis, evidently related to the first, tended to reduce moral features, in particular those evident in the Homeric poems, or at least (more generously) to explain aspects of them as social functions. The thesis has become well known through its appearance in Alasdair MacIntyre's *After Virtue* (1981). As did the advocates of the shame-guilt antithesis, MacIntyre made much use of the influential description of Homeric society found in Moses Finley's *The World of Odysseus* (1954). Adopting Finley´s view of the heroic society, MacIntyre held that "morality and social structure are in fact one and the same in heroic society. There is only one set of social bonds. Morality as something distinct does not yet exist. Evaluative questions are questions of social fact."[5] He also generalised: "What Finley says of Homeric society is equally true of heroic society in Iceland or in Ireland."[6] In fact, the Icelandic sagas are analogous to the Homeric poems in MacIntyre's view, forming as they did (or so he maintains) "a moral background to contemporary debate in classical societies,"[7] which includes the world of Attic tragedy and philosophy of the Classical age. It is significant, I believe, that he does not explain what is analogous to that debate in the case of Iceland.[8]

The third thesis emerged forcefully in 1993 with the appearance of two studies that undermined reasons for believing in the usefulness of the shame-guilt distinction and the soundness of MacIntyre's picture of the moral landscape of shame-cultures, or at least the inferences he drew. These studies were *Aidōs: The Psychology and Ethics of Honour and Shame in Ancient Greek Literature* by Douglas Cairns, and *Shame and Necessity* by Bernard Williams. Although no one has seriously doubted that in ancient Greece, in particular the Homeric world, honour and shame were emphasised to such an extent that these concepts played a major role in the moral

---

[5] Alasdair MacIntyre, *After Virtue: A Study in Moral Theory* (London: Duckworth, 2007³ [1981]), 123.

[6] *Ibid.*, 122. He emphasises the roles of honour and shame (125).

[7] *Ibid.*, 121.

[8] For more on the heroic elements common to the Homeric poems and the sagas, see Preben Meulengracht Sørensen, *Fortælling og ære: Studier i islændingesagaerne* (Aarhus: Aarhus Universitetsforlag, 1993), 291–94. One could ask about the relation of Eddic poetry to the sagas, with regard to the heroic element. Further, one could suggest that, if Eddic poetry provides the proper counterpart to Homeric poetry with regard to the heroic element, are the sagas not better understood as the counterpart to what MacIntyre calls the "contemporary debate in classical societies". (*Ibid.*, 121).

outlook, their significance for explaining the difference between an ancient Greek moral outlook and a modern one is subject to doubt; the easy distinction between internal and external sanctions implied by the use of the concepts was rejected in this revised consideration: "Concern for honour, even when it is acute, betokens no simple reliance on external sanctions alone."[9] When living within a society shaped by such sanctions, internal motivation can always play a role even through shame by the presence of an internalised other: "The internalised other is ... potentially somebody rather than nobody, and somebody other than me. He can provide the focus of real social expectations, of how I shall live if I act in one way rather than another, of how my actions and reactions will alter my relations to the world about me."[10] While Cairns showed what was unhelpful about branding Archaic and Classical Greece a shame-culture, Williams sought depth in the concept of shame absent from that of guilt; the latter is the more confining notion, for shame, as opposed to guilt, "embodies conceptions of what one is and how one is related to others."[11] This was part of Williams' critique of modern moral thought and an attempt to liberate the ancients, in order to draw lessons for the modern world. But the ancients he referred to were emphatically not the philosophers; Aristotle is in fact on the other side of the divide, along with other 'progressives': "Plato, Aristotle, Kant, Hegel are all on the same side, all believing in one way or another that the universe or history or the structure of human reason can, when properly understood, yield a pattern that makes sense of human life and human aspirations."[12] In short, on the one hand the usefulness of the established shame-guilt antithesis for an understanding of the moral outlook of the ancient Greeks was all but rejected, and on the other, shame (together with honour) was introduced as a moral concept of depth which actually had something to offer the modern reader.

[9] Douglas L. Cairns, *Aidōs: The Psychology and Ethics of Honour and Shame in Ancient Greek Literature* (Oxford: Clarendon, 1993), 43.
[10] Bernard Williams, *Shame and Necessity* (Berkeley and Los Angeles: University of California Press, 1993), 84.
[11] *Ibid.*, 94. Chapter IV of Williams' study is mostly concerned with shame. For a useful analysis of Williams' theses, see Michael Stocker, "Shame, Guilt, and Pathological Guilt: A Discussion of Bernard Williams," *Bernard Williams*, ed. Alan Thomas (Cambridge: Cambridge University Press, 2007), 135–54, and A.A. Long, "Williams on Greek Literature and Philosophy," *ibid.*, 155–80.
[12] Williams, *Shame and Necessity*, 163.

This thesis emphasises the qualified rejection of the supposed moral progression of the moderns beyond the ancients, and outdoes the fourth thesis in its effort to liberate Greek antiquity from the exotic and foreign.[13] That thesis, or set of theses, involves the resurgence of Aristotelian ethics, also known (with a wider scope of reference) as virtue ethics, in the wake of various damning criticisms of current ethics, and its defence as a serious alternative; its emphasis on virtues of character and a conception of a well-lived life were offered either as alternatives to contemporary normative ethics or as a persuasive moral psychology. Arguably prompted by G. S. E. Anscombe's seminal "Modern Moral Philosophy" (1958), virtue ethics gained ground through the elucidating efforts of, amongst others, the aforementioned Bernard Williams and Alasdair MacIntyre. The role these latter scholars played in this particular re-emergence of classical ideas is evidently quite different from their work on Homeric literature and Attic tragedy; one of the important points is that the earlier literature was pre-ethical. But, while Aristotle is much concerned with virtue and the good life, his account in the *Nicomachean Ethics* places weight on honour; it plays a role in Aristotle that it has definitely lost in modern moral theory.

II. Clarification and liberation of honour

At the outset I articulated two aims of comparing medieval Icelandic and ancient Greek notions of honour and shame: on the one hand, a clarification of a moral outlook in terms of social structure, and on the other, an endeavour to liberate these notions for the modern world. These are distinct projects, in a way opposed to one another, since the first explains honour in terms of its social embeddedness, from which the second attempts to pry it loose.

Consider first the aim of clarification. The second thesis mentioned in the previous section, MacIntyre's claim that morality and social structure are the same in heroic society (Greek and Icelandic), when adapted to the social world of medieval Iceland is fully compatible with a sociological approach to the sagas, which has not least been championed by Jesse

---

[13] The title of the first chapter of Williams' *Shame and Necessity* is "The Liberation of Antiquity".

Byock.[14] Vilhjálmur Árnason has made use of Byock's work and seems to accept MacIntyre's basic idea: "we need to understand [the morality of the sagas] in terms of the social structure of the sagas."[15] Utilising the Hegelian distinction between reflective *Moralität* and unreflective *Sittlichkeit*, the institutionalised ethical order of saga society, he argues that "the saga *Sittlichkeit* is characterized by an aporia that creates a sociomoral conflict which is of the essence in the sagas."[16] This conflict seems generated by the dominance, within this institutionalised ethical order, of competitive virtues created by the demands of honour, at the cost of cooperative virtues: "the conflict that exists between the unconditional morality of personal honor and the social need for peace which promotes more conciliatory values".[17] While MacIntyre is concerned with addressing the ancient Greek moral outlook and explicitly compares it with the medieval Icelandic one, neither Byock nor Vilhjálmur place any weight on comparing the medieval Icelandic social world to an ancient Greek one. What I shall suggest in the next section, however, is that MacIntyre's conception of heroic societies, indebted as it is to accounts of honour in Homeric society, is conceptually flawed in a manner that seemingly tends to mark discussions of cultures of honour.

Now for the ambitious aim of liberating honour and shame for the modern world. The first thesis of the previous section laid down a distinction between shame-cultures and guilt-cultures. This distinction was based on the conspicuous role that honour played in Archaic Greek culture, a role no less conspicuous in medieval Icelandic culture. That role has been clear for a long time, as it has in the case of the Greeks, although the inferences drawn in the case of medieval Icelandic culture have varied.[18] Presenting

---

[14] See Jesse Byock, *Feud in the Icelandic Sagas* (Berkeley and Los Angeles: University of California Press, 1982), and *Viking Age Iceland* (London: Penguin, 2001); see also William Ian Miller, *Bloodtaking and Peacemaking: Feud, Law, and Society in Saga Iceland* (Chicago: University of Chicago Press, 1990).

[15] Vilhjálmur Árnason, "Morality and Social Structure in the Icelandic Sagas," *Journal of English and Germanic Philology* 90/2 (1991): 157–74, at 162), and see also his "Saga og siðferði: Hugleiðingar um túlkun á siðfræði Íslendingasagna," *Tímarit Máls og menningar* 46 (1985): 21–37.

[16] Vilhjálmur Árnason, "Morality and Social Structure in the Icelandic Sagas," 164.

[17] Ibid., 168.

[18] See Meulengracht Sørensen, *Fortælling og ære*, especially ch. 9, and Helgi Þorláksson, who offers an overview in his "Inngangur" in *Sæmdarmenn*, eds. Helgi Þorláksson *et al.* (Reykjavík: Hugvísindastofnun Háskóla Íslands, 2001), 7–13.

shame (and honour), however, by contrasting it with guilt (and conscience) is a more recent phenomenon. William Ian Miller utilises the concept in a particularly clear manner: "The core belief at the heart of most revenge cultures is that man is more naturally a chicken than a wolf. Thus [sic] revenge cultures are invariably shame cultures ...".[19] Miller is explicit in his application of the terms shame and honour to characterise medieval Icelandic culture and he cites Kant to explain the difference between dignity and anything with a price, like honour.[20]

The first move of those who aim at liberating honour, as found in saga literature, is to undermine this distinction. Hence they embrace the third thesis outlined above and argue against the usefulness and even the legitimacy of the shame-guilt antithesis. As one of the objectives of this thesis is to make ancient Greek morality more readily intelligible to modern readers, or even an alternative to modern conceptions, so, when applied to Icelandic medieval morality, the aim is to rehabilitate the positive notion of honour (rather than the negative one of shame, interestingly enough). Þorsteinn Gylfason, eschewing completely the sociological approach, argues for a timeless conception of honour, according to which it is in fact understood in the same way in the modern world (particularly Iceland) as it is in the world of the sagas. Further, he argues along the lines of Bernard Williams that "[t]here is, in Greek tragedy as well as in an Icelandic saga, plenty of room for a higher honour, independent of received opinion. In our time too."[21] A similar idea informs the work of Kristján Kristjánsson in his attempt to portray the saga moral outlook "as an atemporal, universal moral outlook".[22] He takes over Williams' repudiation of the guilt-shame antithesis but goes further than Williams and in a rather surprising direction, as will presently become clear.

Here we approach the use made of the fourth thesis, that of utilising Aristotelian virtue ethics in an effort to understand and liberate saga morality. In short, saga morality bears a resemblance to the morality championed by Aristotle in his *Nicomachean Ethics*, in particular Aristotle's description

---

[19] William Ian Miller, *Eye for an Eye* (Cambridge: Cambridge University Press, 2006), 96; cf. his *Bloodtaking and Peacemaking*, 29, 302–3.
[20] William Ian Miller, *Eye for an Eye*, 99–100 and 130–32.
[21] Þorsteinn Gylfason, "Introduction," *Njal's Saga* (Ware: Wordsworth, 1998), xxviii–xxx.
[22] Kristján Kristjánsson, "Liberating Moral Traditions: Saga Morality and Aristotle's *Megalopsychia*," *Ethical Theory and Moral Practice* 1 (1998): 407.

of *megalopsychia* or magnanimity. In a manner analogous to that of Williams, Kristján attempts to "dive in at the deep end". He does this by comparing Aristotle's magnanimous person to the *mikilmenni* of saga literature. Honour is central to that account, as it is to saga morality: in both, "honour and dishonour counted as the external criteria of a person's greatness."[23]

This attempt to liberate the honour found in saga literature, an attempt which quite explicitly makes use of analogous attempts within ancient Greek studies, seems to me incoherent. I turn to it in section IV below.

III. Competition and cooperation

While the idea of there being a chasm between the shame cultures of old and modern guilt cultures tends to put any relevance of a morality based on shame and honour beyond retrieval, attempts either to downplay the difference or even to elevate the morality of shame cultures aim at retrieving them. The philosophical complexities (pointed out by Bernard Williams) of the difference between shame and guilt notwithstanding, the emphatic role played by honour in both ancient Greece and medieval Iceland nevertheless seems to invite a characterisation of both as shame cultures, or honour cultures. Hence the persuasiveness of sociological accounts that entrench the morality of honour in social institutions. My misgivings about this project do not pertain to the general idea of such accounts, which I find convincing, but only to apparent connotations of the notion of honour in them.

The social worlds in question are characterised by shame rather than guilt, or honour rather than conscience, as evidenced by the overriding importance of honour which is also to be understood as the social force that determines questions of value. Before venturing further, it is important to distinguish *shame* (*aidōs*) from the *dishonour* (*atimia*) that brings about the shame; shame in turn causes action for the sake of honour (*timē*); hence the social worlds in question are variously called shame- or honour-cultures. But now the role of honour, we are at least often led to believe, makes for a *competitive* social world, in which competitive virtues dominate

---

[23] Ibid., 410.

at the cost of co-operative virtues which, within the institutionalised ethical framework, are at best secondary and at worst nonexistent; hence calamities ensue.[24] But the undoubted importance of honour and shame does not by itself entail the subjection of co-operative virtues to competitive ones, even within the institutionalised ethical framework; the entailment is contingent. Shame can just as easily be created by "a failure to act in some expected self-sacrificing or co-operative manner", as Williams claimed.[25] In order to establish that the one entails the other, we need specific testimonies that simply record the dominance of competitive virtues. In the case of ancient Greece, it had indeed long been held that as a culture of honour it was ruled by competitive virtues.[26] Later, it was forcefully and persuasively argued that the record showed no such thing.[27] Likewise, I submit, in the case of medieval Iceland: the importance of co-operative virtues at all levels seems incontestable, *within* the institutional framework of honour.[28] That they often lose out gives the saga narratives their peculiar poignancy. Tying honour especially to competition, as opposed to co-operation, simply seems fallacious: "... like so many features of Icelandic culture, honour is repeatedly tied to competition," Jesse Byock says, implying that there is a closer connection between honour and competition than honour and co-operation.[29] But he also convincingly maintains when analysing feud as an organising principle that: "Rather than a socially destructive force to be controlled by sheriffs, bailiffs and royal agents, as in many contemporaneous European societies, feud in Iceland became a formalized and culturally stabilizing element. Respected men served as negotiators, and feuding became the major vehicle for channelling violence into the moderating arenas of the courts and into the hands of informal arbitrators,

---

[24] For ancient Greece, see Moses I. Finley, *The World of Odysseus* (Harmondsworth: Penguin, 1979² [1954]), and Arthur Adkins, *Merit and Responsibility*; also, albeit more guardedly, MacIntyre, *After Virtue*, 125, 133–34, 138–39.

[25] Williams, *Shame and Necessity*, 38.

[26] Finley, who claimed that "[o]f necessity ... the world of Odysseus was fiercely competitive, as each hero strove to outdo the others" (*The World of Odysseus*, 118), is clearly echoed by Adkins and MacIntyre.

[27] See especially Cairns, *Aidōs*, 50–51.

[28] This seems especially evident from the account of the feud system in Jesse Byock, *Feud in the Icelandic Sagas*, and in his *Viking Age Iceland*, as indeed from that of Miller's *Bloodtaking and Peacemaking*.

[29] Byock, *Viking Age Iceland*, 14.

where public pressure was applied. In Iceland's single 'great village' environment *goðar* found honour in containing disruptive behaviour. Leaders gained prestige and standing by publicly playing the role of men of moderation (*hófsmenn*) and goodwill (*góðviljamenn*)."[30] Honour in saga literature, it seems, is as much tied to co-operative virtues as to competitive ones, or so I would suggest, just as in the Homeric poems.

MacIntyre's thesis in particular emphasises what Bernard Williams has termed the *moral thickness* of a culture dominated by the institutionalisation of honour, its unreflective character, where questions of value are questions of fact. The idea of 'thick moral concepts' is useful. In short, thick moral concepts unite fact and value: "We can say ... that the application of these concepts is at the same time world-guided and action-guiding."[31] Examples of such concepts would be *coward, lie, brutality, gratitude*. Hume is one of many philosophers who have been quoted in this connection. He discusses words "whose very names force an avowal of their merit, there are many others, to which the most determined scepticism cannot for a moment refuse the tribute of praise and approbation."[32] The sagas, I submit, frequently introduce persons by descriptions that use precisely such thick terms and therefore forestall the possibility of misunderstanding the person's character; by a few strokes the authors make clear as a matter of fact the virtues or vices of the players.

This use of thick terms characterises traditional and homogeneous societies, Williams suggests, that are not particularly given to ethical reflection.[33] They are the offspring of moralities without second order ethical theory. Thin moral concepts, in contrast, like *right, just*, and *good*, are held to characterise reflective moralities, moral communities that have evolved an ethical theory in the sense that they have a second order ethics on the

---

[30] Ibid., 79. But then Byock says again (208): "The taking of vengeance was understood as action that satisfied honour ... The exchanges ... were rooted in competition." The emphasis is also explicit in Helgi Þorláksson, "Vitrir menn og vel metnir," *Sæmdarmenn*, ed. by Helgi Þorláksson *et al.* (Reykjavík: Hugvísindastofnun Háskóla Íslands, 2001), 20–21.

[31] Bernard Williams, *Ethics and the Limits of Philosophy* (Cambridge, Mass.: Harvard University Press, 1985), 141, cf. 140–45. See also the lucid and critical exegesis of Mark P. Jenkins, *Bernard Williams* (Chesham: Acumen, 2006), 133–40. He traces the ancestry of the idea to the "thick description" of anthropologist Clifford Geertz (in *The Interpretation of Cultures* (1973)), who in turn claims indebtedness to philosopher Gilbert Ryle.

[32] *An Inquiry Concerning the Principles of Morals* VI.1 *ad fin*.

[33] See Williams, *Limits*, 148.

truth of their first order moral judgments: "The very general kind of judgment that is in question here — a judgment using a very general concept — is essentially a product of reflection, and it comes into question when someone stands back from the practices of the society and its use of these concepts and asks whether this is the right way to go on, whether these are good ways in which to assess action, whether the kinds of character that are admired are rightly admired."[34] The ethics of Plato would be a case in point, Kantian ethics another. The sagas do not include an external viewpoint from which a character's action can be assessed; no moral judgment is passed on actions, as Halldór Laxness noted long ago, calling their spirit amoral or morally pessimistic.[35] Now, if this distinction is tenable in general, and in this context in particular (as a conceptual instrument with which to clarify the moral landscape of the sagas — and hence to elucidate the morality that gave birth to them) it seems to me that a morality, like that found in the saga-literature, can gain its distinctiveness in one of two ways. Either, and more likely to my mind, saga morality is very thick, although not just teeming with competitive virtues, but also co-operative ones. As such it may have much in common with Archaic and to some extent Classical Greek morality. Or, its distinctiveness is due to its being on the borderline between the two, the thick and the thin, in transition, so to speak. According to MacIntyre, the Greek tragedians and philosophers of the Classical period might be regarded as such borderline cases.[36] That position would then be the determining factor, and would explain the elusiveness of the morality portrayed in the sagas; the idea is that moralities in transition, from the thick to the thin, are fertile grounds for unique cultural products.

Vilhjálmur Árnason advances the latter idea, namely that within the *Sittlichkeit* of the Icelandic republic an *aporia* is created when social conditions demand co-operative virtues in place of the dominant competitive

---

[34] Ibid., 146.

[35] Halldór Laxness, "Minnisgreinar um fornsögur," *Sjálfsagðir hlutir* (Reykjavík: Helgafell 1980, 3rd pr. [1946]), 43: "... í þeim skáldverkum íslenskum sem eru af hreinustum toga og sterkast teingd norrænni fornöld, þarámeðal Egla Njála Gretla Laxdæla og konúngasögur Snorra, er yfirleitt ekki lagður dómur á verk manna ... Andi þessara verka er, þrátt fyrir kristilegt yfirborð hér og hvar, ýmist siðblinda eða siðferðileg bölsýni. Þannig gerast í fornsögum vorum þeir feiknstafir ... að bestu mennirnir ... vinna að jafnaði verstu verkin og hinir verstu menn ... eru fyrirvaralaust farnir að vinna þrifnaðarverk."

[36] See MacIntyre, *After Virtue*, ch. 11.

virtues. But now, if Vilhjálmur is correct, we are faced with a problem. Either the *aporia* is internal to saga *Sittlichkeit*, and the co-operative virtues are as thick as the competitive ones, or the *aporia* is created from without, arising from the need of exchanging competition for co-operation. While the latter possibility seems to demand a *reflective* ethics that is nowhere to be found in the saga culture, the former admits the co-operative virtues into the moral realm dominated by honour. Since Vilhjálmur argues for the latter interpretation, he seems hard pressed to explain the fact that the morality of honour surely includes virtues of co-operation, in medieval Iceland just as in Archaic Greece, as I already suggested. Within such a culture, the dominant moral concepts employed depend on honour as a kind of focal concept. But if moral concepts that denote co-operation are just as weighty as those that denote competition, the tension generated by their clash is internal to the culture itself. And insofar as it is internal, it is part of the unreflective moral thickness of the culture. For moral (or political) reflection to upset this culture one would expect an external view to be needed, as in the case of the Greeks.[37] The thick values of Homeric culture tumbled down first through constitutional changes (by the gradual devaluation of aristocratic ideals of manly excellence in pursuit of honour, especially associated with democratic Athens), and then forcefully through the moral and political reflection culminating in the works of Plato and Aristotle.[38] There does not seem to be anything quite analogous to that process in medieval Iceland. Eventually, the republic crashes through internal paradoxes, no doubt generated by clashes between competitive and cooperative virtues. The sagas, however, do not seem to reflect *on* the inadequacy of this culture to deal with internal problems, but rather simply to reflect the thick moral world of the culture.[39] Here we return to a previously mentioned flaw in MacIntyre's comparisons of Homeric literature and that of the sagas. While for the Classical Greeks, the Homeric poems

[37] Vilhjálmur finds reflection in the importance of advocacy itself ("Morality and Social Structure in the Icelandic Sagas," 173). But that is internal to the culture itself.

[38] For a study on the changes in the Greek conception of honour, see Gabriel Herman, *Morality and Behaviour in Democratic Athens: A Social History* (Cambridge: Cambridge University Press, 2006), 194–203, 258–68.

[39] Gunnar Harðarson has suggested to me that the reflection needed was supplied by Christian ethics, in a way explained most conspicuously by Hermann Pálsson. Although this interpretation remains an option, it does strain the notion of *reflection*; cf. Meulengracht Sørensen, *Fortælling og ære*, ch. 12.

did without doubt provide a moral background, the sagas do not provide a similar background to any later similarly classical age, and they cannot be their own background.

IV. Liberating honour

Consider now the aim of liberating honour as found in ancient Greece and medieval Iceland. Here, too, there is room for misgivings. Fundamental to this project is either debunking the shame-guilt antithesis or elevating shame (and honour) as a moral notion at the cost of guilt. Within the study of medieval Iceland, Þorsteinn Gylfason and Kristján Kristjánsson have attempted to return to honour its due importance, wrenching it as it were from its (previous) embeddedness in (misconceived) shame cultures, and endowing it with a timeless quality, depriving it of its contingency. I suggested that this attempt is incoherent.

First, such an aspiration is at odds with its inspiration, the work of Bernard Williams. One of his fundamental points in arguing for the relevance of shame as a moral notion is precisely its embeddedness in cultures that are characterised by thick moral concepts and an aversion to what he repeatedly and rather antagonistically calls that peculiar institution of morality.[40] Williams' point is – and he is surely right – that the value of honour in these contexts resides in its embeddedness. His objection – more controversial – is against the ambitions of moral theory, that of Aristotle just as that of Kant, to ground morality in a reflective system by employing thin moral concepts, and thus alienating the individual from his own life's project. But that seems to be precisely what scholars seek to do when they elevate honour to a timeless moral concept; they attempt to thin it out. That is also the reason why this approach is opposed to that of MacIntyre and others who attempt to explain the thickness of this concept of honour.

Secondly, Aristotle, to whom Kristján appeals when he offers honour as a moral concept of choice, has a very different idea of honour and shame than that found either in the sagas or Archaic and most Classical Greek

---

[40] This is one of the main points of his *Ethics and the Limits of Philosophy*. MacIntyre makes similar points (*After Virtue*, 126–27).

literature. Honour, although the most important of external goods, is what the virtuous person deserves; correctly judging his desert, the virtuous person is *ipso facto* magnanimous and conscious of his own great worth. But he does not act for the sake of his honour in any straightforward sense, nor does *dishonour* move him in the least; it creates no shame. To be sure, shame would move him (just insofar as he would fail to be virtuous – *per impossibile*), but that shame has little to do with social expectations; dishonour does not affect him, but that is precisely what affects the characters of the sagas (as it does those of the Homeric poems).[41] Hence, when Bernard Williams defends the importance of shame, Aristotle is only mentioned as one of the builders of that peculiar institution of morality.

The analytical tools of moral thickness and thinness that Bernard Williams has used on Greek culture have not gone unchallenged; their soundness as philosophical concepts has been questioned.[42] Their usefulness, however, is to my mind clear. They help scholars to navigate unfamiliar seas, such as the morality of saga culture. They help to expose the social embeddedness of moral terms, how matters of value are, within that culture, matters of fact. But why should gaining an insight into that culture, for example by being clearer on the social embeddedness of honour, encourage one to make its values one's own or rue their disappearance? In fact, awareness of this embeddedness should (if anything) prompt one to circumspection regarding the social embeddedness of contemporary values. But more importantly for the study of medieval Icelandic culture, these insights offer the opportunity of clarifying the roles of competitive *and* co-operative virtues within the framework of honour, the tensions between them, and their resolutions.[43]

---

[41] See especially the *Nicomachean Ethics* IV.3.1124a4–29.
[42] See Jenkins, *Bernard Williams*, 135–40.
[43] Thanks to Gunnar Harðarson and Vilhjálmur Árnason for corrections and criticisms, as well as to the journal's anonymous readers.

REFERENCES

Adkins, Arthur W.H. *Merit and Responsibility: A Study in Greek Values*. Oxford: Clarendon Press, 1960.
Benedict, Ruth. *The Chrysanthemum and the Sword: Patterns of Japanese Culture*. Boston: Turtle, 2003 [1946].
Byock, Jesse. *Feud in the Icelandic Sagas*. Berkeley and Los Angeles: University of California Press, 1982.
Byock, Jesse. *Viking Age Iceland*. London: Penguin, 2001.
Cairns, Douglas L. *Aidōs: The Psychology and Ethics of Honour and Shame in Ancient Greek Literature*. Oxford: Clarendon, 1993.
Dodds, E.R. *The Greeks and the Irrational*. Berkeley and Los Angeles: University of California Press, 1951.
Finley, Moses I. *The World of Odysseus*. Harmondsworth: Penguin, 1979, 2nd pr. [1954].
N.R.E. Fisher. *Hybris: A Study in the Values of Honour and Shame in Ancient Greece*. Warminster: Aris and Phillips, 1992.
Halldór Laxness. "Minnisgreinar um fornsögur." *Sjálfsagðir hlutir*. Reykjavík: Helgafell 1980, 3rd pr. [1946], 7–74.
Helgi Þorláksson. "Inngangur." *Sæmdarmenn*, ed. by Helgi Þorláksson *et al.* Reykjavík: Hugvísindastofnun Háskóla Íslands, 2001, 7–14.
Helgi Þorláksson. "Virtir menn og vel metnir." *Sæmdarmenn*, ed. by Helgi Þorláksson *et al.* Reykjavík: Hugvísindastofnun Háskóla Íslands, 2001, 15–22.
Herman, Gabriel. *Morality and Behaviour in Democratic Athens: A Social History*. Cambridge: Cambridge University Press, 2006.
Jenkins, Mark P. *Bernard Williams*. Chesham: Acumen, 2006.
Kristján Kristjánsson, "Liberating Moral Traditions: Saga Morality and Aristotle's *Megalopsychia*." *Ethical Theory and Moral Practice* 1 (1998): 397–422.
Lloyd-Jones, Hugh. *The Justice of Zeus*. Berkeley and Los Angeles: University of California Press, 1971.
Long, A.A. "Williams on Greek Literature and Philosophy." *Bernard Williams*, ed. by Alan Thomas. Cambridge: Cambridge University Press, 2007, 155–80.
MacIntyre, Alasdair. *After Virtue: A Study in Moral Theory*. London: Duckworth, 2007³ [1981].
Meulengracht Sørensen, Preben. *Fortælling og ære: Studier i islændingesagaerne*. Aarhus: Aarhus Universitetsforlag, 1993.
Miller, William Ian. *Bloodtaking and Peacemaking: Feud, Law, and Society in Saga Iceland*. Chicago: University of Chicago Press, 1990.
Miller, William Ian. *Eye for an Eye*. Cambridge: Cambridge University Press, 2006.
Stocker, Michael. "Shame, Guilt, and Pathological Guilt: A Discussion of Bernard

Williams." *Bernard Williams*, ed. by Alan Thomas. Cambridge: Cambridge University Press, 2007, 135–54.

Vilhjálmur Árnason. "Saga og siðferði: Hugleiðingar um túlkun á siðfræði Íslendingasagna." *Tímarit Máls og menningar* 46 (1985): 21–37.

Vilhjálmur Árnason. "Morality and Social Structure in the Icelandic Sagas." *Journal of English and Germanic Philology* 90/2 (1991): 157–74.

Williams, Bernard. "The Legacy of Greek Philosophy." [1981] *The Sense of the Past: Essays in the History of Philosophy*. Princeton: Princeton University Press, 2006, 3–48.

Williams, Bernard. *Ethics and the Limits of Philosophy*. Cambridge, Mass.: Harvard University Press, 1985.

Williams, Bernard. *Shame and Necessity*. Berkeley and Los Angeles: University of California Press, 1993.

Þorsteinn Gylfason, "Introduction." *Njal's Saga*. Ware: Wordsworth, 1998, xi–xxxi.

SUMMARY

This paper explores two approaches to the literary history of the Icelandic commonwealth. Each uses the concepts of honour and shame to analyse morality and society; and each compares the respective roles of these concepts in the medieval Icelandic commonwealth and in Greek antiquity. One approach seeks to identify those elements in the two literatures which give expression to their respective understandings of ethics/morality and society; by doing so the role of 'thick-morality' within each society is explained. The other approach seeks to dehistoricize these particular notions, arguing (perhaps with limited success) for the timelessness of these moral concepts.

Svavar Hrafn Svavarsson
Department of History and Philosophy,
School of Humanities
University of Iceland
svahra@hi.is

J. HARRIS

PHILOLOGY, ELEGY, AND CULTURAL CHANGE

PHILOLOGY'S concern with minutiae – one rune, one line, an individual poem, at most a group of similar poems, a genre – seems to occupy the opposite end of a spectrum from the grand form of historical generalization known as civilizational analysis.[1] Yet in the hands of a master of both ends of the spectrum, such as Sigurður Nordal, philology's small steps have sometimes led to cultural panoramas that can contribute at the highest level of the study of comparative civilizations, for the bold sweep of *Íslenzk menning* relies on intense case studies such as Nordal's seminal investigation of the religion of Egill Skalla-Grímsson.[2] Without attempting to emulate Nordal, my paper will implicitly argue a continuity from the building blocks of the particular (philology) through the controlled generalization of genre (elegy) to a limited window on an aspect of cultural dynamic; along the way we make a brief pause where genre leads in to literary interpretation. At every point, however, the philologist in me will cling as closely as possible to texts and for the most part to a ninth-century Swedish runic inscription, the Rök stone. My text and free translation stand as an appendix to this article, and I refer throughout to that text.[3]

Philology

My understanding of the Rök inscription as a whole is heavily indebted to Lars Lönnroth's article of 1977, the first effort in this realm by a modern literary historian and literary critic.[4] The whole inscription consists of an

[1] See the historical contributions to this volume, especially the essay of Jóhann Páll Árnason.
[2] Sigurður Nordal 1942/1990. Cf. the reception of *Íslenzk menning* in the contributions of Jóhann Páll Árnason.
[3] The Rök text and translation here and much of the discussion in this article depend on: Harris 2006b, 2009, and forthcoming.
[4] Harris 2006b, especially 45–55; for his part, Lönnroth 1977 owes much to Wessén 1958.

opening memorial formula of two lines followed by three sections of narrative materials, each structured as two teasing Questions followed by an Answer. The first two sections consist of somewhat less controversial heroic materials while the third and climactic section, which is constructed around a sacred story, is little understood and heavily contested. Lönnroth's structural analysis, while basically very revealing, turned out to be too strict in some details. We differ, for example, on the intended arrangement of the three sections and on the damaged l. 20, which I believe constitutes a meta-level introduction to Section 3 rather than a concluding frame.[5]

Underlying the Rök inscription is almost certainly an oral genre, a traditional question-and-answer routine in skaldic verse known as *greppaminni*. Remarkably enough, all three scholars responsible for this important development in modern Rök scholarship were present at the reading of this paper.[6] In fact, however, Sophus Bugge, the founding father of Rök scholarship, had already noticed this analogy before 1910,[7] but, unlike Lönnroth, Bugge did not integrate his insight into a larger interpretative structure where it could enter the chain of inference. In another of his proleptic insights, Bugge interpreted runic **mukmini** as *mǫg-minni*, which he translated 'Erinnerung an den Sohn'; later he retracted this suggestion in view of the preserved final *-u* after a short stressed vowel in *sunu* and *fiaru*, assuming that the language of Rök would require a form like **maguminni*; but Bugge never accepted *múg-minni* 'Volkserinnerung' or *ungmenni* 'dem jungen Mann' (or later 'the youth') – the two main interpretive variants after Bugge's period – and at the time of his death was working on a new explanation.[8] In recent years Prof. Gun Widmark has revived

---

My Rök articles were produced independently of, but contemporaneously with, a "new wave" of writings on this earliest masterpiece of Swedish literature, including: Andersson 2006; Barnes 2007; Ralph 2007a, 2007b; Schulte 2008; Malm 2008. I hope in the near future to take positions on these and a few other recent studies not noticed in Harris 2006b, 2009 (including: Lönnqvist 1999; Widmark 2001; Petersson 1991); I should mention already, however, that the far-reaching arguments of Bo Ralph (in 2007a, 2007b) are incompatible with my beliefs and assumptions though a closer engagement is not possible here.

5 Harris 2006b and forthcoming.
6 Vésteinn Ólason (1969); Lars Lönnroth (1977); Margaret Clunies Ross (Lönnroth 1977, 17, n. 21).
7 Bugge 1910, 39, 244–45.
8 Bugge 1910, 13–15 and Olrik's editorial addition 15, n. 1.

mǫgminni, rescuing Bugge's very early intuition with a theory based on history of the language: the earliest loss of final *-u* would have occurred precisely in a compound, and the spelling with **u** instead of **a** is justified by the u-umlaut which would have set in with the syncope of *u*.[9] I find this a convincing explanation, and in any case, *mǫgminni* is a great improvement from the literary and hermeneutic point of view, establishing a nexus between occasion and content that had been conspicuously absent.

The only line not translated in the Appendix is l. 20. In a forthcoming article I attempt to reconstruct this damaged line; while my efforts yielded a range of possible readings rather than a single most probable result, the one I favor is: *nu'k minni meðr allu sagi einn: huaR iðgjald þa sunu aftir, fra* – which I translate freely as: "Now, speaking for myself (*einn*), I shall tell a *minni* in conclusion (*meðr allu*): Who received recompense after a son's death, I know" (Harris forthcoming). The thematically crucial word here is *iðgjald*, but the theoretical point brought out by the effort at reconstruction confirms the validity of Leo Spitzer's famous 'philological circle': everything in the line depends on the whole, and the whole is comprised of 28 lines with the same part-to-whole relationship. Hermeneutic progress is achieved by a movement back and forth between the whole and the part. This is definitely not 'science' in the usual English meaning of the word, and it provides only the remotest atoms of a larger historical point of view; but it is interesting to me that a rescue operation like reconstruction simply exaggerates and lays bare the basic hermeneutic circle.

I will return to Rök to discuss the content and meaning of this unique inscription, but it seems appropriate first to follow the trail adumbrated by the word *iðgjǫld*. The word is drawn from *Sonatorrek*, Egill Skallagrímsson's famous poem 'The Irreparable Loss of Sons.'[10] This oral poem, composed in Iceland about 961,[11] has a number of interesting features in common with the inscription in stone from the western edge of Östergötland in the

---

[9] Widmark 1992 [1993], 29–31; Grønvik 2003, 48–49 also offers arguments against *múgr*; cf. Harris 2009, 39–40, n. 70.

[10] *Sonatorrek* has been edited many times; I mention as especially significant: Sigurður Nordal 1933, 243–57 (with the whole saga), Jón Helgason 1962, 29–38, Turville-Petre 1976, 24–41, and Jón Hnefill Aðalsteinsson 2001. I quote from Jón Helgason's edition.

[11] I cannot do full justice to very recent skeptical discussion of *Sonatorrek* and its dating, but I cite as two major instances Baldur Hafstað 1995 (see index and especially p. 160) and Torfi Tulinius 2004 (see index) and, as an able reassertion of the older understanding of Egill, Jónas Kristjánsson 2006.

first half of the ninth century, despite the time and space separating them and despite great formal differences. Both of course are a father's memorial for a predeceased son. Unlike many later memorial stones, Rök tells nothing about the deeds of the honored dead, Vámóðr,[12] nothing even about his character except that he was 'death-doomed,' *faigian*, ON *feigr*, while Egill's Bǫðvarr is characterized vaguely as a support to his father but principally by the negative fact that the 'stuff,' *efni*, of a bad man had not grown in him.[13] Neither of these paternal monuments fulfills our modern stereotyped expectation that a funeral elegy should elaborate on the accomplishments and good qualities of the dead, and both authors could be said to treat their early-dead son mainly in terms of *potential*: Bǫðvarr had 'the makings of a man' or was *mannsefni*– if only he had been allowed to grow up before Odin plucked him – while Vámóðr was fated, perhaps from the outset.

Sonatorrek offers clues to a few specific words of Rök. Egill's title itself looks to be a nonce creation on the basis of the word *torrek*, which appears elsewhere only once but then in an intensely elegiac context where it is interpreted by Finnur Jónsson as 'heavy loss' or 'something difficult to replace'.[14] Varinn's *mǫgminni* may have been such a nonce formation based on *greppaminni*, but could Varinn also have intended it as a kind of theme word or even a title? More reliable is the help *Sonatorrek*'s phrase *vamma varr* offers in explanation of Rök's *via vari* (l. 27); in both cases we have the adjective *varr* complemented by a gen. pl., and since *Sonatorrek*'s is also the only example of this structure among the many instances of *varr* in *Lexicon Poeticum*, it may well be an archaic formula.[15]

The richest verbal connections between the two works are to be found in comparison with *Sonatorrek*'s crucial st. 17 (Jón Helgason 1962, 36):

Þat er ok mælt
at engi geti

---

[12] I adopt this form of the name from Widmark 1993 with the further etymology offered in Harris 2009, 13, n. 7.
[13] Sonatorrek 11: *Veit ek þat siálfr / at í syni mínum / vara ills þegns / efni vaxit, / ef sá randviðr / rǿskvask næði / unz her-Gauts / hendr of tǿki.* See the discussion in Harris 2009, 43, n. and 81.
[14] Finnur Jónsson 1931, s.v. *torrek*: "en vanskelig erstattelig genstand, svært tab."
[15] Finnur Jónsson 1931, s.v.; Harris 2006b, 71–73.

sonar iðgiǫld
nema sialfr ali
enn þann nið
er ǫðrum sé
borinn maðr
í bróður stað.

Here the word *iðgjǫld* occurs in the context of Egill's contemptuous rejection of an old saying or proverb that allows one recompense, but only one, for a lost son, namely another born to replace him. Translated literally: 'This also is said, that no one may get recompense for a son unless he himself begets again the descendant who will be a man born for the other one, in the place of his brother.'[16] Of course *iðgjǫld* itself appears in Rök only as a conjecture in l. 20, but the source verb is found in a pregnant context in ll. 21–22 in the question *hvaR vaRi guldinn at kvanaR husli* 'who was compensated for by the sacrifice of a woman.' The verb *gjalda* is multivalent and the syntax debated, but the *Sonatorrek* parallel helps to focus on an understanding of compensation as propagation of the family.[17] While *gjalda* in such a situation could refer to the 'compensation' provided by revenge, *iðgjǫld* in *Sonatorrek* 17 shows that rebirth or its weaker form in birth of a dedicated fraternal substitute will not have been far from the minds of the members of the archaic, family-dominated societies under discussion. Egill's stanza shares other significant vocabulary with Rök: *sonr* 'son,' *niðr* 'descendant,' and *ala* 'to beget' are all important words in Rök, essential to its realization of a theme similar to that of *Sonatorrek* 17. Two further words from this stanza, *borinn* 'born' from *bera* and *bróðir* 'brother,' are also found in Rök though in another context.

More remarkable than the lexical sharing is an illuminating syntactic parallel. For st. 17 not only matches Rök's locution *vera borinn* + dat. but in addition shares the syntactic oddity of placing the past participle before the subject, so that we get parallels of sense and syntax like the following:

[16] I first published this interpretation, which diverges significantly from Turville-Petre 1976, 36–37, in Harris 1994, 54–55, but it goes back to a longer manuscript I circulated widely before 1982.
[17] Cf. Grønvik 1990 and Harris 2006b, 61–62.

1	2	3	4	5
hvaim	se	burinn	niðr	drængi
5	2	3	4	5

er ǫðrum sé borinn maðr í sonar stað

I have argued that *Sonatorrek*, along with some neglected grammar, can help us to disambiguate this sentence in Rök, and with that clarification to move a step nearer to understanding the mythic content.[18]

Genre

For all its difficulties, *Sonatorrek* is much better understood than Rök. From *Egils saga* and from his large body of authentic verse, we know Egill as we will never know Varinn; from the saga context, analogues elsewhere in the sagas, and other poems with similar occasion we can begin to say something about the genre and function of *Sonatorrek*, even if Egill's poem towers over other poems of its kind like the leek among the grasses. It is the saga author, not Egill, who calls the poem an *erfikvæði*, and this occurrence of the word is unique; still, it is rightly taken as a genre term, along with *erfidrápa* and *erfiflokkr*, though less specific as to form. Ottar Grønvik in particular has been successful in exploring the word family of *erfi* and the institutions of inheritance, but the actual institutional or ritual role of the *erfikvæði* itself remains obscure (Grønvik 1982; 1981, 162–89). *Egils saga* implies that no proper funeral could happen without such a poem, but the small number of remains of the genre from the private sphere throws a doubtful light on that claim. Bjarne Fidjestøl is the author of the only standard treatment of *erfikvæði*, an article that is a model of philological workmanship. But to achieve such clarity, Fidjestøl narrowed the conception of the genre to a collection mostly restricted to early Christian court poems on the death of the Norwegian king (Fidjestøl 1989). In a recently published article, I followed in his wake but tried to reopen the focus to consider both private poems such as *Sonatorrek* and also the royal *erfidrápur*, which, I argued, shared a continuous generic space (Harris 2006a). Some of the private poems, for example, Vǫlu-Steinn's *Ǫgmundardrápa*,

---

[18] Harris 2006b, 57–61, 86–89.

have been received by tradition in the context of a narrative paradigm – a 'myth', if you like – in which a father suffers such grief for his early-dead son that he wishes to die – until recalled to life, poetry, and/or revenge by a relative. The story's turn from death to life is in some cases attributed to salutary effects of poetry itself.[19] The full form of this narrative pattern as we find it in *Hávarðar saga Ísfirðings*, as well as twice in *Egils saga*, specifies that the old man *takes to his bed to die*. It would be hard to imagine this story outside the family, yet even the much cooler court poems harbor some expressions of emotion: Sigvatr exclaims *Ólmr erumk harmr* 'violent is my grief' in his *Ólafsdrápa*, precisely in the tradition of Egill's interjection *helnauð es þat* after the burial of his brother.[20] Meanwhile, some myth-based terminal motifs – desolation of the land; no better will be born; and this latter often linked to a separate apocalyptic motif – are scattered through much of the larger corpus of *erfikvæði*.

A related red thread of this kind is a pattern of allusions to Baldr and to Ragnarök. It was Magnus Olsen who first traced the Baldr thread through Eyvindr's *Hákonarmál* of c. 961, and, somewhat less certainly, in Sigvatr's *Ólafsdrápa* of about 1040 (Olsen 1924; 1929). I continued that exercise with the anonymous *Eiríksmál* of c. 954 and the *Ólafserfidrápa* of Hallfreðr vandræðaskald, 1001 (Harris 1999). If these results hold, we can say that allusions to Baldr and Ragnarök constitute a *basso continuo* through the whole extant series of royal funeral poems from late pagan into early Christian times. But are these merely superficial allusive imitations, or were they signs of something deeper, something constitutive of the genre in early times? *Sonatorrek*, generically related but private rather than royal in setting, might tip the balance in answer to that question.

I have argued that the Baldr myth, Odinic language, and the Ragnarök theme run through much of *Sonatorrek* as a submerged but easily reachable metaphor. I attempted to explain Egill's use of the myth in terms of the relationship of archaic religious man to the divine pattern, a relationship made famous in the writings of Mircea Eliade and now almost synonymous with his name (Harris 1999). Applied to our materials, the Eliade hypothesis might run thus: since in the mythology the death of Baldr was the archetypal death and the archetypal sacrifice, the pattern set there by

[19] Discussed mainly in Harris 1994b.
[20] References in Harris 2006b.

Odin formed the model of paternal grief in real life, at least in circles of Odin worshippers. Egill's Odinic language, the ritual occasion of performance, and the situation of events – all suggest that Egill's own grief was a *re-presentatio* of the first death and first grief, that his poem and actions are modeled on a paradigm of religious tradition wherein he cast himself as a shadow of Odin and his lost sons as reflections of Baldr. This hypothesis gets us close to a possible explanation of the persistence of the Baldr allusions even into the court *erfikvæði*, though with changes of emphasis, diminishment and eventual disappearance in the increasingly formal poetry of the Christian courts. But how *old* and how widespread might these connections between myth and elegy be?

Strange to say, there is a clear reflection of this web of connections in the OE *Beowulf*, where, bafflingly, we find not only an echo of the proverb Egill quoted in st. 17 of *Sonatorrek* and find it in connection with a version of the Baldr myth, but we find even the extra-poetic narrative pattern of the bereaved father who takes to bed to die. After nearly thirty years of writing about this suggestive nexus, I still cannot explain it simply and without metaphor; but the analogues in *Beowulf*, which, after all, stem not from English legend but from Gautish, southern Swedish sources, at least support the idea that in pre-Christian Scandinavia, myth, and especially the Baldr myth, was felt to be relevant to real-life grief and its expression in poetry. I will not go into more detail on *Beowulf* in the present context, but with all this in mind I would like to return to Rök and ask now about the content and plan of the little anthology of stories Varinn dedicated to Vámóðr.

Literary interpretation

There are of course many debatable spots in my interpretation of the Rök text, but for the moment we are occupied here only with basic content. Section One concerns Theoderic the Great, and its Question Two gives us the teller's basic slant on the Theoderic material. It is a form of wonder perhaps specific to an oral culture: how can Theoderic have died nine generations ago but still be talked about. The Answer repeats the 'then-and-now' opposition of Question 2, but the stanza, the only strict verse in the inscription, is aptly characterized by Andreas Heusler as a *Denkmalepigramm*, a brief exercise in ekphrasis based on an eye-witness visit to the equestrian statue of Theoderic which Charlemagne had installed in the courtyard of his palace in Aachen; the date of this event, 801, gives us the earliest possible date for the inscription (Harris 2009, 34–35; Heusler 1941, 85). That, at least, is the belief I share with the majority of students of Rök; I realize that this specific source, like many other details, is debatable – *and debated* – but the source of the Theoderic verse, while important for a historical understanding of Rök and of its date, is oddly unimportant for a gross literary explication.[21]

In the hermeneutically more difficult Section 2, Question 2 asks the names of twenty kings who once ruled in Zealand and now lie dead on a battlefield there. The Answer lists their names in four groups of five 'brothers' with their four 'fathers'; the brothers all bear the same name, 'five Valkar sons of Ráðulfr' and so on. Lönnroth had proposed as background something like an early oral *fornaldarsaga* featuring berserk 'brothers' with an especially good parallel in story and thula in the incident on Sámsey known from *Hervarar saga*, *Ǫrvar-Odds saga*, and Saxo. Though this is definitely the best constellation of *medieval* texts so far offered to complete and make intelligible the cryptic *early Viking Age* source, I criticized various details and tried to establish the anachronism as a disabling general critique. I offered an alternative based on earlier historical conditions (discussed below), but again the differences are not crucial to the kind of broad thematic interpretation we are advancing toward.

The third section, the bearer of Olrik's weighty *Achtergewicht* (narrative emphasis on the last of a series), is the most important for interpretation.[22] After torturous examination of ll. 21–28, I proposed that in these Questions and their Answer we have a local Swedish variation of the myth of the death of a young god, best known in West Nordic as attached to Baldr, his father Odin, his 'accidental' slayer, his brother Hǫðr, and a newborn brother Váli or Bous, dedicated to avenge Baldr and specially engendered through the rape of a giant maiden Rindr (Harris 2006b). Equivalents

---

[21] Thus Lönnroth and I disagree sharply on the importance for Rök of the statue and on many other details but seem to be in broad agreement about the theme or meaning or message of this segment of the inscription.

[22] Olrik 1909; and cf. Harris 2006b, 51, 98.

of all five of these actors appear in the Gautish story, where the slaying of Vilinn, the local name of the Baldr-figure, occurs at the hands of an actor denominated *jǫtunn*, but the focus of the story is not on the slaying or on revenge but on the compensation for Vilinn, namely the engendering of a brother, dedicated (as in *Sonatorrek* 17) to replace him and in Östergötland named Thor. The bereaved father, the Odin-figure is not named directly but called 'the fane-respecting kinsman' in the climactic line of the inscription, and his miraculous act of fathering the replacement brother happens at the ripe age of ninety. Of the sacred rape of Rindr we learn only through the phrase *at kvanaR husli* 'through the sacrifice of a woman'; but von Friesen tells us that a local place name *Vrindarvé* makes it probable that Rindr was known in Östergötland under her West Nordic name.[23]

For a literary critic such a collection of narrative materials immediately poses the question, why just *these* stories and why in just *this* collocation. The numbering of *minni*'s in the heroic material shows that a selection was made, and the lack of numbering in the myth section suggests a different source. In any case, it is axiomatic that every inclusion implies exclusions, selection. This question, the why of selection and arrangement, only became available to scholars with Wessén's 1958 break with the older, predominantly functional readings; Wessén gave us a shapely literary collection instead of fragmentary myths and incitements, but to my knowledge Lönnroth in 1977 was the first to ask the literary why-question and has been the most successful at answering it. Up to a point, I agree with him that "All three legends ... were concerned with *posterity* ..." (Lönnroth 1977, 50). But my understanding of the contents of the sections, especially Section 3, ended up being sufficiently different to elicit an alternative and less 'heroic' variant analysis that emphasized the elementary facts of life and death as understood through a myth shaped within the archaic family – concerned, that is, with the wonder of genetic continuity after the death of the beloved son. In the absence of any facts about Vámóðr, I suggested that Eliade's paradigm of *homo religiosus*, while it could teach nothing concrete about Vámóðr, could at least reveal a mentality in the perceived homology between the real and mythical fathers and sons. The sparse wording of Section 3 cannot offer insight into Varinn's mind comparable to that offered by *Sonatorrek*; still, we do have the expensive monument,

---

[23] On Rindr, Harris 2006b, 83–84; von Friesen 1920, 61.

and Varinn did *choose* this myth and can be credited with the exact emphases of the Rök version. Varinn assigned the myth pride of place in the inscription and selected the jarring word *faigian* in its first lines, a keynote that perhaps casts Vámóðr from the beginning in a role like that of the similarly fated Baldr, though we will never know whether in fact Baldr's dreams of death extended to the local Swedish Vilinn variant. So understood, the myth of Vilinn's death and the compensation for it, the engendering of his replacement brother – these constitute Varinn's consolation.

Thus the idea common to all three sections, bearing in mind that the third is the most decisive, has to do with the elementary continuation of life despite the reign of death: life persists while death comes and goes. I consider this analysis fairly obvious for Section 1 where, however, it is molded by its association with a heroic individual. Section 2 presents a challenge to the critic. Clearly it too deals with life and death and offers certain parallels to Section 1, but its affirmation of life in the midst of death seems to contradict the individuality of Section 1 and instead of *singularity* to reside in *plurality*, specifically in the pseudo-family structure of the *Männerbund*, where, as in the U.S. Marines, there is a sense of continuity between the living and the dead. The individual is submerged in a corporate consciousness that does not directly deny death but assures that the brotherhood will continue. The Lévi-Straussian structure of Rök's treatment of the theme of life and death thus begins to emerge: a classic binary opposition is established between the individual and the group that implies, in the language of myth, a problem, the solution to which, the mediating term, appears in Section 3 as death-and-birth, father-and-son, cyclicity within the blood family.

Cultural position, cultural change

So where does this reading of Rök place it within the realm of literature or, on the other hand, within that of life? Is it an elegy in stone, the crystallization (rather, petrification) of funeral ritual? It certainly has affiliations with *Sonatorrek* and *erfikvæði*, but the few critics who have actually tried to situate Rök have tended rather to place it within a social matrix, thus to find a *sitz-im-leben* (rather than *in der Literatur*). Lönnroth speculates especially about its relevance to social hierarchies and about pedagogical function, while Widmark constructs a Varinn who is a *þulr* – this ancient and not fully understood office being constituted as a guardian of ethnically defined knowledge, tribal tradition. Rök's position among genres and media seems a less speculative matter than its position in society, but the significant fact about Rök in literary history is its uniqueness. Like *Beowulf*, the *Canterbury Tales*, and a few other masterpieces, it can be seen as a kind of *summa litterarum*, but *in parvo*, bringing together elements of the literary past in a form so new that it produces no significant heirs.[24] Does that mean it is insulated from cultural change?

One model of cultural change already applied to our field, but less well known than it deserves to be, is embodied in a modest booklet by an anthropologist of the sixties, Rosalie Wax, who wrote on "the changing ethos of the Vikings." Wax derived the model from the anthropologist of peasant cultures James Redfield and explains it briefly:

> The Little Tradition refers to the little community and to that which is transmitted informally (predominantly orally) from generation to generation; while the Great Tradition refers to the corps of disciples within a civilized society and to special wisdom, preserved in scriptures, which they guard and transmit (Wax 1969, 15).

This quotation leaves to the imagination the dynamic between Great and Little, and the explanatory power of this simple model of big fish eating little fish may have its limits. In the age of globalization, however, we do not require much subtlety on this subject. Students of Old Scandinavian literature have long been accustomed to triumphalist presentations of the Continental Great Tradition and to demonstrations that apparent survivals of Scandinavian Little Traditions are in fact *invented* traditions. Instinctively I would like to celebrate the local and instances of resistance to progress, but the resistance – for example the Thor's hammers cast alongside crosses – may be based on imitation and so be sad signs of the inexorable homogenization, the cultural equivalent of loss of species. Long ago I tried to advance an argument that it was later awareness of this kind of cultural

---

[24] Argued for *Beowulf* in Harris 1991, for Rök in Harris 2009.

change that made 'saga' a kind of 'historical novel' and so an analogue of the literary phenomenon known since the Romantic period (Harris 1986). Today, though, I would like to ask whether anything can be learned about cultural change in the early Viking Age through one of its *failures*. The Rök Stone continues to be my example.

In her article on the social background of Rök, Gun Widmark pointed out that Varinn's lifetime was the flourishing time of the Swedish trading town of Birka and that the Carolingian missionary Ansgar, who preached in Birka and ministered to its Christian population, was Varinn's contemporary (Widmark 1997). Widmark imagined Varinn as fearing that a new age was at hand which would espouse different ideals and that soon enough many of his countrymen would lose interest in the ancient local traditions he saw it as his duty to pass on, and Rök was his solution to this anxiety. In short, her Varinn saw his early ninth century as a time of cultural crisis when influences from the South seemed to threaten the Little Tradition. Normally I might have applauded this hypothesis of resistance, but I read Widmark while engaged in completing a study focused, partly, on the West Germanic elements – Frankish, Frisian, and English – in Rök, a study which envisions Varinn rather as a man ahead of his time. Let me summarize the elements that contrast with Widmark's fearful, conservative Varinn (Harris 2009).

Old English sources offer a few striking artistic analogues of the stone's multi-stranded, anthology-like lay-out, notably in the Franks Casket (c. 700) and the (probably) early OE poems *Deor* and *Widsith*. Though all may be regarded as examples of 'panel structure,' the arrangements are not mechanical; in Rök, as in the English works, subject matter may not be fully contained within its 'panel.' For the Anglo-Saxonist, Rök's triadic progression within a two-part structure echoes *Beowulf*; more generally the idea of the ordered collection (as in the *Beowulf* manuscript) has a familiar feel. But ON also has its mythic-heroic order in the Codex Regius of the Elder Edda and such order literally arranged in panels in the Gotlandic picture stones, and aesthetic patterns probably convince few readers of cultural affiliations. The ultimately West Germanic source of the narrative material of the Theoderic section is, however, hardly in dispute in the broad sense that information about the master of Italy from 493 to 526 will have entered Scandinavia via the West. The *Hreiðgotar* are familiar to Anglo-Saxonists from *Widsith*; but though *Widsith* knows the Goths, it does not mention Theoderic. Rök's connection with *Deor* is closer. The Þjóðrekr of Rök was *skati Mæringa* 'lord of the Mærings' while *Deor*'s Þeodric 'ruled for thirty winters the fortress of the Mærings' (ll.18-19a).[25] These Mærings are difficult to place, but the connection between Rök and *Deor* is an intimate one. A further parallel may perhaps be seen between *dæmir enn um sakar* and *Deor*'s *þæt wæs monegum cuð* 'that was known to many' (l. 19), both perhaps referring not just to Theoderic's lasting fame but to the mixture of blame and praise in that great reputation – the blame of course ultimately stemming from his heresy. The identity of both Theoderics with each other and with Theoderic the Great, the later Dietrich von Bern, is, in my opinion, conclusive, and I have already revealed that I am convinced by the argument, which goes back at least as far as 1889, that Rök's *fornyrðislag* stanza is ultimately traceable to an eyewitness of the famous statue in Aachen. Varinn's knowledge that Theoderic the Great died "nine ages ago" was remarkably accurate; counting from 526 at 30 years per generation we arrive at 796. Despite the folk-poetic ring of 'nine ages ago,' this cannot be an accident, and elements of possible Carolingian origin begin to accumulate.

Section 2 continues this accumulation. There the Answer is a *Widsith*-like thula of eight names, which show at the very least a strong West Germanic strain. Two of the fathers' names are probably West Germanic, while the other two are attested in both North and West; the sons show two definitely West Germanic names and two where the evidence is inconclusive but compatible with West Germanic origin. Von Friesen, whose extensive work on the names I have depended on – perhaps too much, but not blindly – sifted the onomastic evidence carefully and concluded that in general the names could be explained as "af icke-nordisk börd" (1920, 81, 76–81), possibly Frisian.

In my article I follow von Friesen (and to an extent Höfler 1952, 308–17) in imagining an historical background in Frisian trade along the Birka-Haithabu-Dorstad axis and in positing a foreground in the kind of *Männerbund* that was the foundation of such trading-and-raiding companies of the earliest Viking Age. The placement of events on Zealand brings the numerical symmetries of the brother-bands into contact with the simi-

---

[25] *Deor* and *Widsith* are cited from Krappe 1936.

larly symmetrical organization of early Viking Age fortresses of the Trelleborg type, though I have not been able to use this insight of Höfler's in any very exact way. I sought an oral literary milieu that, unlike Lönnroth's West Nordic *fornaldarsaga*, looked south and west and found some similarities worth mentioning in praise poetry, Heusler's *Preislied/ Zeitgedicht*. This imagined West Germanic origin requires, I would argue, no *more* unmoored belief than any other attempt to explain this puzzling material. All are speculations into the void of an oral period, but the whole nature of Rök presumes that this foreign material was not entirely new but already existed as stories in the memory of the audience of the inscription.

The West Germanic elements that appear in the Rök text can all be attributed to 'oral tradition,' but oral tradition need not be a disembodied ('superorganic,' in the idiom of folkloristics) force moving in mysterious waves; one conceptualizes it so vaguely only when no actual *traditionbearers* are available as its vectors. With many other Rök scholars I believe a more direct connection, ultimately an eye-witness, is implicit in the relationship of the Theoderic verse and the Aachen statue. Other features, such as the Swedish monument's apparent allusion to Theoderic's compromised fame or when he lived, *could* have been brought from the land of the Franks and Frisians by the kind of individual Swedish traveler to Dorstad whom we meet and hear quoted in Rimbert's *Life of St. Ansgar* (1884, 58).

Is it possible that Varinn's unique decision to record his selection of legends in writing – "eine revolutionierende Idee," as Meulengracht Sørensen calls it (2001, 133) – could have been one of the West Germanic, specifically Frankish, influences? Some later runic memorials quote bits of appropriate verse, and myths and legends were rendered pictorially in the North; but no other rune stone attempts to record a collection of such *minni* in writing. Our hypothetical Swedish visitor, setting out from Birka, will have traveled after 801 to Dorstad and further, up the Maas to Aachen. He will have been curious enough about the great emperor to admire the newly arrived statue of his famous and controversial predecessor, Theoderic. Perhaps among the things he learned there (Theoderic's bad reputation, how long ago he lived?) one concerned the emperor's activities after 800 in improvement of native law, including having the oral laws written down. Perhaps he heard that the emperor was even having ancient story-telling poems collected and reduced to writing – in Einhard's famous words: '[Karl] also had the old rude songs that celebrate the deeds and wars of the ancient kings written out for transmission to posterity' – *barbara et antiquissima carmina, quibus veterum regum actus et bella canebantur, scripsit memoriaeque mandavit*. In the context of such a collection perhaps references to *memoria* reminded him of his native *minni* with a somewhat similar range of meanings centering on 'memory, remembrance.' Einhard's *memoriae mandare* is debated by specialists; but in context its meaning cannot have been far from 'preserve for posterity (in letters).'[26] For the Swede – whose stories *were* 'memory' and 'memory' story – the possibility of *writing* stories or poems *pro memoria* was a new idea and one from an authoritative source. But it did have a partial analogue at home where runic writing was already associated with monumentalization, often to preserve the memory of individuals in stones and runes that were to last until Ragnarök. Ideas, like seeds, may fall on ready ground, or not. Did our imaginary Swedish visitor carry his new idea back with him to Östergötland, where, sometime after the death of young Vámóðr, Varinn applied it to a memorial, resulting in a monument unique in literary history but one with a familiar feeling for the Anglo-Saxonist?

So I disagree with Widmark about the conservative impulses to be read out of the Rök monument. Yet she and Meulengracht Sørensen were rightly – though only implicitly – groping toward a placement of Rök not just in relation to society and culture, as Wessén and Lönnroth do, but in relation to *different* cultures and their interactions. Concerning the anxious Varinn's decision "att anförtro sina minnen åt det beständigaste av allt: sten" (Widmark 1997, 172), Widmark asked: "Ristade kanske Varin egentligen inte alls för någon läsare utan såg i stenen en sorts robot som på något magiskt plan för all evighet fyller den uppgift som hade varit hans?" (173). In other words, the motivation is resistance to cultural change and the technology, though new, is home-grown. Meulengracht Sørensen was closer to my understanding of the matter when he emphasized the utter uniqueness of Rök, the implausibility of Varinn's experiment with extensive writing on stone, and the lack of any evidence of reception: "und tatsächlich fand das großangelegte Schriftexperiment von Rök auch nirgens,

---

[26] On *Vita Karoli*, ch. 29, and the *Heldenliederbuch*, see Haubrichs 1989 and Harris 2009, 45 n. 85.

soviel wir wissen, Nachahmung" (2001, 133). Meulengracht Sørensen's principal concern in this article was, however, quite a different one, in fact about source criticism and allowable anachronism; these remarks on mediality are a fruitful digression, but the word 'revolutionizing,' without a prefix such as 'potential' or 'would-be,' hardly seems to describe Varinn's idea in its results.[27]

*

Rök is a cul-de-sac, a dead end with regard to cultural change, but can anything about the larger subject be learned from such a failure? A philologist is likely to have little confidence at this level of generalization. Nevertheless, some closing axioms present themselves. When a cultural anomaly appears in situations of potential intercultural influence, hasty embrace of the foreign may be a likely hypothesis, along with maladaptation to the receiving culture. Technology is a main vector of change, along with prestige and fashion, but native common sense may resist even an apparently bright idea. In terms of broadest cultural history, Rök should be portrayed as an early stage in the battle of literacy with orality where, clearly, orality won out. Yet scholars naturally see it not as something novel, but as a witness to an archaic time – both points of view have their value, the Little Tradition and the glimpse into the uneven progress of the Great Tradition.

[27] On memory and the mediality of Rök see now also Schulte 2008 and Malm 2008.

APPENDIX: THE RÖK INSCRIPTION, A REFERENCE TEXT

[The letters A-E refer to sides of the stone. The line numbering, however, is sequential 1–28, following Wessén 1958; OSw normalization also follows Wessén. Transcription of l. 20 (with underdotting indicating conjectural runes) is that of Grønvik 2003, 67. The reversal of Wessén's order in lines 27–28 is argued for in Harris 2006b.]

Dedication (lines 1–2, side A):
Aft Vamoð standa runaʀ þaʀ. / Æn Varinn faði, faðiʀ aft faigian sunu.
In memory of Vámóðr stand these runes. But Varinn wrote them, a father in memory of his death-doomed son.

Narrative Section one (3–11, A–B; Theoderic section):
First Question/hint (3–5): *Sagum mogminni þat: hværiaʀ valraubaʀ vaʀin tvaʀ / þaʀ, svað tvalf sinnum vaʀin numnaʀ at valraubu, / baðaʀ saman a ymissum mannum?*
    I pronounce this hint for the lad: Which were the two war-spoils which, both together, were taken twelve times in booty-taking from different men?
Second Question/hint (5–8): *Þat sagum anna/rt: hvaʀ fur niu aldum an urði fiaru / meðr Hraiðgutum, auk do/miʀ æn umb sakaʀ?*
    This I pronounce as second: Who became without life (died) among the Hreið-Goths nine ages ago, and yet his affairs are still under discussion?
Answer (A9–B11): *Reð Þjoðrikʀ hinn þurmoði,*
        stilliʀ / flutna, strandu Hraiðmaraʀ.
        Sitiʀ nu garuʀ a [B] guta sinum,
        skialdi umb fatlaðʀ, skati Mæringa.
    Þjóðrikr the bold, ruler of sea-warriors, (once) ruled the shore of the Gothic Sea. Now he sits outfitted on his Gothic steed, with his shield buckled on, prince of the Mærings.

Narrative Section two (12–19; side C; the twenty kings):
First Question/hint (12–14): *Þat sagum tvalfta, hvar hæstʀ se Gu/nnaʀ etu vettvangi a, kunungaʀ tvaiʀ tigiʀ sva/ð a liggia?*
    This I pronounce as twelfth: Where does the steed of Gunnr see food on the battlefield that twenty kings are lying on?

Second Question/hint (14–17): *Þat sagum þrettaunda, hvariʀ t/vaiʀ tigiʀ kunungaʀ satin at Siolundi fia/gura vintur at fiagurum nampnum, burn/iʀ fiagurum brøðrum?*

This I pronounce as thirteenth: Which twenty kings sat on Zealand for four winters under four names, sons of four brothers?

Answer (17–19): *Valkaʀ fim, Raðulfs sy/niʀ, Hraiðulfaʀ fim, Rugulfs syniʀ, Haislaʀ fim, Haruð/s syniʀ, Kynmundaʀ fim, Bernaʀ synir.*

Five Valkar, sons of Ráðulfr; five Hreiðulfar, sons of Rugulfr; five Haislar, sons of Hǫrðr; five Kynmundar, sons of Bjǫrn.

Line 20 (after Grønvik): **nukmin̥im̥iʀ̥alus̥ak̥iainhuaʀ[...]ftiʀfra**

Narrative Section three (21–26, 28, 27; C, D, C top, E):

First Question/hint (21–22): *Sagum mǫgminni þat: hvaʀ Inguld/inga vaʀi guldinn at kvanaʀ husli?*

I pronounce this hint for the lad: Who among the descendants of Ing-Valdr was compensated for through the sacrifice of a woman?

Second Question/hint (23–24): *Sagum mǫgminni: [h]vaim se burinn nið/ʀ drængi?*

I pronounce a (further) hint for the lad: To whom was a son born for a gallant young man?

Answer (24–26, 28, 27): *Vilinn es þat • knua knatt/i iatun. Vilinn es þat • Nyti. / Sagum mǫgminni: Þor / ol nirøðʀ, / sefi via vari.*

Vilinn it is, whom the enemy slew. Vilinn it is: may he enjoy (this monument). I pronounce a (final?) hint for the lad: At ninety, the Kinsman, respecter of shrines, engendered Þórr.

REFERENCES

Andersson, Thorsten. 2006. "Varin och Vamod – och Sibbe." *Namn och runor. Uppsalastudier i onomastik och runologi till Lennart Elmevik på 70-årsdagen 2 februari 2006*, eds. Lena Peterson, Svante Strandberg, and Henrik Williams. (Namn och samhälle 17.) Uppsala: Uppsala universitet, 1–9.

Baldur Hafstað. 1995. *Die Egils saga und ihr Verhältnis zu anderen Werken des nordischen Mittelalters*. Reykjavík: Rannsóknarstofnun Kennaraháskóla Íslands.

Barnes, Michael. 2007. "Rök-steinen – noen runologiske og språklige overveielser." *Maal og minne*: 120–132.

Brate, Erik. 1911–18. *Östergötlands runinskrifter*. Sveriges runinskrifter 2. Stockholm: Norstedt, 231–55 [fascicule 3].

Bugge, Sophus. 1910. *Der Runenstein von Rök in Östergötland, Schweden*, ed. Magnus Olsen, with contributions by Axel Olrik and Erik Brate. Stockholm: Hæggström.

Fidjestøl, Bjarne. 1989. "Erfidrápa (Erblied)." *Reallexikon der Germanischen Altertumskunde* 7. Berlin: de Gruyter, 482–86.

Finnur Jónsson. 1931. *Lexicon poeticum antiquæ linguæ septentrionalis: Ordbog over det norsk-islandske skjaldesprog oprindelig forfattet af Sveinbjörn Egilsson*. 2nd ed. Copenhagen: Møller. Rpt. 1966.

von Friesen, Otto. 1920. *Rökstenen. Runstenen vid Röks kyrka Lysings härad Östergötland*. Stockholm: K. Vitterhets historie och antikvitets akademien.

Grønvik, Ottar. 1981. *Runene på Tunesteinen. Alfabet, språkform, budskap*. Oslo: Universitetsforlaget.

Grønvik, Ottar. 1982. *The words for 'heir', 'inheritance' and 'funeral feast' in early Germanic: An etymological study of ON* arfr *m,* arfi *m,* erfi *n,* erfa *vb and the corresponding words in the other Old Germanic dialects*. Det Norske Videnskaps-Akademi, II. Hist.-Filos. Klasse, Afhandlinger, new series 18. Oslo: Universitetsforlaget.

Grønvik, Ottar. 1983. "Runeinnskriften på Rök-steinen." *Maal og minne*: 101–50.

Grønvik, Ottar. 1990. "To viktige ord i Rök-innskriften: norr. gjalda vb og minni n." *Arkiv för nordisk filologi* 105: 1–40.

Grønvik, Ottar. 1992. "Rök-innskriftens *sibbi*." *Maal og minne*: 145–49.

Grønvik, Ottar. 2003. *Der Rökstein. Über die religiöse Bestimmung und das weltliche Schicksal eines Helden aus der frühen Wikingerzeit*. Osloer Beiträge zur Germanistik 33. Frankfurt am Main, etc.: Peter Lang.

Harris, Joseph. 1986. "Saga as Historical Novel." *Structure and Meaning in Old Norse Literature: New Approaches to Textual Analysis and Literary Criticism*, ed. by John Lindow et al. Odense: Odense University Press, 187–219.

Harris, Joseph. 1991. "*Beowulf* in Literary History." *Interpretations of Beowulf: A Critical Anthology*, ed. by R. D. Fulk. Bloomington: Indiana University Press, 235–241. (Orig. publ. 1982.)

Harris, Joseph. 1994a. "A Nativist Approach to *Beowulf*. The Case of Germanic Elegy." *Companion to Old English Poetry*, ed. by H. Aertsen and R. Bremmer. Amsterdam: VU University Press, 45–62.
Harris, Joseph. 1994b. "Sacrifice and Guilt in *Sonatorrek*." *Studien zum Altgermanischen. Festschrift für Heinrich Beck*, ed. Heiko Uecker. Ergänzungsbände zum Reallexikon der Germanischen Altertumskunde 11. Berlin & New York: de Gruyter, 173–96.
Harris, Joseph. 1999. "'Goðsögn sem hjálp til að lifa af' í Sonatorreki." *Heiðin minni. Greinar um fornar bókmenntir*, ed. by Haraldur Bessason and Baldur Hafstað. Reykjavík: Heimskringla, 47–70.
Harris, Joseph. 2006a. "*Erfikvæði*–myth, ritual, elegy." *Old Norse religion in long-term perspectives: Origins, changes and interactions. An international conference in Lund, Sweden, June 3–7, 2004*, eds. Anders Andrén, Kristina Jennbert, and Catharina Raudvere. Vägar till Midgård 8. Lund: Nordic Academic Press, 267–71.
Harris, Joseph. 2006b. "Myth and Meaning in the Rök Inscription." *Viking and Medieval Scandinavia* 2: 45–109.
Harris, Joseph. 2009. "The Rök Stone through Anglo-Saxon Eyes." *The Anglo-Saxons and the North*, ed. by Matti Kilpiö, Jane Roberts, and Leena Kahlas-Tarkka. Tempe, Arizona: Medieval and Renaissance Texts and Studies, 11–45.
Harris, Joseph. Forthcoming. "The Rök Inscription, l. 20." *Mediaeval Scandinavia* 16 [guest editor Daniel Melia].
Haubrichs, Wolfgang. 1989. "*Veterum regum actus et bella* – Zur sog. Heldenliedersammlung Karls des Großen." *Aspekte der Germanistik: Festschrift für Hans-Friedrich Rosenfeld zum 90. Geburtstag*, ed. Walter Tauber. Göppinger Arbeiten zur Germanistik 521. Göppingen: Kümmerle, 17–46.
Heusler, Andreas. 1941. *Die altgermanische Dichtung*, 2nd ed. rev. Potsdam: Athenaion.
Höfler, Otto. 1952. *Der Runenstein von Rök und die germanische Individualweihe*. Germanisches Sakralkönigtum I. Tübingen: Niemeyer; Münster: Böhlau.
Jón Helgason, ed. 1962. *Skjaldevers*. Nordisk filologi, A: 12. Copenhagen: Munksgaard, etc.
Jón Hnefill Aðalsteinsson. 2001. *Trúarhugmyndir í Sontorreki*. Studia Islandica 57. Reykjavík: Bókmenntafræðistofnun Háskóla Íslands.
Jónas Kristjánsson. 2006. "Kveðskapur Egils Skallagrímssonar." *Gripla* 17: 7–35.
Krappe, George Philip and Elliott van Kirk Dobbie, eds. 1936. *The Exeter Book*. The Anglo-Saxon Poetic Records 3. N.Y.: Columbia University Press.
Lönnqvist, Olov. 1999. "Vilken väg valde Varin: Läsvägar på Rökstenen." *Saga och Sed. Kungl. Gustav Adolfs akademiens årsbok* 1999 (Annales academiae regiae Gustavi Adolphi 1999): 117–36.
Lönnroth, Lars. 1977. "The Riddles of the Rök-Stone: A Structural Approach." *Arkiv för nordisk filologi* 92: 1–57.
Malm, Mats. 2008. "Rökstenens tilltal." *'Vi ska alla vara välkomna!' Nordiska*

studier tillägnade Kristinn Jóhannesson, ed. by Auður Magnúsdóttir, Henrik Janson, Karl G. Johansson, Mats Malm, and Lena Rogström. Meijerbergs arkiv för svensk ordforskning 35. Göteborg: Meijerbergs institut för svensk etymologisk forskning, 243–257.

Meulengracht Sørensen, Preben. 2001. "Der Runen-Stein von Rök und Snorri Sturluson – oder 'Wie aussagekräftig sind unsere Quellen zur Religionsgeschichte der Wikingerzeit?'" PMS. *At fortælle Historien / Telling History: Studier i den gamle nordiske litteratur / Studies in Norse Literature*. Trieste: Parnaso, 131–41. (Orig. publ. 1990.)

Olrik, Axel. 1909. "Epische Gesetze der Volksdichtung." *Zeitschrift für deutsches Altertum* 51: 1–12.

Olsen, Magnus. 1924. "Om Balder-digtning og Balder-kultus." *Arkiv för nordisk filologi* 40: 148–75.

Olsen, Magnus. 1929. "En iakttagelse vedkommende Balder-diktningen." *Studier tillägnade Axel Kock*. Lund: Gleerup, 169–77 (= *Arkiv för nordisk filologi*, supplement to vol. 40, n.s.)

Petersson, Conny. 1991. *Rökstenen – Varins besvärjelse*. Klockrike.

Ralph, Bo. 2007a. "Gåtan som lösning. Ett bidrag till förståelsen av Rökstenens runinskrift." *Maal og minne*: 133–57.

Ralph, Bo. 2007b. "Rökstenen och språkhistorien." *Nya perspektiv inom nordisk språkhistoria. Föredrag hållna vid ett symposium i Uppsala 20–22 januari 2006.* Ed. Lennart Elmevik. (Acta Academiae Regiae Gustavi Adolphi 97.) Uppsala: Kungl. Gustav Adolphs Akademien för svensk folkkultur, 121–43.

Rimbertus. 1884. *Vita Anskarii autore Rimberto*, ed. G. Waitz. Scriptores rerum germanicarum in usum scholarum ex Monumentis Germaniae Historicis recusi. Hannover: Hahn. Rpt. 1977.

Schulte, Michael. 2008. "Memory culture in the Viking Age. The runic evidence of formulaic patterns." *Scripta Islandica* 59: 57–73.

Sigurður Nordal, ed. 1933. *Egils saga Skalla-Grímssonar*. Íslenzk fornrit 2. Reykjavík: Hið íslenzka fornritafélag.

Sigurður Nordal. 1942 (1990). *Íslensk menning*. I. Reykjavík: Mál og menning. (*Icelandic Culture*, trans. with notes by Vilhjálmur T. Bjarnar. Ithaca: Cornell University Library, 1990.)

Torfi H. Tulinius. 2004. *Skáldið í skriftinni – Snorri Sturluson og Egils saga.* Reykjavík: Hið íslenska bókmenntafélag and Reykjavíkur Akademían.

Turville-Petre, E. O. G. 1976. *Scaldic Poetry*. Oxford: Clarendon.

Vésteinn Ólason. 1969. "Greppaminni." *Afmælisrit Jóns Helgasonar 30. júní 1969*, ed. by Jakob Benediktsson et al. Reykjavík: Heimskringla, 189–205.

Wax, Rosalie. 1969. *Magic, Fate, and History: The Changing Ethos of the Vikings*. Lawrence, KS: Coronado.

Wessén, Elias. 1958. *Runstenen vid Röks kyrka*. Kungl. vitterhets historie och antikvitets akademiens handlingar, filologisk-filosofiska serien 5. Stockholm: Almqvist & Wiksell.

Widmark, Gun. 1992 [1993]. "Varför ristade Varin runor? Tankar kring Rökstenen." *Saga och Sed: Kungl. Gustav Adolfs Akademiens årsbok 1992* [publ. 1993]: 25–43.

Widmark, Gun. 1993. "Vamod eller Vämod." *Nordiska orter och ord. Festskrift till Bengt Pamp på 65-årsdagen den 3 november 1993.* Lund: Dialekt- och ortnamnsarkivet i Lund, 210–12.

Widmark, Gun. 1997. "Tolkningen som social konstruktion. Rökstenens inskrift." *Runor och ABC. Elva föreläsningar från ett symposium i Stockholm våren 1995,* ed. by Steffan Nyström. Stockholm: Sällskapet Runica et Mediævalia, Riksantikvarieämbetet, 165–75.

Widmark, Gun. 2001. "Rökstenen – ett fornminne av världsarvsklass." *Det språk som blev vårt: Ursprung och utveckling i svenskan. Urtid – Runtid – Riddartid.* Acta Academiae Regiae Gustavi Adolphi XXXVI. Uppsala: Kungl. Gustav Adolfs Akademien för svensk folkkultur, 115–20.

SUMMARY

Citing Sigurður Nordal as a model, the article attempts to bring philology, with its concern with minutiae, into dialogue with the grand sweep of Nordic civilizational analysis that formed the focus of the workshop as a whole. The paper argues a continuity from the building blocks of the particular through the controlled generalization of genre (and interpretation) to a limited window on one aspect of cultural dynamic. The examples of philology ascending toward broad cultural history are supplied by Egill Skalla-Grímsson's *Sonatorrek* and the Swedish Rök inscription. The genre in question is *erfikvæði*, which, however, is treated as a form of cross-cultural 'elegy,' thus opening toward the memorial inscription. The Rök inscription is, in conclusion, assessed in its relation to hegemonic influence from the Continent, advancing communications technology, and possible nativistic resistance.

J. Harris
Harvard University
harris@fas.harvard.edu

HANDRIT

Stofnun Árna Magnússonar í íslenskum fræðum, Reykjavík

AM 249 b fol 189

AM 194 4to 187
AM 673 a 4to 189
AM 748 I 4to 194
AM 748 II 4to 194
AM 757 a 4to 194

GKS 1812 4to 187, 188, 189
GKS 2365 4to (Codex regius) 194
GKS 2367 4to (Codex regius) 194

Den Arnamagnæanske samling, Københavns universitet, København

AM 47 fol 193
AM 242 fol (Codex Wormianus) 194

AM 544 4to 188, 193
AM 685 d 4to 184, 187
AM 736 I 4to 188, 189
AM 764 4to 187, 188, 193

Uppsala universitetsbibliotek, Uppsala
DG 11 8vo (Codex Upsaliensis) 194

Universiteitsbibliotheek, Rijksuniversiteit te Utrecht
MS No. 1374 (Codex Trajectinus) 194